RESTORING AMERICA
The Path to Liberty

Written By: Greg Masceri

This book is dedicated to my children and grandchildren. For it is their world that they have loaned to our generation and our generation that has helped saddle them with too much debt for that I am sorry.

Masceri, Greg, -

RESTORING AMERICA - The Path to Liberty

ISBN 978-1466407640

United States Politics

Government

Political Theory

RESTORING AMERICA....The PATH TO LIBERTY

907 N Greece Rd

Rochester, NY 14626

www.thepathtoliberty.com

Contents

Chapter One - Conceived in Freedom

The American credo of liberty and justice for all and government of, by and for the people has a long and rich tradition. Protecting and guarding that tradition has been the duty of patriots for 235 years. Alexander Fraser Tytler, Lord Woodhouselee was a Scottish born British lawyer and writer during the enlightenment period. His words written hundreds of years ago apply to us today:

"A democracy is always temporary in nature; it simply cannot exist as a permanent form of government. A democracy will continue until the time that voters discover that they can vote themselves generous gifts from the public treasury. From that moment on, the majority always votes for the candidates who promise the most benefits from the public treasury, with the result that every democracy will finally collapse because of loose fiscal policy, which is always followed by a dictatorship. The average age of the world's greatest civilizations from the beginning of history has been about 200 years. During those 200 years, these nations always progressed through the following sequence: From bondage to spiritual faith; From spiritual faith to great courage; From courage to liberty; From liberty to abundance; From abundance to complacency; From complacency to apathy; From apathy to dependence; From dependence back into bondage."

This historic quotation is compelling given the nature of the ills that currently face America and its people. These words by Lord Woodhouselee about the fall of the Athenian Republic some 2,000 years before his remarks at the University of Edinburgh in 1787. The future is unavoidable but just what does our future hold is the real question. Are we now living in a state between complacency and apathy, with nearly forty percent of our population dependent on the government?

Where we are today is a result of a journey that started around the time that Lord Woodhouselee framed those words of wisdom some 235 years ago. The problems and challenges that face our country have roots back about 100 years but we could go back to the founding of our nation to gain true perspective. By examining our past and reviewing our history as a nation we can discover where we started to lose our liberty.

I make the assumption that where we are as a nation today is unacceptable with the economy, human welfare, societal relations, foreign relations and national defense.

We will examine the history of and results of issues that have impacted us as a people. We will look at economic issues such as employment, central banking, inflation and finance. For human welfare we will look at poverty, welfare, education, social security, health care and how these have impacted where we are and how we should continue in the future. In our examination we will consider societal issues such as crime, drug abuse, violence, immigration and racism. As far as international relations we mean foreign relations, treaties and trade. Finally how we as a people prepare to defend ourselves from terrorism, aggression and how we use our military.

Law stems from our right to defend ourselves and our property, not from the power of the state. If law was merely whatever the state decreed, then the ideas of the rule of law and of legitimacy could not have the meaning that they plainly do have. The idea of actions being lawful and unlawful would not have the emotional significance that it does have.

John Locke made a major advance to our understanding of natural law, by stressing the nature of man as a maker of things, and a property owning animal. From the right to self-defense comes the right to the rule of law, but from the right to property comes a multitude of like rights, such as the right to privacy "An Englishman's home is his castle."

Further, Locke repeatedly reminds us that a ruler is legitimate so far as he upholds the law. A ruler that violates natural law is illegitimate. He has no right to be obeyed; his commands are mere force and coercion.

Rulers who act lawlessly, whose laws are unlawful, are mere criminals, and should be dealt with under natural law. As applied in nature, in other words they and their servants should be killed as the opportunity presents, like the dangerous animals that they are the common enemies of all civilization.

John Locke's writings were a call to arms, an assertion of the right and duty to forcibly and violently remove illegitimate rulers and their servants. Locke argued the legal authority of the state was granted to it by civil society, the state existed by the power of civil society, that this was its source of power morally and in fact.

Until the twentieth century Locke's position was widely accepted as self-evident. When the state was unarmed and the people armed, as in eighteenth century England and America, it was indeed self-evident.

People came to believe that civil society only existed by fiat of the state, the state existed because its army and police were armed. The people being unarmed gave impression the state existed by force. Now a change in the collective mind-set was beginning to take place.

During the first five Presidential administrations that lasted about 35 years we were led by our founding fathers. The founders didn't all agree on every aspect of the constitution but as they hammered it out they all came together to embrace it. When the convention ended them did all agree on the constitution as the document that they were all guided by? So issues whether economic or societal they were all guided by that instrument that provided a limited central government and no possibility of a King or tyrannical leader.

In the next period of roughly another 35 years we were led by the sons of founding fathers who led us in the years up to the American Civil War. These men led a nation that became more democratic with average citizens voting. They also contemplated issues of slavery and human welfare that would continue to be postponed to keep our nation together. The executive branch still remained a coequal branch of government.

The third period would last for about 50 years from the Civil War to just after the turn of the century when Woodrow Wilson took the reins of the executive office. There were some extraordinary times that found President Lincoln faced with decisions that led him to increase federal power unlike ever before, during the Civil War. Little did anyone realize but the early seeding of liberty occurred under the Lincoln administration during the Civil War.

His experiment with an income tax which was later ruled unconstitutional is an excellent example of the American people losing liberty. Another example would be the first time that military conscription was used to force people into military service.

After that fairly brief period post Civil War Presidents returned to a less aggressive Presidency. In fact even though an argument could be made that Teddy Roosevelt began the Imperial Presidency I think we will see that it was Wilson and his administration that was to blame for us moving in that direction.

Let's first take a look at our economy over the first 125 years. Of course there were ups and downs; there were financial panics, wars and crisis. Each time we were faced with these challenges we could overcome them with a limited government and little taxation of the citizenry. No President thought it proper that one citizen should have to pay the way for another citizen. If charity was to be granted by one to another it certainly wasn't the purview of government.

In looking at societal issues in that period we also note that little to no government interference existed to regulate their citizens. Crime was handled for the most part by local law enforcement which carried out the wishes of their citizens.

Of course there was no prohibition of drugs or alcohol in those days except in certain local communities. Immigration did face some trials and tribulations during this preWilson period and they were dealt with, without the federal government imposing its will on the states. Of course the issue of slavery was blight on our nation and finally the federal government did impose its will on the secessionist states of the Confederacy.

As far as issues such as Social Security, health care and poverty and welfare these were not issues that were ever considered by the federal government. All welfare was local and voluntary through charities and churches. Finally about foreign relations and defense that was handled by the federal government with much assistance from state militias in the early years and through the Civil War.

In fact the United States didn't ever need a standing army as part of federal policy until the Lincoln and the Civil War. Since World War II though we have had and continue to build an awesome standing army.

From the beginning of the ratification of the constitution in each colony that ratified the document one thing was stressed time and again. The premise that the role of government would be limited to protect liberty, it was well agreed there was a direct correlation to the increase in government and limiting liberty. However the founders understood that some loss of liberty for the common good was necessary to protect people from harm by others.

To help people from being compelled to do one thing or another was at the constitution's essence. The founders understood the role of government lay in providing a strong national defense and to provide laws to regulate commerce. The people couldn't be harmed or property interfered with was most important. This is central to protecting life, liberty and the pursuit of happiness.

It was men like Adams, Jefferson, Madison and others who wrote of the ideas of liberty and the guarding of it by a limited federal government. The founders were careful to spell out that while the constitution could be amended it was no easy task in that 2/3 majority would prevent tyranny by a simple majority. They also understood that it was the role of the federal government not to limit liberty, but allow its free expression without injury to others.

Most issues of moral consequence were left to local authority where citizens could regulate and enforce their own laws. There were no laws on a federal level to regulate the use of drugs, alcohol, tobacco or most anything else.

No federal laws that suggested that prostitution, gambling or riding horses without a helmet was illegal. In short the role of the local government was to regulate these things as the communities saw fit. It is simply not the role of government to regulate morality or societal issues that should be governed by ones own character and moral judgment.

The genius of the founding fathers has been the essence of our very governmental structure. In a coequal trinity of government branches; the executive, legislative and judicial branches to be specific. It was up to Congress to make laws on behalf of the people that they served. Courts were to interpret the constitution in deciding what was lawful, not to make laws. Only Congress could make war and pass legislation and they were elected by the people.

What was never planned for by the founding fathers was that a party system would spring up to kidnap and corrupt this democracy. When George Washington was elected our first President he represented no party. Although he was co-opted by the Federalists Washington never imagined factionalism would rule the day. In the beginning there were

Federalists such as Adams and Hamilton who stood opposed by Democrat-Republicans led by Jefferson and Madison. At the start the differences were slight but still important, however all still agreed on a small federal government.

After all even though Jefferson and Madison weren't part of the Federalist Party they helped design the Federalist government. It was in fact Madison who was a chief architect of Federalism through his co authorship of the Federalist papers.

In the first real division of political power it was the Andrew Jackson Democrats and the old Federalist or anti – Jackson Republicans that began to take shape. While Jackson acted often like a tyrant he was he believed a benevolent one. Never the less he was perhaps the first American President to suggest that he spoke for the people and began to wield excessive executive power. He knew what the people wanted and he was going to do their bidding. He unlike any one before him used the Presidency and expanding his powers and often usurping Congress as well as the Supreme Court. As a response to this simple majority tyranny the Whig Party began to rise. After Jackson things settled back and a series of Presidents were elected to preside over the nation. It wasn't until the Civil War that Americans would see another flare up of the tyranny of the federal government.

While I would never argue for the rights of one man to enslave another I can also not trade the rights of my neighbor for mine. President Abraham Lincoln changed the Presidency to a strong almost dictatorial position to preserve the union.

Suspending Habeas Corpus, The invasion of privacy of its citizens, the manner in which we held a draft. All were illegal actions by an out of control federal government. I might even argue that all of this was necessary to preserve the union. However once the union was preserved its power was returned to the people and their rights were restored.

For the first time in our history, war proved to be horrible, tragic and a big engine for an economy and profitable for war profiteers. A model of a new way was emerging within the American experience. A model that would be used to gain foreign lands during the administration of Teddy Roosevelt as he tested the limits of Presidential power through nation building. Under the guise of manifest destiny America was beginning to embark on a new Imperialism as we began to spread democracy around the world. Still the role of the federal government in the lives of its citizens was limited. Laws and regulations were still mostly the business of local areas.

All of this would begin to change irrevocably after the Presidential election of 1912 which elected Woodrow Wilson to the Presidency. During his administration the executive, legislative and judicial branches of government began to see the government as a vehicle of change. That by the expanse of government it could ensure control of the people as well as loyalty from the people. This principle helped to foment the idea that somehow government was an alternative to mankind itself. People even began to see the government as having provided our inalienable rights.

Of course the founders knew that our rights to life, liberty and happiness come from our creator and are inherent in all men and not granted by the government. Therefore the nature of the increase in government power has the effect of lessening our natural rights.

A review of the last hundred years shows some interesting and telling demographics. A hundred years ago, most people living in the U.S. were male, under 23 years old, lived-in the country and rented their homes.

Almost half of all the people in the U.S. lived-in households with five or more other people. Today, most people in the U.S. are female, 35 years old or older and live in metropolitan areas where they own their home.

Most people in the U.S. now either live alone or in a household with no more than two other people.

These are just the top-level changes reported by the Census Bureau in their 240-page report titled Demographic Trends in the 20th Century. The report tracks trends in population, housing and household data for the nation, regions and states.

In the past 100 years the U.S. population grew by some 225 million people, more than tripling from 75 million in 1900 to 300 million in 2010.

In every decade of the century, the West's population grew faster than the populations of the other three regions. Florida's population rank rose more than that of any other state, catapulting it from 33rd to 4th place in state rankings. Iowa's population ranking plummeted the furthest, from 10th in the nation in 1900 to 30th in 2010.

Children under 5 years old represented the largest five-year age group in 1900 and again in 1950; but in 2010 the largest groups were 35 to 39 and 40 to 44. The percentage of the U.S. population age 65 and over increased in every census from 1900 (4.1 percent) to 1990 (12.6 percent), then declined for the first time in Census 2000 to 12.4 percent.

From 1900 to 1960, the South had the highest proportion of children under 15 and the lowest proportion of people 65 and over, making it the country's "youngest" region. The West grabbed that title in the latter part of the century.

The black population remained concentrated in the South and the Asian and Pacific Islander population in the West through the century, but these regional concentrations declined sharply by 2010. In fact there was a dramatic shift in black Southerners moving to the North and West which occurred during the great migration from 1910 to 1970. Among the races, the American Indian and Alaska Native population had the highest percentage under age 15 for most of the 20th century.

From 1980 to 2000, the Hispanic-origin population, which may be of any race, more than doubled.

The total minority population people of Hispanic origin or of races other than white increased by 88 percent between 1980 and 2000 while the nonHispanic white population grew by only 7.9 percent.

In 1950, for the first time, more than half of all occupied housing units were owned instead of rented. The homeownership rate increased until 1980, decreased slightly in the 1980s and then rose again to its highest level of the century in 2000 at 66 percent. The 1930s was the only decade when the proportion of owner-occupied housing units declined in every region. The largest increase in homeownership rates for each region then occurred in the next decade when the economy recovered from the Depression and experienced post-World War II prosperity.

Between 1950 and 2000, married-couple households declined from more than three-fourths of all households to just over one-half. The proportional share of one-person households increased more than households of any other size. In 1950, one-person households represented 1-in-10 households; by 2000, they comprised 1-in-4.

Over the past hundred years our nation has changed greatly in its diversity, age, ethnic makeup and population. With these changes old and new issues have arisen that as Americans we've had to face. One example is the issue of Abortion in the United States since our founding. In the United States, abortion laws began to appear in states and localities in the 1820s, forbidding abortion after the fourth month of pregnancy. Through the efforts primarily of doctors, the American Medical Association, and legislators, most abortions in the US had been outlawed by 1900. Illegal abortions were still frequent, though they became less frequent during the reign of the Comstock Law in the late nineteenth century which essentially banned birth control information and devices.

The Comstock Law, passed in the United States in 1873, was part of a campaign for legislating public morality in the United States. In reality, the Comstock Law was targeted not only at obscenity but at birth control devices and information on abortion and at information on sexuality and on sexually transmitted diseases.

Some early feminists, like Susan B. Anthony, wrote against abortion. They opposed abortion which at the time was an unsafe medical procedure for women, endangering their health and life. These feminists believed that only the achievement of women's equality and freedom would end the need for abortion. Historically, the impulse early nineteenth-century legislatures were to pass laws only when necessary and generally only after near unanimity was achieved. Social pressure and education had been effective abortion deterrents in the past, but as the morality of America grew more relaxed, "nongovernmental means of containment seemed inadequate. Abortion gained a larger foothold in American life, so lawmakers had to start dealing with it specifically and clearly.

In 1821, the first abortion legislation was passed in Connecticut, and lawmakers elsewhere did their best to keep up (New York legislation changed on abortion 10 times between 1828 and 1881). The frequency of abortion, however, continued to increase.

During the 1840's and 1850's, 13 states passed laws forbidding abortion at any stage. Three others made abortion illegal after quickening. In 1856, the Iowa Supreme Court held that prequickening abortion was not a crime, but in the next legislature, the prohibitions against prequickening abortions were restored 27-0 and 53-1. Despite this newfound devotion to legislative intervention, abortionists continued to make inroads. They began advertising heavily in the *Penny Press*, though never using the word "abortion".

Women were offered instant relief from "menstrual suppression", or were told of pills that were so effective at restoring a woman's monthly cycle that they should never be taken by pregnant women (wink, wink).

On top of the public pressure applied both by the medical community and by the major media outlets, there also was a growing commitment to establishing more practical support measures to help pregnant, unmarried women. In 1895, Chicago, itself was known to have dozens of shelters for just such women. Eventually, though, the victories gained by the pro-life movement began to be undermined and reversed.

The settling of America began with an idea. The idea was that people can join and agree to govern themselves by making laws for the common good. In the mid-1840s, a wave of Swedish migration began with the landing of a group of migrant farmers in New York and continued up to World War I.

During the colonial era most of the immigrants to the U.S. came from Northern Europe. Their numbers declined during the 1770s, but picked up during the mid 1800s. New arrivals came from several countries, but mostly from Germany and Ireland where crop failures caused many to leave their homelands.

The Naturalization Act of 1790 Stipulated that any alien, being a free white person, may be admitted to become a citizen of the United States. In 1875 the Supreme Court declared that regulation of US immigration is the responsibility of the Federal Government. By 1882 The Chinese Exclusion Act: Prohibited certain laborers from immigrating to the United States. In 1885 and 1887: Alien Contract Labor laws which prohibited certain laborers from immigrating to the United States. 1891: The Federal Government assumed the task of inspecting, admitting, rejecting, and processing all immigrants seeking admission to the U.S. 1892: On January 2, a new Federal US immigration station opened on Ellis Island in New York Harbor. 1903: This Act restated the 1891 provisions about land borders and called for rules covering entry as well as inspection of aliens crossing the Mexican border. 1907 The US immigration Act of 1907:

Reorganized the states bordering Mexico Arizona, New Mexico and a large part of Texas into Mexican Border District to stem the flow of immigrants into the United States.

American immigration history can be viewed in four epochs: the colonial period, the midnineteenth century, the turn of the twentieth, and post-1965. Each epoch brought distinct national groups, races, and ethnicities to the United States.

During the seventeenth century, about 175,000 Englishmen migrated to Colonial America. Over half of all European immigrants to Colonial America during the 17th and 18th centuries arrived as indentured servants.

The midnineteenth century saw mainly an influx from northern Europe; the early twentieth-century mainly from Southern and Eastern Europe; post-1965 mostly from Latin America and Asia.

Historians estimate that less than one million immigrants—perhaps as few as 400,000—crossed the Atlantic during the 17th and 18th centuries. The 1790 Act limited naturalization to "free white persons"; it was expanded to include blacks in the 1860s and Asians in the 1950s. In the early years of the United States, immigration was fewer than 8,000 people a year, including French refugees from the slave revolt in Haiti. After 1820, immigration gradually increased. From 1836 to 1914, over 30 million Europeans migrated to the United States.

In 1875, the nation passed its first immigration law until then immigration wasn't even regulated or controlled. The peak year of European immigration was in 1907, when 1,285,349 persons entered the country. By 1910, 13.5 million immigrants were living in the United States.

The first banks in the United States were the brainchild of one of our nations leading Federalists Alexander Hamilton. In most states of the early federal union, bank organizers needed special permission from the state government to open and run. For a while, an added layer of oversight was provided by the Bank of the United States, a central bank founded in 1791. Its Congressional charter expired in 1811. A second Bank of the United States was created in 1816 and operated until 1832.

In those days, city bankers tended to be cautious about to whom they lent and for how long. To make sure they had enough cash available to meet unexpected demands from depositors, bankers made short-term loans only. Thirty to sixty days was the norm. Typically manufacturers and shopkeepers would use these funds to pay their suppliers and workers until they could sell the goods to customers. After that sale they would pay off the bank loan. In less settled parts of the country, lending standards tended to be more liberal. There farmers could often get bank loans to buy land and equipment and finance the shipment of farm products to market. Because of the unpredictability of weather and market conditions, loan losses tended to be higher too.

When the second Bank of the United States went out of business in 1832, state governments took over the job of supervising banks. In those days banks made loans by issuing their own currency. These banknotes were supposed to be convertible, on demand, to cash—that is, to gold or silver. It was the job of the bank examiner to visit the bank and certify that it had enough cash to redeem its outstanding currency. Because this was not always done, many banknote holders found themselves stuck with worthless paper. It was sometimes difficult or impossible to detect which notes were sound and were not, because of their staggering variety.

By 1860 more than 10,000 different banknotes circulated throughout the country. Commerce suffered as a result. Counterfeiting was epidemic. Hundreds of banks failed. Throughout the country there was an insistent demand for a uniform national currency acceptable anywhere without risk. In response, Congress passed the National Currency Act in 1863.

In 1864, President Lincoln signed a revision of that law, the National Bank Act. These laws showed a new system of national banks and a new government agency headed by a Comptroller of the Currency. The Comptroller's job was to organize and supervise the new banking system through regulations and periodic examinations.

The new system worked well. National banks bought U.S. government securities, deposited them with the Comptroller, and received national banknotes in return.

By being lent to borrowers, the notes gradually entered circulation. On the rare occasion that a national bank failed, the government sold the securities held on deposit and reimbursed the note holders. No owner of a national banknote ever lost his or her money. National banknotes were produced and distributed through an involved process.

Next, the notes were sent to the bank whose name appeared on them, where they were signed by two senior bank officers. The notes were then ready for circulation. National banknotes were the mainstay of the nation's money supply until Federal Reserve notes appeared in 1914. National banknotes featured elaborate scenes and portraits drawn from American history. The complexity of their design was intended to foil counterfeiters. Today, collectors prize national banknotes as outstanding examples of the engraver's art.

The nation had few taxes in its early history. From 1791 to 1802, the United States government was supported by internal taxes on distilled spirits, carriages, refined sugar, tobacco and snuff, property sold at auction, corporate bonds, and slaves. The high cost of the War of 1812 brought about the nation's first sales taxes on gold, silverware, jewelry, and watches. In 1817, however, Congress did away with all internal taxes, relying on tariffs on imported goods to provide enough funds for running the government.

In 1862, to support the Civil War effort, Congress enacted the nation's first income tax law. It was a forerunner of our modern income tax in that it was based on the principles of graduated, or progressive, taxation and of withholding income at the source. During the Civil War, a person earning from $600 to $10,000 per year paid tax at the rate of 3%.

Those with incomes of more than $10,000 paid taxes at a higher rate. Added sales and excise taxes were added, and an "inheritance" tax also made its debut. In 1866, internal revenue collections reached their highest point in the nation's 90-year history—more than $310 million, an amount not reached until 1911.

The Act of 1862 set up the office of Commissioner of Internal Revenue. The Commissioner was given the power to assess, levy, and collect taxes, and the right to enforce the tax laws through seizure of property and income and through prosecution. The powers and authority remain much the same today.

In 1868, Congress again focused its taxation efforts on tobacco and distilled spirits and eliminated the income tax in 1872.

It had a short-lived revival in 1894 and 1895. In the latter year, the U.S. Supreme Court decided the income tax was unconstitutional because it was not apportioned among the states in conformity with the Constitution.

Perhaps the most famous historical incident that relates to the resistance to taxes was the Boston Tea Party in Colonial America. In 1773, a group of colonists, dressed as Native Americans, boarded three English ships moored in Boston Harbor.

These colonists then spent hours smashing the ships' cargo, wooden chests filled with tea, and then throwing the damaged boxes over the side of the ships. American colonists had been heavily taxed for over a decade with such legislation from Great Britain as the Stamp Act of 1765 and the Townsend Act of 1767.

The colonists threw the tea over the side of the ships to protest what they saw as the very unfair practice of taxation without representation.

Taxation, one might argue, was one of the major injustices that led directly to the American War for Independence. Thus, the leaders of the newly created United States had to be careful about how and exactly what they taxed. Alexander Hamilton, the new U.S. Secretary of the Treasury, needed to find a way to collect money to lower the national debt, created by the American Revolution.

In 1791, Hamilton, balancing the need of the federal government to collect money and the sensitivity of the American people, decided to create a "sin tax," a tax placed on an item society feels is a vice. The item chosen for the tax was distilled spirits.

Unfortunately, the tax was seen as unfair by those on the frontier who distilled more alcohol, especially whiskey, than their eastern counterparts. Along the frontier, isolated protests eventually led to an armed revolt, known as the Whiskey Rebellion.

Alexander Hamilton was not the first man in history with the dilemma of how to raise money to pay for war. The need for a government to be able to pay for troops and supplies in wartime had been a major reason for ancient Egyptians, Romans, medieval kings, and governments around the world to increase taxes or to create new ones. Although these governments had often been creative in their new taxes, an income tax had to wait for the modern era.

Income taxes (requiring individuals to pay a percentage of their income to the government, often on a graduated scale) required the ability to retain detailed records. Throughout most of history, keeping track of individual records would have been a logistical impossibility. Thus, implementing an income tax was not found until 1799 in Great Britain. The new tax, viewed as a temporary one, was needed to help the British raise money to fight the French forces led by Napoleon.

The U.S. government faced a similar problem during the War of 1812. Based on the British model, the U.S. government considered raising money for the war through an income tax. However, the war ended before the income tax was officially enacted.

The idea of creating an income tax resurfaced during the American Civil War. Again considered a temporary tax to raise money for a war, Congress passed the Revenue Act of 1861 which instituted an income tax. However, there were so many problems with the details of the income tax law that income taxes were not collected until the law was revised the following year in the Tax Act of 1862. The income tax law was amended several times over the next few years and eventually fully repealed in 1872.

In the 1890s, the U.S. federal government was beginning to rethink its general taxation plan. Historically, most of its revenue had been from taxing imported and exported goods as well as taxes on the sale of specific products.

Realizing that these taxes were increasingly bearing on only a select portion of the population, mostly the less affluent, and the U.S. federal government began looking for a more even way to spread the tax burden. Thinking that a graduated-scale income tax placed upon all citizens of the United States would be a fair way to collect taxes, the federal government attempted to enact a country-wide income tax in 1894. However, because then all federal taxes had to be based on state population, the income tax law was found unconstitutional by the U.S. Supreme Court in 1895.

Our system of checks and balances works in the great American experiment of democracy especially when each branch of government is treated as coequal to the other. Up and until Woodrow Wilson became President the first twenty seven Presidents of the United States were coequal executives acting in concert with Congress and the Supreme Court. With the glaring exceptions of Jackson, Lincoln and Teddy Roosevelt, who all exceeded their authority under the constitution the other twenty four Presidents were great examples of coequal partners in our democracy.

For the balance of our history from Woodrow Wilson through Barrack Obama it would more often than not become the rule of the President to exceed his authority under the constitution.

It also became more incumbent on the Congress to treat their re election as the primary goal of holding office as opposed to the citizen legislator which had been the original intent of government.

Chapter 2 – Losing Liberty

Woodrow Wilson

Wilson was the first president to criticize the Constitution and the Declaration of Independence. Wilson criticized spreading government power over the different branches in his most famous book *Congressional Government*. In this work he confessed, "I cannot imagine power as a thing negative and not positive." His love and worship of power was a prime characteristic of what drove him internally. If any trait bubbles up in all one reads about Wilson it is this, "he loved, craved, and in a sense glorified power," writes historian Walter McDougall. It should not surprise us that his idols were Abraham Lincoln and Otto von Bismarck.

"No doubt much nonsense has been talked about the inalienable rights of the individual, and a great deal that was mere sentiment. Pleasing speculation has been put forward as fundamental principle," wrote Wilson, attacking the individual rights that have made America great.

He rejected the principles of "separation of powers" and "checks and balances" that are the foundation of American government: "Government does now whatever experience permits or the times demand…." wrote Wilson in *The State*.

He was no fan of democracy or constitutional government, he wrote the following in *Constitutional Government in the United States*: "The President is at liberty, both in law and conscience, to be as big a man as he can. His capacity will set the limit…." If this sounds a bit totalitarian like a devotee of the imperial presidency that would be correct.

Indeed, in a disturbing 1890 essay entitled *Leaders of Men*, Wilson said that a "true leader" uses the masses of people like "tools." He writes, "The competent leader of men cares little for the internal niceties of other people's characters: he cares much–everything–for the external uses to which they may be put…. He supplies the power; others supply only the materials on which that power operates….

It is the power which dictates, dominates; the materials yield. Men are as clay in the hands of the consummate leader." So much for the dignity of each person!

"Woe is to the man or group of men that seeks to stand in our way," said Wilson in June 1917 to counter protests to the fascist regime that he created upon entering WW I. Wilson rejects the Jeffersonian individualism that has defined the Founding and American conservatism.

"While we are followers of Jefferson, there is one principle of Jefferson's which no longer can obtain in the practical politics of America. You know that it was Jefferson who said that the best government is that which does as little governing as possible…. But that time is passed. America is not now and cannot in the future be a place for unrestricted individual enterprise." In this very pointed statement Wilson is in fact acknowledging the need for a growing more powerful federal government.

Wilson sought war with Germany and purposefully drew the US into World War I.

"I am an advocate of peace, but there are some splendid things that come to a nation through the discipline of war," said Wilson. And he would seek after those progressive "splendid things" when the opportunity of the Great War arose.

It is an often overlooked fact of WW I that Great Britain's powerful navy blockaded Germany and in so doing starved the German population. And guess who led the British in this distant blockade which was against international law at the time? It was none other than the beloved Winston Churchill, the First Lord of the Admiralty. This blockade drove the Germans to retaliate with submarine warfare. And they warned that "neutral ships will be exposed to danger" and it would be "impossible to avoid attacks being made on neutral ships in mistake for those of the enemy." Wilson all the while claimed neutrality but was actually pro-British. The British blockade and the German unrestricted submarine warfare both violated the rights of neutral nations under international law. But he refused to acknowledge that the former had led to the latter.

German misdeeds against vessels carrying Americans received swift denunciation from Wilson, but the terrible British blockade that starved hundreds of thousands of Germans to death got a slap on the wrist. The Germans even proposed to end their unrestricted sub warfare if the British would end the blockade; the British refused. It was this double standard that would drive Wilson to bring the US into the war.

Britain aimed to lure America into the war. Indeed, by making it dangerous for the German submarines to surface, Churchill would increase his chances of success: "The submerged U-boat had to rely increasingly on underwater attack and thus ran the greater risk of mistaking neutral for British ships and of drowning neutral crews and thus embroiling Germany with other Great Powers." By that time, the US was the only great power left that had remained neutral.

The most famous incident was the sinking of the *Lusitania*. But you will seldom read in school textbooks that the German government actually published warnings in major newspapers not to book passage on the great vessel. But most passengers ignored the warning. The German U-boat only fired one torpedo at the *Lusitania* and, to the surprise of the German captain Walter Schwieger, that was all it took. The liner went down quickly and a total of 124 Americans died.

What was the American reaction to this tragedy? Hardly any of the newspapers favored that declaring war was the proper response. Secretary of State William Jennings Bryan had no desire to go to war over it and challenged Wilson's double standard head on: "Why be shocked by the drowning of a few people, if there is no objection to a starving nation?" It was of no use and Bryan resigned in protest. The resignation of the Secretary of State was an unheard-of reaction to Wilson's cry for war. Senators Wesley Jones of Washington and Robert Follette of Wisconsin urged the President to exercise restraint. Congressional leaders on both the left and right had great disagreement with entering the Great War.

Wilson was determined for war to spread his version of democracy to a new world order. His vision was to create a global government and the first step to that end would be his League of Nations idea. Bryan's replacement, Robert Lansing, reveals the Wilson administration was determined to go to war: "In dealing with the British government, there was always in my mind the conviction that we would ultimately become an ally of Great Britain.

Then Wilson did the most irresponsible act that brought us into war: he ordered that merchant ships be armed with US Navy guns and staffed with US Navy crews and that they fire on any surfacing submarines they encountered. Under such circumstances, the ships sailed into the war zone. Wilson sent out ships with the purpose of sacrificing them in order to push America into war! Four of them had been sunk by the time Wilson requested a declaration of war from Congress. It was only after the war that Congress would realize how dangerous Wilson was and actually stood up to him in rejecting the Treaty of Versailles, especially Article 10 the League of Nations. This article obligated each League member to preserve the territorial integrity of the other member states. Why should the US sacrifice blood and treasure for obscure border disputes in Europe? Congress was not advocating isolationism as many have asserted but rather defending its own constitutional authority to decide when America goes to war. Over the years we have always learned that isolationism was some kind of crime, when in fact that was our last best hope against empire. Only Congress can declare war according to the constitution although Wilson was no great fan of the constitution.

No American interest was at stake in WW I, and yet a total of 116,516 men died and 204,002 were wounded. In fact, Wilson bragged about fighting a war with no national interests at stake! "There is not a single selfish element, so far as I can see, in the cause we are fighting for," he declared. It was a war to satisfy his own idealism that he could remake the world in his "progressive" ideology.

War was an instrument for perverse social engineering that would remake the world: "As head of a nation participating in the war, the president of the United States would have a seat at the peace table, but…if he remained the representative of a neutral country; he could at best only 'call through a crack in the door.'"

Wilson created the first official propaganda department in the US. A week after Congress declared war on Germany, Wilson created a government apparatus whose sole purpose was to lie to the American people, the first modern ministry for propaganda in the West. It was called the Committee on Public Information and was led by journalist George Creel. Edward Bernays, an adviser to Wilson and participant in CPI operations, characterized the mission of CPI as the "engineering of consent" and "the conscious manipulation of the organized habits and opinions of the masses."

A typical poster for Liberty Bonds read: "I am Public Opinion. All men fear me! If you have money to buy and do not buy, I will make this No Man's Land for you!" Other posters were created to mobilize the public and silence dissent. A trained group of nearly a hundred thousand men gave four minute speeches to any audience that would listen. They portrayed Wilson as a larger-than-life leader and the Germans as less-than-human Huns, emphasizing fabricated German war crimes and horrors. CPI released propaganda films entitled *The Claws of the Hun*, *The Prussian Cur*, and *To Hell with the Kaiser*, and *The Kaiser, the Beast of Berlin*.

Wilson harshly suppressed dissent and resistance among citizens and the press.

At Wilson's urging, a Sedition Act (not unlike the Alien and Sedition Acts of 1798) forbade Americans from criticizing their own government in a time of war. Citizens could not "utter, print, write or publish any disloyal, profane, scurrilous, or abusive language" about the government or the military.

The Postmaster General was given the authority to revoke the mailing privileges of those who disobeyed. About 75 periodicals were shut down by the government in this way and many others were given warnings.

In the fashion of a police state, the Department of Justice arrested tens of thousands of individuals without just cause. One was not safe even within the walls of one's own home to criticize the Wilson administration. A letter to federal attorneys and marshals said that citizens had nothing to fear as long as they "Obey the law; keep your mouth shut." In fact, the Justice Department created the forerunner to the Gestapo called the American Protective League. Its job was to spy on fellow citizens and turn in "seditious" persons or draft dodgers. In September of 1918 in NYC, the APL rounded up about 50,000 people. This doesn't even include the famous Palmer Raids named after Wilson's attorney general that occurred after the war.

In 1915, in his address to Congress, Wilson declared, "The gravest threats against our national peace and safety have been uttered within our own borders. There are citizens of the United States; I blush to admit, born under other flags. Who have poured the poison of disloyalty into the arteries of our national life. They have sought to bring the authority and good name of our Government into contempt, to destroy our industries wherever they thought it effective for their vindictive purposes...."

All in all it is estimated that about 175,000 Americans were arrested for failing to demonstrate their patriotism in one-way or another.

Wilson took over the US economy. He charged Bernard Baruch with running the War Industries Board, which would try to control all industry in-service to the state. It would serve as a forerunner to the corporatist policies of Mussolini and Hitler.

Grosvenor Clarkson, a member and later historian of the WIB, would characterize the WIB as follows: "It was an industrial dictatorship without parallel–a dictatorship by force of necessity and common consent which step-by-step at least encompassed the Nation and united it into a coordinated and mobile whole."

He would also later say there was "a story of the conversion of a hundred million combatively individualistic people into a vast cooperative effort in which the good of the unit was sacrificed to the good of the whole." The government weakened the spirit of the people to resist government tyranny.

Under the War Industries Board, industrial production in the U.S. increased 20 percent. The War Industries Board was decommissioned by an executive order on January 1, 1919. With the war mobilization conducted under the supervision of the War Industries Board unprecedented fortunes fell upon war producers and certain holders of raw materials and patents. Hearings in 1934 by the Nye Committee led by U.S. Senator Gerald Nye were intended to hold war profiteers to account. Rationing and price-fixing characterized the wartime command economy. **Wilson himself was a major cause of the outbreak of World War II.**

It is a well-accepted fact that the extremely harsh and unfair terms of the Treaty of Versailles were the incipient cause of WW II. Wilson's Fourteen Points were fair and persuaded the Germans to surrender before the allies devastated Germany.

Wilson had the opportunity to make sure Europe did not take revenge on Germany, but he let is slip away.

He threw Germany to the dogs so he could have his worthless, utopian League of Nations. He deluded himself into thinking the League could make up for the other thirteen points.

This stab in the back of Germany would give rise to Hitler and allow him to rouse the German people to war a mere two decades or so later. Therefore, in a very real sense, Wilson is responsible for all the horrors of WW II.

Wilson took over the US economy, infringed on American civil liberties especially by suppressing dissent, oppressed the "unpatriotic," and purposefully sought to drag the US into war. He worshiped the power of the state, and such misuse of power is exactly what fascism is.

I don't think President George W. Bush is a fascist, but his Wilsonian idealism for spreading democracy should disturb any conservative. America was attacked on 9/11; no such thing happened during Wilson's presidency. The Patriot Act is no where near as harmful to civil liberties as Wilson's Sedition Act was. When people surrender their rights to the nation they are surrendering liberty.

Though the Democratic Party is largely dominated by anti-war people now even though Soviet communism and radical Islam have been actual threats to national security unlike the Kaiser's Germany, Wilson's fascism still remains with the party, especially with regard to economics and expanding the power of the federal government in general whenever possible.

This should not be surprising since fascism is a product of the Left, not the Right, side of the political spectrum.

Begin with his election in 1912. Wilson received barely forty percent of the popular vote, with the two Republicans (T.R., of course, as a Bull Moose) collecting sixty percent of the vote. But that understates Wilson's utter lack of any mandate. The vote that Wilson received came largely from the South, where blacks could not vote and where Republicans were a threatened group.

How much of a one party state was the South then? Consider that while Theodore Roosevelt in 1904 was receiving almost sixty percent of the national vote, in some states of the South T.R. received less than ten percent of the vote, even less than five percent of the vote.

Wilson almost immediately began undoing the good work of past Republican administrations on black civil rights. The Leftist notion that Republicans once supported black civil rights and then stopped is just patently false: Republicans, if anything, were more solicitous of black rights in the period from 1876 to 1920 than they had been before then. Blacks could, and did, serve as delegates to the Republican National Convention, as federal officers appointed by Republican presidents, and even as Republican congressmen.

Wilson resegregated the civil service. W.E.B. Dubois had broken ranks with other blacks to support a Democrat, rather than a Republican, in 1912. Dubois soon regretted his decision. Wilson reneged on his promise to create a national race commission something that his Republican successor, the ever maligned Warren Harding, would do.

Wilson's bigotry was not confined to blacks. He also loathed what he called Orientals. His two Republican predecessors had carefully intervened to prevent anti-Japanese legislation from being passed in West Coast states. They urged, properly, that slapping Japan - a growing industrial power that sought friendly relations with America - was a national security question.

Woodrow, however, made no such effort. As a result, the combination of strength and fairness which Theodore Roosevelt had used to improve relations with Japan. This was complemented by Taft - who was familiar with the Orient -, was all squandered by Wilson.

Even after the horror of the Great War when all decent people were grappling with ways to prevent another war, Wilson was destroying the possibility of bringing Japan into the company of western nations, a principal reason in the Second World War.

Japan in 1919 proposed to insert a reasonable clause inserted into the covenant of the League of Nations supporting the principle of racial equality.

Alternatives to the proposed clause were rejected as unsatisfactory by the Japanese. Japan, like America, had been one of the major allied powers.

They forced a vote, and President Wilson, chairman of the League of Nations Commission, again tried to avoid a vote. When it passed by a vote of eleven to six, Wilson claimed the amendment had failed since the vote was not unanimous.

Wilson ran for reelection in 1916, campaigning on the slogan "He Kept Us out of War." After he won and after he took his oath of office the second time, Wilson asked Congress to declare war on the Central Powers. In retrospect, we see Imperial Germany as a bad nation like Nazi Germany. Even though the comparison is ridiculous given that Imperial Germany was no less imperial than Imperial England or America for that matter. While Hitler represented a true monster loose on the entire world. But in the Great War, there was no moral high ground. If ever there was a war in which America needed to remain neutral, and use its wealth and good offices to provide a lasting peace, this was the war.

By entering the war, however, Wilson insured that Germans would view America as hostile to Germany. As a result, the ghastly Treaty of Versailles caused quiet rage in Germany, deep cynicism in Italy, indifference in Communist Russia, apathy in France, and alienation in Japan. The three totalitarianism systems of the Twentieth Century - Fascism, Communism, and National Socialism - each were helped mightily by Wilson's arrogance and ignorance.

Wilson, who thought himself indispensable to mankind, concealed his mental incapacity just when the future of the human race was being hammered out in the salons of Europe. He failed, utterly completely and totally. Even honorable progressives, like LaGuardia, had almost unbridled contempt for Woodrow Wilson.

Charles Evans Hughes, who would later serve as one of the best Chief Justices in American history, almost won the 1916 election. Indeed, if blacks in the South had been allowed to vote, Hughes would have won a landslide in the popular vote. Had Hughes won the presidency, a hundred million or so lives may have been saved because the ridiculous punishing Treaty of Versailles could have been watered down.

The Federal Reserve

What can be said about Wilson? One of the most damaging parts of his awful eight years happened at the beginning, when the Sixteenth Amendment was adopted, allowing a federal income tax. Rhode Island Senator Nelson Aldrich, the Republican leader in the Senate, headed a Commission personally, with the aid of a team of economists.

They went to Europe and were impressed at how well they believed the central banks in Britain and Germany handled stabilizing the overall economy and the promotion of international trade. Aldrich's investigation led to his plan in 1912 to bring central banking to the United States, with promises of financial stability, expanded international roles, control by fair experts and no political meddling in finance. Aldrich asserted that a central bank had to be decentralized somehow, or it would be attacked by local politicians and bankers as had the First and Second Banks of the United States. The Aldrich plan was introduced in Congress in 1912 and 1913, but never gained much traction as the Democrats in 1912 won control of the House and the Senate as well as the White House.

President, Woodrow Wilson, then became the principal mover for banking and currency reform in the 63rd Congress, working with the two chairs of the House and Senate Banking and Currency Committees, Rep. Carter Glass of Virginia and Sen. Robert L. Owen of Oklahoma.

William Jennings Bryan, now Secretary of State, longtime enemy of Wall Street and still a power in the Democratic Party, threatened to destroy the bill. Wilson masterfully came up with a compromise plan that pleased bankers and Bryan alike. The Bryanites were happy that Federal Reserve currency became liabilities of the government rather than of private banks and by terms for federal loans to farmers. The Bryanite demand to restrict interlocking directorates did not pass.

Wilson convinced the antibank Congressmen that because Federal Reserve notes were obligations of the government, the plan fit their demands. Wilson assured southerners and westerners the system was decentralized into 12 districts, and thus would weaken New York City's Wall Street influence and strengthen the hinterlands.

After much debate and many amendments Congress passed the Federal Reserve Act or Glass-Owen Act, as it was sometimes called at the time, in late 1913. President Wilson signed the Act into law on December 23, 1913.

The Fed's power developed slowly in part due to an understanding at its creation that it was to work primarily as a reserve. It was a money-creator of last resort to prevent the downward spiral of withdrawal of funds which characterizes a monetary panic. At the outbreak of World War I, the Fed was better positioned than the Treasury to issue war bonds, and so became the primary retailer for war bonds under the direction of the Treasury. After the war, the Fed, led by Paul Warburg and Benjamin Strong, convinced Congress to modify its powers, giving it the ability to both create money, as the 1913 Act intended, and destroy money, as a central bank could. As time progressed the power of the Fed became greater and greater.

During the 1920s, the Fed experimented with a number of approaches, alternatively creating and then destroying money which, in the eyes of many scholars notably Milton Friedman, helped create the late-1920s stock market bubble.

In 1928, Strong died, leaving a tremendous vacuum in Fed governance, from which did not recover in time to react to the 1929 collapse, unlike after 1987's Black Monday. Because of this power vacuum, the Fed adopted what most would consider a restrictive policy by today's standards, worsening the crash.

The Federal Reserve is the central banking system of the United States. It began in 1913 with enacting the Federal Reserve Act, largely in response to a series of financial panics, particularly a severe panic in 1907. Events such as the Great Depression were major reasons leading to changes in the system. Its duties today, according to official Federal Reserve documentation, are to conduct the nation's monetary policy, supervise and regulate banking institutions, preserve the stability of the financial system and provide financial services to depository institutions, the U.S. government, and foreign official institutions.

The Federal Reserve System's structure is composed of the presidentially appointed Board of Governors (or Federal Reserve Board), the Federal Open Market Committee (FOMC), twelve regional Federal Reserve Banks located in major cities throughout the nation, numerous privately owned U.S. member banks and various advisory councils.

The FOMC is the committee responsible for setting monetary policy and consists of all seven members of the Board of Governors and the twelve regional bank presidents, though only five bank presidents vote at any given time. The Federal Reserve has both private and public parts, and was designed to serve the interests of both the public and private bankers.

The result is a structure that is considered unique among central banks. It is also unusual in that an entity outside the central bank, namely the

United States Department of the Treasury, creates the currency used. If you're starting to ask yourself if the fox is guarding the henhouse, you're right it is.

According to the Board of Governors, the Federal Reserve is independent within government in that its decisions do not have to be approved by the President. No one else in the executive or legislative branch of government need to ratify either.

The government also exercises some control over the Federal Reserve by appointing and setting the salaries of the system's highest-level employees.

Considered a leading intellectual, with the degrees and background to prove it, Wilson's work was central to the intellectual and historical justification for the racist policies he set up in 1912. Wilson gave new life to violent racist organizations. So powerful were his words that they were used in *"The Birth of a Nation"* one of the earliest and most acclaimed motion pictures.

Wilson was also anti-immigrant, and had written much on the subject. In 1910, however, considering his political career, he integrated particular immigrants into the Democratic Party and the army.

His first term was spent blocking Women's rights and trying to keep America out of the First World War. Neither action strenuous. The major crisis of his time was sinking the Titanic. This was responded to by demanding extra lifeboats on all ships.

Wilson ran for reelection in 1916 on the platform; *"He kept us Out of War."* The election between Wilson and Charles Evans Hughes was close, and for several days, uncertain. The idea that Wilson was popular or the nation was behind him is a myth.

Wilson asked for a declaration of War on April 2, 1917, five months after beginning his second term. To gain soldiers, Woodrow Wilson imposed the Draft. Considering people voted for him on his antiwar platform there was opposition. Wilson pushed the *Espionage Act of 1917* and the *Sedition Act of 1918* through Congress to suppress anti-British, pro-German, and antiwar opinions. Provisions in the *Espionage Act* had U.S. Post Office refused to carry written materials that could be believed critical of the U. S. war effort. A number of newspapers were denied second-class mailing rights.

Wilson set up a propaganda office, *the United States Committee on Public Information.* This was the first overt use of propaganda by the American Government. When America entered WWI, it was almost over. America took credit for Victory though it had not participated in most of the battles.

An interesting aside, on American foreign policy 1914 - 1918; was the intervention by the United States in South America and the Caribbean, going so far to install Presidents in Haiti, Nicaragua and the Dominican Republic.

Wilson's view of himself as an almost Messianic figure arose after the War. He spent his last year's believing that what he stood for would come about. "You can't fight God!" He would say. Remarkably, Wilson received the Nobel Peace Prize in 1919. Wilson spoke for National women's suffrage, late in his Second term. It came after years of pressure, protest, and publicity. Far from being a supporter of Women's rights, he had been a barrier.

Wilson suffered a debilitating stroke in 1919 and his wife virtually became President. She decided who saw him, what matters were brought to his attention. What Wilson's incumbency can be credited with is enforcing segregation.

It inspired the Ku Klux Klan to resurgence, delaying women's suffrage, and the participation in the Treaty of Versailles which almost guaranteed World War II. History has been kind to Woodrow Wilson.

In summary it was Woodrow Wilson perhaps more than any other President who set the stage for Empire and began us down the road to disintegrating Republic. His views pointed a new ruling class toward a paternalism that mimicked fascism and socialism. None of the New Deal, Great Society or other wealth distribution programs would be possible without his fingerprints on them.

The Roaring Twenties

The 1920s era went by such names as the Jazz Age, the Age of Intolerance, and the Age of Wonderful Nonsense. Under any name the era embodied the beginning of modern America. Many Americans felt buoyed up following World War I in 1918.

America had survived a deadly worldwide influenza epidemic as well. The new decade of the roaring twenties would be a time of change for everyone, not all of it good.

The close of World War I saw the United States recede into an inward-looking stance. Despite President Woodrow Wilson's tyrannical efforts, the Senate refused to approve the Versailles Peace Treaty that ended World War I, and the U.S. failed to join the League of Nations. Early in the 1920s the U.S. raised tariffs on imported goods, and free immigration ended. Also women now had the right to vote and prohibition of alcohol became the law of the land. Government intrusion into the life of its citizens was on the rise as they would legislate the morality of taking a drink. The government also created the biggest black market for liquor in history as they helped bootleggers into business.

These unintended consequences would be just the beginning in a virtual parade of unintended consequences of paternalism and federal intervention into the lives of its citizens in the coming years.

Government spending has been out of control for so long, it's hard to imagine how big cuts in taxes and spending, actual cuts, not baseline cuts could ever be achieved. True, John F. Kennedy and Ronald Reagan achieved epic personal income tax cuts, but neither controlled spending, and both incurred budget shortfalls every year of their administrations. The federal government has incurred budget deficits more than 80% of the time since 1930, a period when the number of governmental functions increased dramatically.

Elected president in 1920, Warren G. Harding promoted a "return to normalcy," which signaled a resurgence of nativism, isolationism, and rejection of the progressive era's governmental activism. Overall, Harding's policies reflected a conservative, laissez-faire attitude.

Great success cutting both taxes and spending involved President Warren G. Harding who inherited one of the worst depressions in American history. It happened in 1921, after World War I as the government canceled orders for war materials.

Unemployment doubled, and wholesale prices plunged about one third. Harding shrewdly believed that if tough adjustments must be made, such from wartime economy to a peacetime economy the most humane policy is to get through the certain adjustments as fast as possible. Although the intent of bailouts and relief programs is to relieve misery, Harding recognized that such policies undermine incentives to adjust rapidly and can end prolonging misery.

Harding cut spending about 50%, he cut taxes about 40%, and he started paying down the debt. There were no bailouts, no "stimulus" programs, no entitlements, and no government employee unions, none of the things that made it difficult for later presidents to cut spending.

His administration was blighted by scandals, but most of them did not surface until following his death of a stroke in office in August 1923. One of the most notorious of them was the Teapot Dome Scandal, which appalled the public for years after Harding's death.

Calvin Coolidge was Harding's vice president (1921-23). When the presidency fell to his lot with Harding's death, he moved swiftly to sew up the 1924 nomination and mend the effects of the administration's scandals. Coolidge was elected handily over Democrat John W. Davis and Progressive Robert M. La Follette. He declined to run for reelection and in 1929 and left politics for good. Coolidge retired to live a life of quiet and as he faded to a distant memory so did any chance of a small government mind-set or at least one that didn't look to government for all the answers.

Such Coolidge administration policies as high tariffs and federal tax cuts were approved of during his four years, but they would become unpopular during the next decade. Having served as secretary of commerce under both Harding and Coolidge. So, during the 1920s, taxes and spending were cut 50%, and about 30% of the national debt was paid off. There were budget surpluses every year during the 1920s. Unemployment dropped to 1.8%, the lowest in more than a century.

Herbert Hoover was elected to the presidency in 1928, buoyed by the country's prosperity. His personal popularity suffered, however, when he vetoed the Veteran's Bonus proposal.

Hoover had been in office just a few months when the Great Depression began to carve its trough into the nation's economy. His early relief efforts were generally viewed to be inadequate. A banking crisis had seized the nation and in 1932, he lost the presidential election to Franklin D. Roosevelt.

The so-called Red Scares during the roaring twenties refer to the fear of Communism in the U.S. just before and during the 1920s. It is estimated there were 150,000 anarchists or Communists in the U.S. in 1920, but they made up only 0.1 percent of the general population. The highly publicized Sacco and Vanzetti Case showed what could happen to people who held radical views.

Amendment 18 to the Constitution (1919) had banned the manufacture, transport and sale of intoxicating liquor. Prohibitionists expected that Prohibition would relieve social problems and bolster the economy. However, many people disliked the law and imbibed in unlawful nightclubs called speakeasies. Gangsters took control of bootlegging and violent lawlessness erupted. Lacking public support, the federal government was almost unable to enforce Prohibition.

The roaring twenties ushered in a rich period of American writing, distinguished by the works of such authors as Sinclair Lewis, Willa Cather, William Faulkner, F. Scott Fitzgerald, Carl Sandburg and Ernest Hemingway.

A uniquely American music form, whose roots lay in African expression, came to be known as jazz. The Jazz Age produced such greats as Louis Armstrong, Duke Ellington and Fletcher Henderson. George Gershwin, Cole Porter and others would bring jazz influences to Broadway and the concert hall. Bessie Smith hallowed the Blues on a sound recording.

Charlie Chaplin and Rudolph Valentino were movie box office draws. Walt Disney would produce his first cartoon, Alice's Wonderland. The lush, ornate style of Art Deco architecture, art, clothing, hairstyles, decor and furnishings flourished in the 1920s.

At the beginning of the roaring twenties, the United States was converting from a war time to peacetime economy. When weapons for World War I were no longer needed, there was a temporary stall in the economy. After a few years, the country prospered. In this decade, America became the richest nation on Earth and a culture of consumerism was born. It was the time of the $5 workday, good worker pay for those days. People spent money for better roads, tourism, and holiday resorts. Real estate booms, most notably in Florida, sent land prices soaring. Technology played a vital part in delivering the economic and cultural good times that most of America enjoyed during the 1920s. Henry Ford blazed the way with his Model T; he sold more 15 million of them by 1927. Ford's assembly line means of production was the key. The automobile's popularity and construction of roads and highways. Pouring fresh public funds into the economy brought tremendous economic prosperity during the roaring twenties.

The radio found its way into almost every home in America. Following the first public station, KDKA, in Pittsburgh, thousands more went on the air across the country. Radio became a national pastime; many listeners would gather in their living rooms to tune in sports, concerts, sermons, and "Red Menace" news.

The year 1922 introduced the first movie made with sound, The Jazz Singer, starring Al Jolson. And in 1926, the arrival of Technicolor made movies more entertaining and memorable. Thus, the movie industry became a major part of American industry in general.

Charles A. Lindbergh's pioneering flight across the Atlantic Ocean in the Spirit of St. Louis in 1927 did much to stimulate the young aviation industry. Canned foods, ready-made clothing and household appliances freed women from much household drudgery. The influence of Ford's methods of mass production and efficiency enabled other industries to produce a huge variety of consumer appliances.

However, not everyone benefited from technology. The number of people living and working on farms reached its peak at well over 32 million back in 1916.

Most of the farms were fairly small operations. New technology in the roaring twenties introduced a number of impacts on the American farm. The use of machinery increased productivity, while decreasing the demand for manual laborers.

While productivity increased, the nation's demand for food remained rather steady. As a result, food prices and profits dropped. Machinery was costly. The small farmer was no longer able to cope because he lacked the capital to buy the equipment. At the same time, the decade's industrial boom lured many workers off the farm to the cities.

Small farms lost their viability, and many farmers were compelled to merge to compete. The lasting effect would be larger, but fewer farms.

The year 1920 was a historic watershed. For the first time in the United States, more people were living in cities than on farms. Science, medicine and health advanced remarkably during the roaring twenties. Albert Einstein was awarded the Nobel Prize in physics in 1921. Diphtheria became better controlled in 1923 by newly introduced immunization.

It seemed as though Dow Jones Industrial Stock Index would never quit increasing. Stock speculation went sky-high in the bull market of 1928-1929. No one suspected that a signal of the end would occur on October 24, 1929, with the infamous stock market crash, and that more than a decade of depression and despair would follow such an era of happiness and prosperity. Until that time, American life seemed fundamentally sound. The typical American was still hardworking and sensible. The coming storms lay unseen beyond the horizon as the twenties roared on.

World War I may not have made the world safe for democracy, but it did help to lay the groundwork for a decade of American economic expansion. The 1920s saw the growth of the culture of consumerism—many Americans began to work fewer hours, earn higher salaries, invest in the stock market, and buy everything from washing machines to Model T Fords. The culture of consumerism of the 1920s changed the politics of American society and set the tone for American attitudes about money in coming decades.

The new role that technology would play in shaping the economy of the 1920s was powerful and compelling. The culture of the 1920s was broadening and changing. The relationship between big business and government grew during the 1920s compared to that of the Gilded Age. The nation's lasting love affair with the automobile and its' affect on American society by helping to create a monster for the American economy.

The decade of the 1920s was marked by prosperity and new opportunity in the aftermath of World War I. The war began in Europe in 1914, and the United States entered the fray in 1917. A significant reason for United States involvement in the war was the nation's economic links to the Allied Powers, and especially to Great Britain. Wall Street financial institutions such as the House of Morgan had given loans to Great Britain totaling over $2.3 billion. As a result, Wall Street feared a British defeat even more than Main Street.

The transition from a war-time to a peacetime economy caused economic dislocation for industrial workers, loss of income for farmers, and renewed racism and nativism against African-Americans and foreign immigrants. Many Americans, however, reveled in the new culture of consumerism.

In search of prosperity, Americans elected three Republican Presidents during this decade. Each of these men promised to promote the politics of prosperity: **Warren G. Harding** (1865-1923). Elected to the Presidency in the 1920s, Harding urged a "return to normalcy." The policies of his administration were conservative, especially about taxes, tariffs, immigration control, labor rights, and business regulation. Harding's administration was marked by corruption and scandal, although most of the scandals did not become public knowledge until after he died of a stroke in office in August 1923.

Calvin Coolidge (1872-1933). Coolidge did little as Warren G. Harding's vice president (1921-23), but when he assumed the presidency after Harding's death, he acted quickly to repair the damage of the Harding administrations scandals and to secure the 1924 presidential nomination.

He was easily elected over Democrat John W. Davis and Progressive Robert M. La Follette. Near the end of his second term, Coolidge decided not to run for president again and retired from politics. Many of Coolidge's policies, including federal tax cuts and high tariffs, were popular during his tenure as president, but lost favor during the Great Depression.

Herbert Hoover (1874-1964). Having served as secretary of commerce under Harding and Coolidge, Hoover was elected to the presidency in 1928, helped by the prevailing prosperity in the country. Hoover had been in office just a few months when the Great Depression began.

In 1932, he lost the presidential election to Franklin D. Roosevelt. On the whole, the United States economy experienced steady growth and expansion during the 1920s. Three reasons fueled this economic growth: Machines, Factories and the process of Mass Production.

As scientific management and new technology increased worker productivity, workers earned higher wages and became better consumers. A new innovation appeared: the installment plan, which encouraged Americans to build up debt to buy consumer goods.

In various ways, Americans wanted to get rich, and to do so with little effort. Thorstein Veblen, an economist, published *The Theory of the Leisure Class* in 1898. The book reached a wide American audience during the 1920s because it spoke directly to the psychology of American consumption. Veblen, in fact, introduced the now-familiar term "conspicuous consumption," which seemed to embody the cultural mind-set of post World War I America.

Radio, the first commercial radio station went on the air in the 1920s in Pittsburgh, while the first public radio station opened on the campus of the University of Wisconsin. By 1922, 3 million American households had radios, and buys of receivers had increased by 2,500%, giving the industry annual sales of S850 million by 1929. **Motion pictures,** A fledgling industry before World War I, motion picture production became one of the ten largest industries in the United States during the 1920s.

In 1922, theaters sold 40 million tickets a week. By 1929, that number had grown to 100 million a week. One of the capitalists who cashed in on Hollywood was Joseph P. Kennedy, patriarch of the Kennedy's, one of the nation's most influential political families. During eight months in Hollywood, he made $6 million.

The Automobile industry nowhere was the psychology of consumption more obvious than in the automobile industry. Annual automobile production rose from 2 million during the 1920s to 5.5 million in 1929. By the late 1920s, there was one automobile for every five Americans, allowing, theoretically, for every person in the United States to be on the road at the same time.

Henry Ford (1863-1947) was the chief figure in this expanding industry. Ford did not invent the automobile, but he did the most to promote the car by developing more efficient and cheaper means of production. He built his first car in his garage in 1896. Symbolic of the American century to come, the door of the shed was too small and he had to remove bricks to make way for the car.

The automobile had a huge impact on American life, both economic and social. It also **promoted growth of other industries,** especially petroleum, rubber, and steel. These industries **helped fuel creating a national system of highways.** Automobiles needed better roads. After WWI, federal funds became available for building highways and a major industry was born. **Created new service facilities.** Filling stations, garages, and roadside restaurants sprang up across the nation. Motels (the word itself is a blend of 'motor' and 'hotel') catering to the needs of motorists began to replace hotels.

Social Affects of the Automobile were many as well. Cars broke down the distinctions between urban and rural America.

With the automobile came the new tradition of the "Sunday drive," and many city folks got their first chance to tour the rural countryside. Rural Americans, on the other hand, drove into cities to shop and to be entertained. Now it was far easier for individual family members to go their own way. Children could escape parental supervision as cars became a sort of "bedroom on wheels."

Many Americans began to equate prosperity with progress. Relationships between businessmen and government had never been closer than they were in the 1920s. Calvin "Silent Cal" Coolidge piped up: "Wealth is the chief end of man!" and "The man, who builds a factory, builds a temple. The man, who works there, worships there." "The American Way"

Businessmen had two major propaganda mills: the Chamber of Commerce and the National Association of Manufacturers. Both groups preached a return to laissez-faire economics, less government regulation of business, and less government support for labor unions. The National Association of Manufacturers labeled this program, "The American Way." President Harding spoke for himself and for his successors, Coolidge and Hoover, when he asked for "less government in business and more business in government."

There were ways in which the federal government supported big business. High tariff policies were one-way. The Fordney-McCumber Act (1922) and the Hawley-Smoot Act (1930) created the highest-ever schedule of tariffs for foreign-made goods. **Andrew Mellon,** Secretary of the Treasury from 1921 to 1932 oversaw much of this transition.

In response to his demands, Congress repealed the excess profits tax and reduced the rates for corporate and personal income taxes. Mellon provided business leaders with a list of tax loopholes which the IRS had drawn up at Mellon's request large **cutbacks in the Federal Trade Commission (FTC).**

In immigration during the period 1917 - 1924: A series of laws were enacted to further limit the number of new immigrants. These laws set up the quota system and imposed passport requirements. They expanded the categories of excludable aliens and banned all Asians except Japanese. 1924 Act: Reduced the number of US immigration visas and shared them based on national origin. In 1921, the Congress passed the Emergency Quota Act, followed by the Immigration Act of 1924. The 1924 Act was aimed at further restricting the Southern and Eastern Europeans, especially Jews, Italians, and Slavs, who had begun to enter the country in large numbers beginning in the 1890s.

In 1921, Congress sought to protect local agriculture as opposed to industry by passing the Emergency Tariff. The tariff increased rates on wheat, sugar, meat, wool and other agricultural products brought into the United States. This placed a burden on foreign nations, which provided protection for domestic producers of those items.

However, one year later Congress passed another tariff, the Fordney-McCumber Tariff, which applied the scientific tariff and the American Selling Price.

The purpose of the scientific tariff was to equalize production costs among countries so no country could undercut the prices charged by American companies. The difference of production costs was calculated by the Tariff Commission.

A second novelty was the American Selling Price. This allowed the president to calculate the duty based on the price of the American price of a good, not the imported good. By 1918, the top rate of the income tax was increased to 77 percent (on income over $1,000,000) to finance World War I. The top marginal tax rate was reduced to 58 percent in 1922, to 25 percent in 1925 and finally to 24 percent in 1929.

Chapter 3 – Dawn of The Nanny State

The Depression

The 1920s "boom" enriched only a fraction of the American people. Earnings for farmers and industrial workers stagnated or fell. While this represented lower production costs for companies, it also precluded growth in consumer demand. Thus, by the mid 1920s the ability of most Americans to buy new automobiles, new houses and other durable goods was beginning to weaken. This weakening demand was masked, however, by the "great bull market" in stocks on the New York Stock Exchange. The ever-growing price for stocks was, in part, the result of greater wealth concentration within the investor class. Eventually the Wall Street stock exchange began to take on a dangerous aura of invincibility, leading investors to ignore less optimistic signs in the economy. Over-investment and speculating in stocks further inflated their prices, contributing to the illusion of a robust economy.

The important point came in the 1920s when banks began to loan money to stock-buyers since stocks were the hottest commodity in the marketplace. Banks allowed Wall Street investors to use the stocks themselves as collateral. If the stocks dropped in value, and investors could not repay the banks, the banks would be left holding near-worthless collateral. Banks would then go broke, pulling productive businesses down with them as they called in loans and foreclosed mortgages in a desperate attempt to stay afloat.

But that doomsday scenario was laughed off by analysts and politicians who argued the U.S. stock market had entered a "New Era" where stock values and prices would always go up. That, of course, did not happen. Stock prices were seriously overpriced when measured in the productivity of the companies they represented making a market "correction" certain.

In October 1929 the New York Stock Exchange's house of cards collapsed in the greatest market crash seen up to that time. Students are often surprised to learn the stock market crash itself did not cause the rest of the economy to collapse. But, because American banks had loaned so heavily for stock purchases, falling stock prices began endangering local banks whose stock-buying borrowers began defaulting on their loans.

Banks are the pumping stations or hearts of the capitalist organism. Not only do banks circulate money, they create new money through making loans. Bank-created credit represents the most elastic element in the supply of money.

As hundreds then thousands of banks failed between 1929 and 1933, the economy's credit and, thus, money supply began to dry up. Also, as banks went down, they often took local businesses with them as they called in business loans in a desperate effort to stay afloat. All of this rippled outward in ever-widening circles of bankruptcies, job layoffs and curtailed consumption.

During the worst years of the Depression, 1933-34, the overall jobless rate was twenty-five percent with another twenty-five percent of breadwinners having their wages and hours cut. Effectively, then, almost one out of every two U.S. households directly experienced unemployment or underemployment. For workers' families already facing hard times, the Depression's unemployment woes wreaked unprecedented, catastrophic havoc.

Scholars view the Depression and New Deal differently depending on their own ideological perspective. Conservative historians place a high value on the ideal of *laissez-faire*. Thus, the Depression was simply a painful but necessary market correction which would have corrected itself if left alone. To conservatives, small government means maximum freedom; and, the New Deal means the beginnings of an irresponsible and/or over-regulatory welfare state.

The overriding theme of the Great Depression that speaks more loudly than anything else is government involvement.

During the major financial panics that filled American life from over the prior 125 years or so the federal government was never thought to be the answer to these problems.

In fact most of the time it was the leaders of business and finance who came to the government with solutions and suggestions. However now as people looked more to their government as they were well encouraged to do by the new emerging ruling class.

This new dynamic was taking hold even in the Conservative administration of Herbert Hoover. Even Hoover seemed to be giving in to the ruling class ideas that would eventually lead to the New Deal.

During the Depression, life was difficult for farmers, but it wasn't much better in the cities, where fourteen million people lived-in crowded, unheated, unsanitary tenements. In a letter to Harry Hopkins, the director of the Civil Works Administration, Martha Gellhorn described the unemployed workers and their families:

"This picture is so grim that whatever words I use will seem hysterical and exaggerated. And I find them all in the same shape - fear, fear driving them into a state of semi-collapse cracking nerves; and an overpowering terror of the future....

They can't pay rent and are evicted. They are watching their children grow thinner and thinner; fearing the cold for children who have neither coats nor shoes; wondering about coal."

As the Depression deepened, cities attracted beaten people from all parts of the country. Farmers whose livelihoods had been foreclosed packed up their families and moved into the cities. Hoboes and other itinerants sought shelter in cities during harsh winters. City dwellers themselves were not immune to the rails of the nation.

Thousands of unemployed residents who could not pay their rent or mortgages were evicted into public assistance and bread lines. At the peak of the Depression, seventeen thousand families were put out on the street each month. Although residents were given priority over newcomers for local aid, there were too many other residents standing in the same lines waiting for a check or a bowl of soup.

Municipal resources were overwhelmed quickly, and city agencies resorted to thinning relief payments to below the cost of living and watering down the soup to help more people over a longer time.

Many cities just ran out of money and were even forced to pay city employees in scrip a temporary voucher, redeemable for food and other products. At the height of the Depression Chicago had half a million unemployed, and in New York the jobless figure topped a million. With so many taxpayers both jobless and homeless, American cities lost a major source of income. Relief budgets meant to last a year were spent in several months.

At President Hoover's calling, charities had stepped in to help ease the load on municipal resources. Hoover was a firm believer in volunteerism.

Feeling that each community was responsible for aiding people in distress, Hoover created programs that bolstered morale and encouraged charity.

But the charities were themselves in trouble because they depended on contributions from a public who could not give any more. In many cities philanthropic groups of businessmen mounted relief drives, but the funds collected dwindled quickly as conditions worsened. So President Hoover used federal funds to help to support private charity.

Crowded living conditions were not uncommon in the working-class home. Extended families were formed who shared the same space, food costs, rent, and even bedding: the "hotbed- was a living arrangement in which night workers slept during the day and day workers used the same beds at night. Furnishings in working-class apartments were sparse. There were a few chairs, tables, and boxes that served as dressers.

There was rarely any carpeting, and not all homes had hot water. In older buildings heat was pro- vided through coal grates, which forced ten- ants to scour the neighborhood for coal or other fuel. Many people planted subsistence gardens in vacant lots or rooftops to feed themselves when grocery money was scarce.

When they could no longer pay the rent and were evicted from their apartments, city dwellers used scraps of lumber and cardboard boxes to build shacks that they could live in. These new shantytowns on the edges of the cities were called Hoovervilles, for President Herbert Hoover, since many blamed him for causing the depression.

In public parks, homeless men slept on benches, covering their bodies with "Hoover blankets," or newspapers. "Hoover hogs" were jackrabbits or gophers caught and cooked to replace the traditional Sunday ham. "Hoover villas" were public latrines used for overnight stays.

Hoovervilles had no electricity or running water but were usually built near rivers or fireplugs. They were not supported by the city or government in any way, so moving into such an encampment required no registration or security deposit. Prospective residents simply looked around and picked a spot. City dumps, construction sites, and trash bins pro- vided materials for building shelters. The gutted husks of old cars made acceptable homes, as did stacks of fruit boxes and worn tires. If a shelter was built well enough, a resident could sell it. There was always turnover, since people continually came and went. A good prebuilt home could easily be worth as much as $50. Despite zoning violations and health hazards, many Hoovervilles were allowed to exist. Some cities even lent tracts of public land for cultivating small gardens.

By 1933 millions of Americans we'll never know how many were desperate. Out of work and with his family depending on him, the breadwinner, the patriarch, the father and husband bore the brunt of the despair. When he couldn't provide for his family, he felt ashamed and humiliated. Many of these men abandoned their families and became what one has called "a generation of wanderers," vagabonds, or hobos. Unable to find work and because each job they applied for had hundreds of seekers, these shabby, disillusioned men wandered aimlessly without funds. They began begging, picking over refuse in city dumps, and finally getting up the courage to stand and be seen publicly - in a breadline for free food. To accommodate these shamed, idle, and malnourished masses, charities, missions, and churches began programs to feed them.

Bread lines often formed as early as 4 a.m. on cold wintry days when men lined up six across to wait as long as two to three hours before they could sit down inside a soup kitchen and share of the meager fare offered. In January 1931, 82 bread lines in New York City served 85,000 "meals" daily! Men who experienced the waiting in line recall the personal shame of asking for a handout, unable to care for oneself or to provide for others. Most men found it difficult to look into the eyes of other men in line, who, if asked, had similar stories to tell.

In 1929, Yale University economist Irving Fisher stated confidently: "The nation is marching along a permanently high plateau of prosperity." Five days later, the bottom dropped out of the stock market and ushered in the Great Depression, the worst economic downturn in American history. Although Americans often believe the Crash was the starting point of the Great Depression, many historians point out that it wasn't the sole cause.

Americans were so confident in the stock market in the years leading up to the Great Depression because they were following the lead of the rich. The Psychology of Consumption shaped the causes and affects of the Crash itself. The stock market investing change during the 1920s was one that was suddenly open to the common man. Average people were in the market and many creative investors were paying for their stock purchases in a risky method of borrowing called margin buying. By 1929, much of the money that was invested in the stock market did not actually exist. It was leveraged from investors buying using borrowed funds called buying on margin. It had become a Vegas style casino like culture.

When Americans elected Herbert Hoover President in 1928, the mood of the public was one of optimism and confidence in the United States economy. Most people believed that national prosperity would continue indefinitely.

In his acceptance speech for the Republican Party nomination for the presidency, Hoover had said: "We in America today are nearer to the final triumph over poverty than ever before in the history of any land. The poorhouse is vanishing from among us."

Many Americans shared Hoover's optimism at the beginning of 1929. An editorial in the New Year's edition of the New York Times on January 1, 1929, for example, stated: "It has been twelve months of unprecedented advance, of wonderful prosperity. If there is any way of judging the future by the past, this new year will be one of felicitation and hopefulness."

That same year, John Jacob Raskob, Chief Executive of General Motors and head of the Democratic National Committee, published an article entitled "Everybody Ought to be Rich" in the *Ladies Home Journal*. Raskob suggested that every American could become wealthy by investing $15 a week in common stocks. He failed to realize, however, the weekly salary of the average American worker was between $17 and $22, but that's not important: the optimism was there.

For five years before 1929, rising prices typified the stock market. During this period, American investors enjoyed an enormous "bull market." The opposite, a market characterized by falling prices, is called a "bear market."

Americans invested in the stock market for six reasons during the 1920s:

Rising stock dividends meant that new investors entering the market, many who viewed it as an easy way to get rich quick, helped inflate stock prices. Economic historians, however, estimate that a relatively small number of Americans—about 4 million—had investments in the market at any one time. Yet, the constant influx of new investors coming in and old investors moving out ensured that new money was always floating around. **An increase in personal savings from h**igher wages meant that even average Americans now had surplus money to put into savings or invest in the stock market. There was also an **easy money policy.** Now, banks made money more readily available at lower interest rates to more and more people. Although economists debate the actual influence of this phenomenon on the stock market, it's conceivable that many people took out loans not only to buy cars, but also to buy stock.

Companies invested their over-production profits in new production. From 1925 on, industry was overproducing. In expectation of eventually selling the surplus, business leaders funneled their profits right back into industry.

They invested in factories and new machinery, and hired more workers, which, in turn, fueled even greater overproduction. This increased production gave the companies an aura of financial soundness, which encouraged Americans to buy more stock.

Now, there were no effective legal guidelines on buying and selling stock. Free from such limits, corporations began printing up more and more common stock. Many investors in the stock market practiced "buying on margin," that is, buying stock on credit.

Confident that a given stock's value would rise, an investor put a down payment on the stock, expecting in a few months to pay off the balance of their initial investment while reaping a hefty profit. This investment strategy turned the stock market into a speculative pyramid game, in which most of the money invested in the market didn't exist. The Psychology of Consumption fed the optimism of investors and gave them unquestioning faith in prosperity. When the Crash did come, it was even more devastating because of this unquestioned faith.

Most economists of the 1920s believed the stock market—not housing starts, sales of durable goods, or the financial health of banks—was the chief indicator of the fiscal health of the United States. In September of 1929, stock prices began to fluctuate, but market analysts dismissed this as temporary. What many of these analysts did not realize—or refused to admit—however, was that stock prices were out of proportion to actual profits. Sales of goods and the construction of factories were falling rapidly while stock values continued to climb. Still, very few were worried; they still accepted Adam Smith's "self-adjusting economy" as dogma and believed the problems would correct themselves.

Historians refer to October 24, 1929 as "Black Thursday." On this day, people began dumping their stocks as quickly as they could. Sell orders inundated market exchanges and the bull market suddenly shifted to a bear market. By that evening, J.P. Morgan and other financiers bought up stock to stop the panic and keep the market afloat. On Friday, October 25, the House of Morgan continued to keep the market stable and it seemed the panic was over. Yet, many investors began to worry during the weekend. George and Martha and thousands of their friends decided to sell whatever stock they still had as soon as the market opened on Monday. As a result, on Monday, October 28, there was another wave of sell orders. The next day, October 29, 1929, "Black Tuesday," was the beginning of the Great Crash.

"Black Tuesday" was the single most devastating financial day in the history of the New York Stock Exchange. Within the first few hours the stock market was open; prices collapsed and wiped out all the financial gains of the previous year.

Since most Americans viewed the stock market as the chief indicator of the health of the American economy, the Great Crash shattered public confidence. Between October 29 and November 13, the day when stock prices hit their lowest point, over $30 billion disappeared from the American economy. This amount was comparable to the total amount of money the federal government had spent to fight the First World War.

Still, optimism persisted and many leaders declared the worst was over. J. D. Rockefeller said: "These are days when many are discouraged. In the 93 years of my life, depressions have come and gone. Prosperity has always returned and will again."

Such optimism, however, did not last long. Popular songs of the day mirrored the transition from optimism to despair. In 1930, people sang "Happy Days Are Here Again" and the national income dropped from $87 billion to $75 billion.

In 1931, more dejectedly, people sang "I've Got Five Dollars" and the nation's income dropped to $59 billion. The song of 1932 was "Brother, Can You Spare a Dime," when the domestic economy fell to $42 billion. Eventually, the American economy bottomed out at $40 billion in 1933.

So as not to alarm the public President Hoover chose his words carefully when he discussed the state of the economy in 1929. American economists and politicians had referred to previous economic downturns as "Panics," such as the "Panic of 1873" and the "Panic of 1893." Hoover, however, called this latest downturn a "Depression" rather than a "Panic," and the name stuck. Of course, America was not alone in the Great Depression; it struck all the industrialized nations of the world, including Germany, Britain, and France. Moreover, Germany still had huge reparation payments to make to the Allies in the aftermath of WWI. These reparation payments fueled spiraling inflation in Germany and crippled that nation's economy. The Allies themselves had borrowed money from the United States during the war, could not pay it all back during the 1920s, and were now not only broke, but in debt.

Farmers armed with guns and pitchforks marched on the local banks to prevent foreclosures. "The Bonus Expeditionary Force." A group of WWI veterans who had been denied their pensions organized the first march on Washington in protest.

In 1932, twenty thousand men set up a tent city, vowing to stay until they got their money. President Hoover overreacted and sent in the army (led by future war heroes Douglas MacArthur and Dwight D. Eisenhower to break up this peaceful demonstration.

The Great Depression hit farmers especially hard. Many had gone into debt to buy machinery and land, and now could not make their payments. Low crop prices wiped out potential profits. In addition to the usual challenges of agriculture, a great drought took place in 1931 and 1932 in the Midwest and the South and turned much of the trans-Mississippi West into a dust bowl. Nevertheless, if farmers couldn't make a profit selling their products, at least they could still eat, so most stayed put. In contrast to popular images of farmers leaving the land, the 1930s actually had the lowest rate of migration from farms to cities.

One-third of Americans were below the poverty line, yet some industries managed to make a profit at the beginning of the 1930s as the public looked for a way to escape.

If Americans couldn't find work, at least they could go for a drive, have a cigarette, or go to a movie. Similarly, sales of oil, gas, cigarettes, and movie tickets all went up.

Humorist Will Rogers remarked, "We're the first nation in the history of the world to go to the poorhouse in an automobile."

However, the Crash was not the immediate cause of the Depression. It alone was not responsible for a decade of worldwide economic catastrophe. But what was responsible for the Depression? And what were the long-term consequences of the Great Depression in the United States?

The Depression itself was responsible for a dramatic transformation in the structure of American politics, for a change in Americans' expectations about government, and for a shift in United States foreign policy during the 1930s.

President Herbert Hoover resisted calls for government intervention for individuals. He reiterated his belief that if left alone the economy would right itself and argued that direct government help to individuals would weaken the moral fiber of the American people. Hoover further believed that during hard times the government should adopt austerity measures, that is, cut spending even further.

Forced by Congress to intervene, Hoover did so reluctantly, concerned about both unbalancing the federal budget, and, even more importantly, violating his *laissez-faire* principles.

Hoover's efforts consisted of spending to stabilize the business community, believing that returning prosperity would eventually "trickle down" to the poor majority. The poor majority proved unwilling to wait. Branded by his many detractors as cold and uncaring, Hoover was easily defeated in the presidential election of 1932 by Democrat Franklin D. Roosevelt.

Roosevelt remained vague on the campaign trail, promising only that under his presidency government would act decisively to end the Depression.

Once in office, FDR said yes to almost every plan put forward by advisors and the Congress said yes to almost every program proposed by the president. In the frantically-paced first few months of his administration, Congress passed scores of new legislation at the president's request.

Historians categorize these efforts as either measures for "relief" short-term programs designed to alleviate immediate suffering. Recovery long-term programs to strengthen the economy back to its pre-crash level. Reform permanent structures meant to prevent future depressions.

Another way of understanding FDR's Depression-fighting efforts is to analyze the politics of the New Deal. Generally speaking, the overall aim of the New Deal was essentially conservative. The New Deal sought to save capitalism and the fundamental institutions of American society from the disaster of the Great Depression.

Within that framework, however, significant differences between New Deal programs existed. The "first" New Deal (1933-35) tended toward a continuation of "trickle down" policies, although better-funded and executed more creatively. Even in the early first New Deal, exceptional programs pointed toward the "second" New Deal's tendency toward "Keynesian" economic policies of revitalizing a mass-consumption based economy by revitalizing the masses ability to consume.

English economist John Maynard Keynes sought both to explain why depressions occurred and what might be done to prevent them. Simply put, he thought government should use its massive financial power (taxing and spending) as a sort of ballast to stabilize the economy. Depressions, then, should be attacked with increased government spending at the bottom of the income pyramid. This position is the opposite of "trickle down." Keynesian economists call this "countercyclical demand management," believing the government's massive financial impact can be used as a counterweight to current market forces.

Born August 10, 1874 in West Branch, Iowa, and Herbert "Bert" Hoover was the middle of three children whose parents were Quakers. In 1908, Herbert Hoover started his own engineering business.

His company specialized in reorganizing failing companies, hunting for new mining prospects, and finding investors to pay for developing the best mines. Hoover's consulting firm employed 175,000 workers all over the world, with offices in England, France, Russia, San Francisco and New York City. He soon became known as the "Great Engineer."

Already a multimillionaire in his early thirties, Herbert Hoover became interested in public service. In 1914, he put other men in charge of his mining business and gave all his time to Belgian relief during World War I. In May 1917, President Woodrow Wilson asked Hoover to come to Washington, D.C., to serve as his wartime food administrator, which, once he accepted the position, Hoover insisted on doing without any salary. With World War I in full swing, the U.S. would have to find enough food to feed itself and its European allies for a longtime. Herbert Hoover urged American households to conserve food, and in so doing, more food was made available to send overseas. Even after the war was over in November 1918, Europe's need for food was as pressing as when the war was still being fought. The war had left European nations without enough food to last the winter. Hoover organized shipment of food for millions of starving people in central Europe, and even extended aid into Soviet Russia in 1921.

For his efforts, he became an important wartime adviser to President Woodrow Wilson, who made Hoover a part of the American delegation to the conference of the Treaty of Versailles.

Herbert Hoover served as secretary of commerce for seven years, under presidents Harding and Coolidge, and became the Republican presidential nominee in 1928.

He was elected by an overwhelming majority. During his first few months as president, Hoover pushed Congress to set aside money for national park land, to reform prisons, and provide better education on American Indian reservations. He also urged Congress to pass the Agricultural Marketing Act, which helped farmers set up cooperatives, control surpluses, and keep the food supply steady.

After just eight months in office, on October 29, 1929, the stock market crashed, fueling a growing depression that became the most severe economic crisis the United States had ever known. Second only to the Civil War as the greatest domestic crisis in the nation's history.

After the crash, Herbert Hoover ordered federal departments to speed up construction projects, cut $160 million in taxes, and doubled the amount spent on public works. By 1933, one-fourth of the nation's workers were unemployed. Besides the high unemployment, the American economy experienced slow economic growth and financial instability. Hoover was criticized for his refusal to authorize large-scale relief programs that might have eased the nation's suffering and hunger, his unwillingness to use a significant amount of federal dollars to stimulate the nation's economy, and his failure to recognize the all-encompassing nature of the Great Depression.

Perhaps the most politically damaging event of Hoover's presidency was the Bonus March, staged by World War I veterans in 1932. Several years earlier, Congress had passed the Soldiers' Bonus Act, which granted veterans Adjusted Compensation Certificates, payable in 1945. In May 1932, the "Bonus Army" converged on the capitol to urge early redemption for the certificates.

More than 17,000 desperate veterans gathered in Washington to force passage of the bill. Herbert Hoover had already made generous provisions for veterans and felt the bill was a huge expense that wouldn't help the countries most needy. In July, the Bonus Bill was defeated in the Senate, although the government offered to pay the fare home for each veteran.

Thousands accepted the offer, but thousands more remained encamped across the Potomac from central Washington in a ramshackle shantytown, dubbed "Hoover Ville." Although the Bonus Army had behaved remarkably peacefully, the police were called in to evict the veterans. A riot broke out and Hoover ordered that federal troops be dispatched to contain the veterans.

The commanding general, Douglas MacArthur, did much more than "contain", however, and ordered the use of tear gas, tanks, and bayonets, and commanded soldiers to set fire to the veterans' shacks. Several veterans and even an infant were killed in the chaos. Herbert Hoover never publicly criticized the general for his excessive conduct, and thus the American people blamed the president as well as MacArthur.

Herbert Hoover was defeated by Franklin D. Roosevelt in the Election of 1932. Only six of the 48 states voted for Hoover. Hoover and Roosevelt did not get along. Hoover strongly opposed Roosevelt's New Deal legislation, in which the federal government assumed responsibility for the welfare of the nation by maintaining a high-level of economic activity - providing for the unemployed and elderly, prohibiting anti-social business practices, protecting natural resources, and developing the Tennessee Valley and other largely undeveloped regions. Roosevelt never consulted Hoover, nor did he involve him in government in any way during his presidential term.

For all of his humanitarian efforts, Hoover is still seen by many as the most unpopular president in American history. The public, and especially the Democratic Party, blamed Hoover for the Great Depression. He was so unpopular in fact, that 1936 presidential nominee Alfred M. Landon did not even want Hoover to give speeches in his behalf. Few Republicans wanted Hoover involved in party politics because of his negative image in the popular mind.

The Great Depression was the beginning of a new story in the history of our Republic. It was the beginning of people looking to the federal government for solutions.

It was the beginning of a ruling class that would decide for its citizens what was best for them. In short it was the beginning of the end of true liberty for Americans.

The New Deal

The New Deal was a series of economic programs set up in the United States between 1933 and 1936. They were passed by Congress during the first term of President Franklin D. Roosevelt. The programs were responses to the Great Depression, and focused on what historians call the "3 Rs": Relief, Recovery, and Reform.

That is, Relief for the unemployed and poor; Recovery of the economy to normal levels; and Reform of the financial system to prevent a repeat depression. The New Deal produced a political realignment, making the Democrat Party the majority.

The Democrat party held the White House for seven out of nine Presidential terms from 1933 to 1969. With its base in liberal ideas, big city machines, and newly empowered labor unions, ethnic minorities, and the white South the Democrat Party knew their customers well. The Republicans were split, either opposing the entire New Deal as an enemy of business and growth, or accepting some of it and promising to make it more efficient.

Historians distinguish a "First New Deal" (1933) and a "Second New Deal" (1934–36). Some programs were declared unconstitutional, and others were repealed during World War II. The "First New Deal" (1933) dealt with groups; from banking and railroads to industry and farming, all of which demanded help for economic recovery. A "Second New Deal" in 1934-36 included the Wagner Act to promote labor unions, the Works Progress Administration (WPA) relief program, the Social Security Act, and new programs to aid tenant farmers and migrant workers. The final major items of New Deal legislation were the creation of the United States Housing Authority and Farm Security Administration both in 1937. Then the Fair Labor Standards Act of 1938, which set maximum hours and minimum wages for most categories of workers and the Agricultural

Adjustment Act of 1938. The New Deal became the largest intrusion into American life by the federal government in its history.

Despite Roosevelt campaigning heavily against anti-New Deal Republicans and anti-New Deal Democrats, Republicans gained many seats in Congress in the 1938 midterm elections. The Democrat opponents of the New Deal retained their seats, resulting in the WPA, CCC and other relief programs being shut down during World War II by the Conservative Coalition; they argued the return of full employment made them unnecessary.

In a measure that garnered popular support for his New Deal, Roosevelt, on March 13, 1933, moved to end one of the most divisive cultural issues of the 1920s. Just nine days later he signed the bill to legalize the manufacture and sale of alcohol, an interim measure pending the repeal of Prohibition, for which a constitutional amendment (the 21st) was already in process. The repeal amendment was ratified later in 1933. States and cities gained additional new revenue, and Roosevelt secured his popularity in the cities, which were overwhelmingly for supporting or permitting the legal production and sale of alcoholic beverages.

Although by now our government had another unintended consequence and that was the rise of organized crime. During the era of Prohibition crime syndicates across the country became more powerful than any corporation in America. By making and selling illegal alcohol which the public demanded a new underground economy had been created. These unintended consequences would have a lasting mark in American society that was eventually graduated to illegal drug use.

Several New Deal programs remain active, with some still operating under the original names, including the Federal Deposit Insurance Corporation (FDIC), the Federal Crop Insurance Corporation (FCIC), the Federal Housing Administration (FHA), and the Tennessee Valley Authority

(TVA). The largest programs still in existence today are the Social Security System and the Securities and Exchange Commission (SEC).

From 1929 to 1933, unemployment in the U.S. increased from 4% to 25%, and manufacturing output decreased by one third. Prices fell by 20%, causing a deflation which made the repayments of debts much harder. The mining, lumber, construction, and farming sectors were hit especially hard, along with railroads and heavy industries such as steel and automobiles. The impact was much less severe in the white-collar and service sectors. Upon accepting the 1932 Democratic nomination for president, Franklin Roosevelt promised "a new deal for the American people".

Throughout the nation men and women, forgotten in the political philosophy of the Government, look to us here for guidance and for more equitable opportunity to share in the distribution of national wealth... I pledge myself to a new deal for the American people. This is more than a political campaign. It is a call to arms.

The Great Depression had devastated the nation. As Roosevelt took the oath of office, the state governors had closed every bank in the nation; no one could cash a check or get at their savings. The unemployment rate was 25% and higher in major industrial and mining centers. Farm income had fallen by over 50% since 1929.

Nearly one million nonfarm mortgages had been foreclosed, 1930–33, out of five million in all. Political and business leaders feared revolution and anarchy. Joseph P. Kennedy, Sr., who remained wealthy during the Depression, stated years later that "in those days I felt and said I would be willing to part with half of what I had if I could be sure of keeping, under law and order, the other half."

Roosevelt entered office without a specific set of plans for dealing with the Great Depression; so he improvised as Congress listened to a very wide variety of voices.

The "First New Deal" (1933–34) encompassed the proposals offered by a wide spectrum of groups. Not included was the Socialist Party, whose influence was all but destroyed.

This first phase of the New Deal was also characterized by fiscal conservatism and experimentation with several different, sometimes contradictory, cures for economic ills.

The consequences were uneven. Some programs, especially the National Recovery Administration (NRA) and the silver program, have been widely seen as failures. Other programs lasted about a decade; some became permanent. The economy shot upward, with FDR's first term marking one of the fastest periods of GDP growth in history. However a downturn in 1937-38 raised questions about just how successful the policies were, with the great majority of economists and historians agreeing they were an overall benefit.

The New Deal policies drew from many different ideas proposed earlier in the 20th century. Some opponents of bigness, led by assistant Attorney General Thurman Arnold, went back to the anti-monopoly tradition that stretched back to Andrew Jackson and Thomas Jefferson. Supreme Court Justice Louis Brandeis, an influential adviser to many New Dealers, argued that bigness was a negative economic force, producing waste and inefficiency.

However, the anti-monopoly group never had a major impact on New Deal policy. Other leaders such as Hugh Johnson of the NRA took ideas from the Woodrow Wilson Administration, advocating techniques used to mobilize the economy for World War I. They brought ideas and experience from the government controls and spending of 1917-18. Other New Deal planners revived experiments suggested in the 1920s, such as the TVA. The Progressives of the earlier decades meet the liberals of the new decade to form an unholy alliance.

Roosevelt listened to an informal "Brain Trust", which advocated more government regulation. The New Deal faced some vocal conservative opposition. The first organized opposition in 1934 came from the American Liberty League led by conservative Democrats such as 1924 and 1928 presidential candidates John W. Davis and Al Smith. There was also a large but loosely affiliated group of New Deal opponents, who are commonly called the Old Right. This group included politicians, intellectuals, writers, and newspaper editors of various philosophical persuasions including classical liberals and conservatives, both Democrats and Republicans. These people from both parties show that this intrusion into American life was far beyond the scope of the federal government.

Roosevelt entered office with enormous political capital. Americans of all political persuasions were demanding immediate action, and Roosevelt responded with a remarkable series of new programs in the "first hundred days" of the administration, in which he met with Congress for 100 days. During those 100 days of lawmaking, Congress granted every request Roosevelt asked, and passed a few programs such as the FDIC to insure bank accounts that he opposed. Ever since, presidents have been judged against FDR for what they accomplished in their first 100 days.

With strident language Roosevelt took credit for dethroning the bankers he alleged had caused the debacle. On March 4, 1933, in his first inaugural address, he proclaimed: "Practices of the unscrupulous money changers stand indicted in the court of public opinion, rejected by the hearts and minds of men. ... The money changers have fled from their high seats in the temple of our civilization." As the new President began to rally the American people with his extraordinary rhetoric we began down a road of paternalism that would do nothing but gather steam for the next nearly half century.

President Roosevelt closed all the banks in the country and kept them all closed until he could pass new legislation. On March 9, Roosevelt sent to Congress the Emergency Banking Act, drafted in large part by Hoover's top advisors. The act was passed and signed into law the same day. It provided for a system of reopening sound banks under Treasury supervision, with federal loans available if needed. Three-quarters of the banks in the Federal Reserve System reopened within the next three days. Billions of dollars in hoarded currency and gold flowed back into them within a month, thus stabilizing the banking system. By the end of 1933, 4,004 small local banks were permanently closed and merged into larger banks. Their depositors eventually received on average 86 cents on the dollar of their deposits; it is a common false myth that they received nothing back.

To deal with deflation, the nation went off the gold standard. In March and April in a series of laws and executive orders, the government suspended the gold standard for United States currency. Anyone holding significant amounts of gold coinage was mandated to exchange it for the existing fixed price of US dollars, after which the US would no longer pay gold on demand for the dollar, and gold would no longer be considered valid legal tender for debts in private and public contracts.

The dollar was allowed to float freely on foreign exchange markets with no guaranteed price in gold, only to be fixed again at a significantly lower level a year later with the passage of the Gold Reserve Act in 1934. Markets immediately responded well to the suspension, in the hope that the decline in prices would finally end.

The economy had hit bottom in March 1933 and then started to expand. Economic indicators show the economy reached bottom in the first days of March, then began a steady, sharp upward recovery. Thus the Federal Reserve Index of Industrial Production sank to its lowest point of 52.8 in July 1932 (with 1935-39 = 100) and was practically unchanged at 54.3 in March 1933; however by July 1933, it reached 85.5, a dramatic rebound of 57% in four months. Recovery was steady and strong until 1937. Except for employment, the economy by 1937 surpassed the levels of the late 1920s.

The Recession of 1937 was a temporary downturn. Private sector employment, especially in manufacturing, recovered to the level of the 1920s but failed to advance further until the war.

The Economy Act, drafted by Budget Director Christian McDonald was passed on March 14, 1933. The act proposed to balance the regular non-emergency federal budget by cutting the salaries of government employees and cutting pensions to veterans by fifteen percent. Roosevelt argued there were two budgets: the "regular" federal budget, which he balanced, and the "emergency budget", which was needed to defeat the depression; it was imbalanced on a temporary basis. This began the shell game of on the record budgets and off record budgets done by our government, now you see it, now you don't!

Roosevelt was initially in favor of balancing the budget, but he soon found himself running spending deficits in order to fund the numerous programs he created. Roosevelt strenuously opposed the Bonus Bill that would give World War I veterans a cash bonus. Finally, Congress passed it over his veto in 1936, and the Treasury distributed $1.5 billion in cash as bonus welfare benefits to 4 million veterans just before the 1936 election. New Dealers never accepted the Keynesian argument for government spending as a vehicle for recovery.

Most economists of the era, along with Henry Morgenthau of the Treasury Department, rejected Keynesian solutions and favored balanced budgets.

Many rural people lived in severe poverty, especially in the South. Major programs addressed to their needs included the Resettlement Administration (RA), the Rural Electrification Administration (REA), rural welfare projects sponsored by the WPA, NYA, Forest Service and CCC, including school lunches, building new schools, opening roads in remote areas, reforestation, and purchase of marginal lands to enlarge national forests.

In 1933, the Administration launched the Tennessee Valley Authority, a project involving dam construction planning on an unprecedented scale in order to curb flooding, generate electricity, and modernize the very poor farms in the Tennessee Valley region of the Southern States.

Roosevelt was keenly interested in farm issues and believed that true prosperity would not return until farming was prosperous. Many different programs were directed at farmers. The first 100 days produced the Farm Security Act to raise farm incomes by raising the prices farmers received, which was achieved by reducing total farm output. The Agricultural Adjustment Act created the Agricultural Adjustment Administration (AAA) in May 1933. The act reflected the demands of leaders of major farm organizations, especially the Farm Bureau, and reflected debates among Roosevelt's farm advisers such as Secretary of Agriculture Henry A. Wallace

In 1936, the Supreme Court declared the AAA to be unconstitutional, stating that a statutory plan to regulate and control agricultural production, a matter beyond the powers delegated to the federal government. The AAA was replaced by a similar program that did win Court approval. This program instead subsidized them for planting soil enriching crops such as alfalfa that would not be sold on the market.

Federal regulation of agricultural production has been modified many times since then, but together with large subsidies it is still in effect in today. The last major New Deal legislation concerning farming was in 1937, when the Farm Tenancy Act was created which in turn created the Farm Security Administration (FSA), replacing the Resettlement Administration.

In 1935, Roosevelt called for a tax program called the Wealth Tax Act to redistribute wealth, in which he proposed to increase inheritance tax, a gift tax, a severely graduated income tax, and a corporate income tax scaled according to income.

However, Congress watered it down, by dropping the inheritance tax and only mildly increased the corporate tax. A tax called the undistributed profits tax was enacted in 1936.

The idea was to force businesses to distribute profits in dividend and wages, instead of saving or reinvesting them. Business profits were taxed on a sliding scale; if a company kept 1% of their net income, 10% of that amount would be taxed under the Undistributed Profits Tax. If a company kept 70% of their net income, the company would be taxed at a rate of 73.91% on that amount. Facing widespread and fierce criticism, the tax was reduced to 2½% in 1938 and completely eliminated in 1939. This constant tug and pull of tax rates kept the discussion on the rates of taxation instead of the constitutionality of taxation which is where the discussion belonged.

Besides all the programs for immediate relief, the federal government embarked quickly on an agenda of long-term reform aimed at avoiding another depression. The New Dealers responded to demands to inflate the currency by a variety of means.

Another group of reformers sought to build consumer and farmer co-ops as a counterweight to big business. The consumer co-ops did not take off, but the Rural Electrification Administration used co-ops to bring electricity to rural areas, many of which still operate. From 1929 to 1933, the industrial economy had been suffering from a vicious cycle of deflation.

The administration insisted that business would have to ensure that the incomes of workers would rise along with their prices. The product of all these impulses and pressures was the National Industrial Recovery Act (NIRA) which was passed by Congress in June 1933. The NIRA established the National Planning Board, also called the National Resources Planning Board (NRPB), to assist in planning the economy by providing recommendations and information.

Fredric A. Delano, the president's uncle, was appointed head of the NRPB. This step toward social justice and now a mechanism to control private business and labor.

The NIRA guaranteed to workers the right of collective bargaining and helped spur some union organizing activity, but much faster growth of union membership came before the 1935 Wagner Act. The NIRA established the National Recovery Administration (NRA), which attempted to stabilize prices and wages through cooperative "code authorities" involving government, business, and labor.

The NRA allowed business to create a multitude of regulations imposing the pricing and production standards for all sorts of goods and services. Most economists were dubious because it was based on fixing prices to reduce competition; the NRA was ended by the Supreme Court in 1935, and no one tried to revive it. During this period the New Deal programs were often shot down by constitutional justices. As the court would change so would the political makeup and therefore the process of producing more judges and legislators loyal to the ruling class would emerge.

To prime the pump and cut unemployment, the NIRA created the Public Works Administration (PWA), a major program of public works. From 1933 to 1935 PWA spent $3.3 billion with private companies to build 34,599 projects, many of them quite large. New Deal economists argued that cut-throat competition had hurt many businesses and that with prices having fallen 20% and more, "deflation" exacerbated the burden of debt and would delay recovery. They rejected a strong move in Congress to limit the workweek to 30 hours. Instead their remedy, designed in cooperation with big business, was the NIRA. It included stimulus funds for the WPA to spend, and sought to raise prices, give more bargaining power for unions (so the workers could purchase more) and reduce harmful competition. At the center of the NIRA was the National Recovery Administration (NRA), headed by former General Hugh

Johnson, who had been a senior economic official in World War I. Johnson called on every business establishment in the nation to accept a stopgap "blanket code": a minimum wage of between 20 and 45 cents per hour, a maximum workweek of 35–45 hours, and the abolition of child labor. Johnson and Roosevelt contended that the "blanket code" would raise consumer purchasing power and increase employment. To mobilize political support for the NRA, Johnson launched the "NRA Blue Eagle" publicity campaign to boost what he called "industrial self-government". The NRA brought together leaders in each industry to design specific sets of codes for that industry; the most important provisions were anti-deflationary floors below which no company would lower prices or wages, and agreements on maintaining employment and production.

In a remarkably short time, the NRA announced agreements from almost every major industry in the nation. By March 1934, industrial production was 45% higher than in March 1933. Donald Richberg, who soon replaced Johnson as the head of the NRA said: There is no choice presented to American business between intelligently planned and uncontrolled industrial operations and a return to the gold-plated anarchy that masqueraded as "rugged individualism"...

Unless industry is sufficiently socialized by its private owners and managers so that great essential industries are operated under public obligation appropriate to the public interest in them, the advance of political control over private industry is inevitable.

By the time NRA ended in May 1935, industrial production was 55% higher than in May 1933. On May 27, 1935, the NRA was found to be unconstitutional by a unanimous decision of the U.S. Supreme Court in the case of Schechter v. United States. On that same day, the Court unanimously struck down the Frazier-Lemke Act portion of the New Deal as unconstitutional. Libertarian Richard Ebeling believes these and other rulings striking down portions of the New Deal prevented the U.S. economic system from becoming a planned economy corporate state.

Governor Huey Long of Louisiana said, "I raise my hand in reverence to the Supreme Court that saved this nation from fascism."

However, soon after, on June 27, 1935, the NLRA was passed, which gave even more power to unions. It forced employees to join unions if a majority of employers voted in favor of unionizing and prohibited business management from declining to engage in collective bargaining with the unions. The Act also established the National Labor Relations Board (NLRB) to enforce the rules of the NLRA and enforce wage agreements.

Employment in private sector factories recovered to the level of the late 1920s by 1937 but did not grow much bigger until the war came and manufacturing employment leaped from 11 million in 1940 to 18 million in 1943.

The New Deal had an important impact in the housing field. The New Deal followed and increased President Hoover's lead and seek measures.

The New Deal sought to stimulate the private home building industry and increase the number of individuals who owned homes. The New Deal implemented two new housing agencies; Home Owners' Loan Corporation (HOLC) and the Federal Housing Administration (FHA). HOLC "facilitated nation-wide lending and encouraged uniform national appraisal methods". The Federal Housing Administration (FHA) created national standards for home construction.

The New Deal helped increase the number of Americans who owned homes. Before the New Deal only four out of 10 Americans owned homes; this was because the standard mortgage lasted only five to 10 years and had interest as high as 8%. These conditions severely limited the accessibility to housing for most Americans. Under the New Deal, Americans had access to 30-year mortgages, the standardized appraisal and construction standards helped open up the housing market to more

Americans. Forty years after the implementation of the New Deal, ⅔ of Americans were home owners.

The number of unemployed in 1929 was estimated at less than 4%, but by 1933 the unemployment rate had jumped up to approximately 25%. The New Deal was designed for complete economic recovery during the depression. However, the New Deal did not achieve full economic recovery. It actually had a limited economic impact. The New Deal failed to lower the unemployment rate below 14%. However, the New Deal did help maintain an average of 17% level the unemployment throughout the 1930s.

By the end of the 1930s, business found itself competing for influence with an increasingly powerful labor movement, with an organized agricultural economy, and occasionally with aroused consumers. This was accomplished by creating a series of government institutions that greatly and permanently expanded the role of the federal government. Thus, perhaps the strongest legacy of the New Deal was to make the federal government a protector of interest groups and a supervisor of competition among them.

As a result of the New Deal, political and economic life became more competitive than before, with workers, farmers, consumers, and others now able to press their demands upon the government in ways that in the past had been available only to the corporate world. If there was more political competition, there was less market competition. Farmers were not allowed to sell for less than the official price.

The transportation industry was tightly regulated so that every firm had a guaranteed market and management and labor had high profits and high wages, all at the cost of high prices and much inefficiency. Quotas in the oil industry were fixed by the Railroad Commission of Texas with Tom Connally's federal Hot Oil Act of 1935, which guaranteed that illegal "hot oil" would not be sold.

To the New Dealers, the free market meant "cut-throat competition" and they considered that evil. It was not until the 1970s and 1980s that most of the New Deal regulations were relaxed.

The Roosevelt Administration was under assault during FDR's second term, which presided over a new dip in the Great Depression in the fall of 1937 that continued through most of 1938. Production declined sharply, as did profits and employment. Unemployment jumped from 14.3% in 1937 to 19.0% in 1938. Keynesian economists speculated that this was a result of a premature effort to curb government spending and balance the budget, while conservatives said it was caused by attacks on business and by the huge strikes caused by the organizing activities of the Congress of Industrial Organizations (CIO) and the American Federation of Labor (AFL).

Roosevelt moved to his left and unleashed a rhetorical campaign against monopoly power, which was cast as the cause of the new crisis. Ickes attacked automaker Henry Ford, steelmaker Tom Girdler, and the superrich "Sixty Families" who supposedly comprised "the living center of the modern industrial oligarchy which dominates the United States".

But the Administration's other response to the 1937 dip that stalled recovery from of the Great Depression had more tangible results. Ignoring the requests of the Treasury Department and responding to the urgings of the converts to Keynesian economics and others in his Administration, Roosevelt embarked on an antidote to the depression, reluctantly abandoning his efforts to balance the budget and launching a $5 billion spending program in the spring of 1938, an effort to increase mass purchasing power.

The New Deal had in fact engaged in deficit spending since 1933. Now they had a theory to justify what they were doing. Roosevelt explained his program in a fireside chat in which he told the American people that it was up to the government to "create an economic upturn" by making "additions to the purchasing power of the nation".

Business-oriented observers explained the recession and recovery in very different terms from the Keynesians. They argued that the New Deal had been very hostile to business expansion in 1935-37, had encouraged massive strikes which had a negative impact on major industries such as automobiles, and had threatened massive anti-trust legal attacks on big corporations. All those threats diminished sharply after 1938. For example, the antitrust efforts fizzled out without major cases.

The CIO and AFL unions started battling each other more than corporations, and tax policy became more favorable to long-term growth.

When the Gallup poll in 1939 asked, do you think the attitude of the Roosevelt administration toward business is delaying business recovery? The American people responded 'yes' by a margin of more than two-to-one. The business community felt even more strongly so." Treasury Secretary Henry Morgenthau, angry at the Keynesian spenders, confided to his diary May 1939: "We have tried spending money.

We are spending more than we have ever spent before and it does not work. And I have just one interest, and now if I am wrong somebody else can have my job. I want to see this country prosper. I want to see people get a job. I want to see people get enough to eat. We have never made good on our promises. I say after eight years of this administration, we have just as much unemployment as when we started, and enormous debt to boot."

Many historians argue that Roosevelt restored hope and self-respect to tens of millions of desperate people, built labor unions, upgraded the national infrastructure and saved capitalism in his first term when he could have destroyed it and easily nationalized the banks and the railroads. Still others have complained that he enlarged the powers of the federal government, built up labor unions, slowed long-term economic growth, and weakened the business community.

The New Deal tried public works, farm subsidies, and other devices to reduce unemployment, but Roosevelt never completely gave up trying to balance the budget. Unemployment remained high throughout the New Deal years though greatly reduced from the much higher rates before the New Deal; business simply would not hire more people, especially the low skilled and supposedly "untrainable" men who had been unemployed for years and lost any job skill they once had. Keynesians later argued that by spending vastly more money — using fiscal policy — the government could provide the needed stimulus through the multiplier effect. Critics of Keynesian economic theories said that government spending would "crowd out" private investment and spending and thus not have any effect on the economy, a proposition known as the Treasury view, which Keynesian economics reject.

In recent years more influential among economists has been the monetarist interpretation of Milton Friedman, which did include a full-scale monetary history of what he calls the "Great Contraction". Friedman concentrated on the failures before 1933, particularly those of the Federal Reserve, and in his memoirs said the relief programs were an appropriate response.

Historians generally agree that apart from building up labor unions, the New Deal did not substantially alter the distribution of power within American capitalism. "The New Deal brought about limited change in the nation's power structure."

Lowell E. Gallaway and Richard K. Vedder argue that the "Great Depression was very significantly prolonged in both its duration and its magnitude by the impact of New Deal programs." They suggest that without Social Security, work relief, unemployment insurance, mandatory minimum wages, and without special government-granted privileges for labor unions, business would have hired more workers and the unemployment rate during the New Deal years would have been 6.7% instead of 17.2%.

Analysts agree the New Deal produced a new political coalition that sustained the Democratic Party as the majority party in national politics for more than a generation after its own end. During Roosevelt's 12 years in office, there was a dramatic increase in the power of the federal government as a whole. Roosevelt also established the presidency as the prominent center of authority within the federal government. Roosevelt created a large array of agencies charged with protecting various groups of citizens, workers, farmers and others who suffered from the crisis.

In this way, the Roosevelt Administration generated a set of political ideas known as New Deal liberalism that remained a source of inspiration and controversy for decades and that helped shape the next great experiment in liberal reform, the Great Society of the 1960s.

Chapter 4 - War As an Economic Model

World War II

For the United States, World War II and the Great Depression constituted the most important economic event of the twentieth century. The war's affects were varied and far-reaching. The war decisively ended the depression itself. The federal government emerged from the war as a potent economic actor. The politico was learning to regulate economic activity and to partially control the economy through spending and consumption. American industry was revitalized by the war, and many sectors were by 1945 either sharply oriented to defense production for example, aerospace and electronics or dependent on it atomic energy. The organized labor movement, strengthened by the war beyond even its depression-era height, became a major counterbalance to both the government and private industry. The war's rapid scientific and technological changes continued and intensified trends begun during the Great Depression and created a permanent expectation of continued innovation by many scientists, engineers, government officials and citizens. Similarly, the substantial increases in personal income and frequently in quality of life during the war led many Americans to foresee permanent improvements to their material circumstances. Even as others feared a postwar return of the depression. Finally, the war's global scale severely damaged every major economy in the world except for the United States, which thus enjoyed unprecedented economic and political power after 1945.

The global conflict which was labeled World War II emerged from the Great Depression, an upheaval which destabilized governments, economies, and entire nations around the world. In Germany, for instance, the rise of Adolph Hitler and the Nazi party occurred at least partly because Hitler claimed to be able to transform a weakened Germany. He promised to create a self-sufficient military and economic power which could control its own destiny in European and world affairs.

Even as liberal powers like the United States and Great Britain were buffeted by the depression as Nazi Germany was rising.

In the United States, President Franklin Roosevelt promised, less dramatically, to enact a "New Deal" which would essentially remake American capitalism and governance on a new basis. As it waxed and waned between 1933 and 1940, Roosevelt's New Deal mitigated some effects of the Great Depression, but did not end the economic crisis.

In 1939, when World War II erupted in Europe with Germany's invasion of Poland, many economic signs suggested the United States was still deeply mired in the depression.

For instance, after 1929 the American gross domestic product declined for four straight years, and then slowly and haltingly climbed back to its 1929 level, which was finally exceeded again in 1936. Unemployment was another measure of the depression's impact. Between 1929 and 1939, the American unemployment rate averaged 13.3 percent. In the summer of 1940, about 5.3 million Americans were still unemployed. Far fewer than the 11.5 million who had been unemployed in 1932 about thirty percent of the American workforce but still a significant pool of unused labor and, often, suffering citizens.

Despite these dismal statistics, the United States was, in other ways, reasonably well prepared for war. The wide array of New Deal programs and agencies which existed in 1939 meant the federal government was markedly larger. It was more actively engaged in social and economic activities than it had been in 1929. Moreover, the New Deal had accustomed Americans to a national government which played a prominent role in national affairs. At least under Roosevelt's leadership, often chose to lead, not follow, private enterprise and to use new capacities to plan and run large-scale endeavors.

As war spread throughout Europe and Asia nowhere was the federal government's leadership more important than in the realm of preparedness. on was the key issue in American economic life in 1940-1942. In many industries, company executives resisted converting to military production because they did not want to lose consumer market share to competitors who did not convert. Conversion thus became a goal pursued by public officials and labor leaders.

In 1940, Walter Reuther, a high-ranking officer in the United Auto Workers labor union, provided impetus for conversion by advocating that the major automakers convert to aircraft production. Though at first rejected by car-company executives and many federal officials, the Reuther Plan effectively called the public's attention to America's lagging readiness for war. Still, the auto companies only fully converted to war production in 1942 and only began substantially contributing to aircraft production in 1943.

Even for contemporary observers, not all industries seemed to be lagging as badly as autos, though. Merchant shipbuilding mobilized early and effectively. The industry was overseen by the U.S. Maritime Commission (USMC), a New Deal agency established in 1936 to revive the moribund shipbuilding industry, which had been in a depression since 1921, and to ensure that American shipyards would be capable of meeting wartime demands. With the USMC supporting and funding the establishment and expansion of shipyards around the country, including especially the Gulf and Pacific coasts, merchant shipbuilding took off.

The entire industry had produced only 71 ships between 1930 and 1936, but from 1938 to 1940, commission-sponsored shipyards turned out 106 ships and then almost that many in 1941 alone. The industry's position in the vanguard of American readiness grew from its strategic import ever more ships were needed to transport American goods to Great Britain and France, among other American allies.

Many of the ships built in Maritime Commission shipyards carried American goods to the European allies as part of the "Lend-Lease" program. It was instituted in 1941 and provided another early indication the United States could and would shoulder a heavy economic burden. By all accounts, Lend-Lease was important to enabling Great Britain and the Soviet Union to fight the Axis, not least before the United States formally entered the war in December 1941.

Though scholars are still assessing the impact of Lend-Lease on these two major allies, it is likely that both countries could have continued to wage war against Germany without American aid. It served largely to augment the British and Soviet armed forces and to have shortened the time necessary to retake the military offensive against Germany.

Between 1941 and 1945, the U.S. exported about $32.5 billion worth of goods through Lend-Lease, of which $13.8 billion went to Great Britain and $9.5 billion went to the Soviet Union. The war dictated that aircraft, ships, military vehicles, and munitions would always rank among the quantitatively most important Lend-Lease goods, but food was also a major export to Britain.

Pearl Harbor was an enormous spur to conversion. The formal declarations of war by the United States on Japan and Germany made plain, oncat the American economy would now need to be transformed into what President Roosevelt had called "the Arsenal of Democracy" a full year before, in December 1940. From the perspective of federal officials in Washington, the first step toward wartime mobilization was establishing an effective administrative bureaucracy.

From the beginning of preparedness through the peak of war production in 1944, American leaders recognized the stakes were too high to let the war economy to grow in an unfettered manner. American manufacturers could not be trusted to stop producing consumer goods and to start producing materiel for the war effort.

To organize the growing economy and to ensure that it produced the goods needed for war, the federal government spawned an array of mobilization agencies. They not only often purchased goods but which in practice closely directed those goods' manufacture and heavily influenced the operation of private companies and whole industries.

Though both the New Deal and mobilization for World War I served as models, the World War II mobilization assumed its own distinctive shape as the war economy expanded. Most importantly, American mobilization was markedly less centralized than mobilization in other belligerent nations.

The war economies of Britain and Germany, for instance, were overseen by war councils which comprised military and civilian officials. In the United States, the Army and Navy were not incorporated into the civilian administrative apparatus, nor was a supreme body created to subsume military and civilian organizations and to direct the vast war economy.

Instead, the military services enjoyed almost-unchecked control over their enormous appetites for equipment and personnel. With respect to the economy, the services were largely able to curtail production destined for civilians and even for war-related but non-military purposes.

In parallel to but never commensurate with the Army and Navy, a succession of top-level civilian mobilization agencies sought to influence Army and Navy procurement of manufactured goods like tanks, planes, and ships, raw materials like steel and aluminum, and even personnel. One way of gauging the scale of the increase in federal spending and the concomitant increase in military spending is through comparison with GDP, which itself rose sharply during the war.

To oversee this growth, President Roosevelt created a number of preparedness agencies beginning in 1939, including the Office for

Emergency Management and its key sub-organization, the National Defense Advisory Commission; the Office of Production Management; and the Supply Priorities Allocation Board. None of these organizations was particularly successful at generating or controlling mobilization because all included two competing parties. On one hand, private-sector executives and managers had joined the federal mobilization bureaucracy but continued to emphasize corporate priorities such as profits and positioning in the marketplace. On the other hand, reform-minded civil servants, who were holdovers from the New Deal, emphasized the state's prerogatives with respect to mobilization and war making. This would change as the two theoretically opposing forces found a natural alliance with one another. This would become the greatest of military industrial complexes ever seen by mankind.

In January 1942, as part of another effort to mesh civilian and military needs, President Roosevelt established a new mobilization agency, the War Production Board, and placed it under the direction of Donald Nelson, a former Sears Roebuck executive.

Nelson understood immediately the staggeringly complex problem of administering the war economy could be reduced to key issues. Balancing the needs of civilians, especially the workers whose efforts sustained the economy, against the needs of the military, especially those of servicemen and women but also their military and civilian leaders.

Though neither Nelson nor other high-ranking civilians ever fully resolved this issue, Nelson did realize several key economic goals. First, in late 1942, Nelson successfully resolved a conflict between civilian administrators and their military counterparts over the extent to which the American economy should be devoted to military needs during 1943. Arguing that all-out production for war would harm America's long-term ability to continue to produce for war after 1943. Nelson convinced the military to scale back its Olympian demands. He thereby also established a precedent for planning war production so as to meet most military and some civilian needs. Second the WPB in late 1942 created the "Controlled Materials Plan," which effectively allocated steel, aluminum, and copper to industrial users. The CMP obtained throughout the war, and helped curtail conflict among the military services and between them and civilian agencies over the growing but still scarce supplies of those three key metals.

By late 1942 it was clear that Nelson and the WPB were unable to fully control the growing war economy and especially to wrangle with the Army and Navy over the necessity of continued civilian production. Accordingly, in May 1943 President Roosevelt created the Office of War Mobilization and in July put James Byrne, a trusted advisor, a former U.S. Supreme Court justice, and the so-called "assistant president" in charge. Though the WPB was not abolished, the OWM soon became the dominant mobilization body in Washington. Unlike Nelson, Byrnes was able to establish an accommodation with the military services over war production by "acting as an arbiter among contending forces in the WPB, settling disputes between the board and the armed services, and dealing with the multiple problems" of the War Manpower Commission, the agency charged with controlling civilian labor markets and with assuring a continuous supply of draftees to the military.

Beneath the highest-level agencies like the WPB and the OWM, a vast array of other federal organizations administered everything from labor the War Manpower Commission to merchant shipbuilding (the Maritime Commission) and from prices the Office of Price Administration to food the War Food Administration.

Given the scale and scope of these agencies' efforts, they did sometimes fail, and especially so when they carried with them the baggage of the New Deal.

By the midpoint of America's involvement in the war, for example, the Civilian Conservation Corps, the Works Progress Administration, and the Rural Electrification Administration. All prominent New Deal organizations which tried and failed to find a purpose in the mobilization bureaucracy had been actually or virtually abolished.

However, these agencies were often quite successful in achieving their respective, narrower aims. The Department of the Treasury, for instance, was remarkably successful at generating money to pay for the war, including the first general income tax in American history and the famous "war bonds" sold to the public. Beginning in 1940, the government extended the income tax to virtually all Americans and began collecting the tax via the now-familiar method of continuous withholdings from paychecks. A practice that continues today. Witholding tax is theft from workers like almost nothing else is. The number of Americans required to pay federal taxes rose from 4 million in 1939 to 43 million in 1945. With such a large pool of taxpayers, the American government took in $45 billion in 1945, an enormous increase over the $8.7 billion collected in 1941 but still far short of the $83 billion spent on the war in 1945.

Over that same period, federal tax revenue grew from about 8 percent of GDP to more than 20 percent. Americans who earned as little as $500 per year paid income tax at a 23 percent rate, while those who earned more than $1 million per year paid a 94 percent rate. The average income tax rate peaked in 1944 at 20.9 percent.

All told, taxes provided about $136.8 billion of the war's total cost of $304 billion. To cover the other $167.2 billion, the Treasury Department also expanded its bond program, creating the famous "war bonds" hawked by celebrities and purchased in vast numbers and enormous values by Americans. The first war bond was purchased by President Roosevelt on May 1, 1941.

Though the bonds returned only 2.9 percent annual interest after a 10-year maturity, they nonetheless served as a valuable source of revenue for the federal government and an extremely important investment for many Americans. Bonds served as a way for citizens to make an economic contribution to the war effort, but because interest on them accumulated slower than consumer prices rose, they could not completely preserve income which could not be readily spent during the war.

By the time war-bond sales ended in 1946, 85 million Americans had purchased more than $185 billion worth of the securities, often through automatic deductions from their paychecks. Commercial institutions like banks also bought billions of dollars of bonds and other treasury paper, holding more than $24 billion at the war's end.

Fiscal and financial matters were also addressed by other federal agencies. For instance, the Office of Price Administration used its "General Maximum Price Regulation" to attempt to curtail inflation by maintaining prices at their March 1942 levels.

In July, the National War Labor Board (NWLB; a successor to a New Deal-era body) limited wartime wage increases to about 15 percent, the factor by which the cost of living rose from January 1941 to May 1942. Neither "General Max" nor the wage-increase limit was entirely successful, though federal efforts did curtail inflation.

Between April 1942 and June 1946, the period of the most stringent federal controls on inflation, the annual rate of inflation was just 3.5 percent; the annual rate had been 10.3 percent in the six months before April 1942 and it soared to 28.0 percent in the six months after June 1946.With wages rising about 65 percent over the course of the war, this limited success in cutting the rate of inflation meant that many American civilians enjoyed a stable or even improving quality of life during the war. Improvement in the standard of living was not ubiquitous, however. In some regions, such as rural areas in the Deep South, living standards stagnated or even declined, and according to some economists, the national living standard barely stayed level or even declined. Never before in history and perhaps never since was there such direct governmental interference in wages in the country.

Labor unions and their members benefited especially. The NWLB's "maintenance-of-membership" rule allowed unions to count all new employees as union members and to draw union dues from those new employees' paychecks, so long as the unions themselves had already been recognized by the employer. Given that most new employment occurred in unionized workplaces, including plants funded by the federal government through defense spending, "the maintenance-of-membership ruling was a fabulous boon for organized labor," for it required employers to accept unions and allowed unions to grow dramatically: organized labor expanded from 10.5 million members in 1941 to 14.75 million in 1945. By 1945, approximately 35.5 percent of the non-agricultural workforce was unionized, a record high.

Despite the almost-continual crises of the civilian war agencies, the American economy expanded at an unprecedented and unduplicated rate between 1941 and 1945. The gross national product of the U.S., measured in constant dollars, grew from $88 billion in 1939. While the country was still suffering from the depression to $135 billion in 1944. War-related production skyrocketed from just two percent of GNP to 40 percent in 1943. The wartime economic boom spurred and benefited from several important social trends.

Foremost among these trends was the expansion of employment, which paralleled the expansion of industrial production. Driven by the federal government's abilities to prevent price inflation and to subsidize high wages through war contracting and by the increase in the size and power of organized labor, incomes rose for virtually all Americans — whites and blacks, men and women, skilled and unskilled. Workers at the lower end of the spectrum gained the most: manufacturing workers enjoyed about a quarter more real income in 1945 than in 1940. These rising incomes were part of a wartime "great compression" of wages which equalized the distribution of incomes across the American population.

While all of the major belligerents were able to tap their scientific and technological resources to develop weapons and other tools of war, the American experience was impressive in that scientific and technological change positively affected virtually every facet of the war economy.

American technology and its innovations mattered most dramatically in "high-tech" sectors which were often hidden from public view by wartime secrecy. For instance, the Manhattan Project to create an atomic weapon was a direct and massive result of a stunning scientific breakthrough: the creation of a controlled nuclear chain reaction by a team of scientists at the University of Chicago in December 1942. Under the direction of the U.S. Army and several private contractors, scientists, engineers, and workers built a nationwide complex of laboratories and plants to manufacture atomic fuel and to fabricate atomic weapons. The Manhattan Project climaxed in August 1945, when the United States dropped two atomic weapons on Hiroshima and Nagasaki, Japan; these attacks likely accelerated Japanese leaders' decision to seek peace with the United States. By that time, the Manhattan Project had become a colossal economic endeavor, costing approximately $2 billion and employing more than 100,000.

Though important and gigantic, the Manhattan Project was an anomaly in the broader war economy. Technological and scientific innovation also transformed less-sophisticated but still complex sectors such as aerospace or shipbuilding.

The United States, as David Kennedy writes, "ultimately proved capable of some epochal scientific and technical breakthroughs, but innovated most characteristically and most tellingly in plant layout, production organization, economies of scale, and process engineering".

Reconversion from military to civilian production had been an issue as early as 1944, when WPB Chairman Nelson began pushing to scale back war production in favor of renewed civilian production. The military's opposition to Nelson had contributed to the accession by James Byrnes and the OWM to the paramount spot in the war-production bureaucracy. Meaningful planning for reconversion was postponed until 1944 and the actual process of reconversion only began in earnest in early 1945, accelerating through V-E Day in May and V-J Day in September.

The high level of defense spending, in turn, contributed to the creation of the "military-industrial complex," the network of private companies, non-governmental organizations, universities, and federal agencies which collectively shaped American national defense policy and activity during the Cold War.

Reconversion spurred the second major restructuring of the American workplace in five years, as returning servicemen flooded back into the workforce and many war workers left, either voluntarily or involuntarily. For instance, many women left the labor force beginning in 1944 sometimes voluntarily and sometimes involuntarily. In 1947, about a quarter of all American women worked outside the home, roughly the same number who had held such jobs in 1940 and far off the wartime peak of 36 percent in 1944.

Servicemen obtained numerous other economic benefits beyond their jobs, including educational assistance from the federal government and guaranteed mortgages and small-business loans via the Serviceman's Readjustment Act of 1944 or "G.I. Bill." Former servicemen thus became a vast and advantaged class of citizens which demanded, among other goods, inexpensive, often suburban housing; vocational training and college educations; and private cars which had been unobtainable during the war.

The U.S. emerged from the war not physically unscathed, but economically strengthened by wartime industrial expansion, which placed the United States at absolute and relative advantage over both its allies and its enemies. Possessed of an economy which was larger and richer than any other in the world, American leaders were determined to make the United States the center of the postwar world economy. American aid to Europe ($13 billion via the Economic Recovery Program (ERP) or "Marshall Plan," 1947-1951) and Japan ($1.8 billion, 1946-1952) furthered this goal by tying the economic reconstruction of West Germany, France, Great Britain, and Japan to American import and export needs, among other factors.

Even before the war ended, the Bretton Woods Conference in 1944 determined key aspects of international economic affairs by establishing standards for currency convertibility and creating institutions such as the International Monetary Fund and the precursor of the World Bank.

In brief, as economic historian Alan Milward writes, "the United States emerged in 1945 in an incomparably stronger position economically than in 1941"... By 1945 the foundations of the United States' economic domination over the next quarter of a century had been secured"... This may have been the most influential consequence of the Second World War for the post-war world".

World War II was followed by a Cold War that pitted the United States and its Allies against the Soviet Union and its supporters. It was called a Cold War, but it would flare into violence in Korea and Vietnam and in many smaller conflicts. The period from 1946 to 1991 was punctuated by a series of East-West confrontations over Germany, Poland, Greece, Czechoslovakia, China, Korea, Vietnam, Cuba, and many other hot spots.

In March 1946, Winston Churchill announced that "an iron curtain has descended across" Europe. On one side was the Communist bloc; on the other side were non-Communist nations.

Post war America

One source of conflict between the United States and the Soviet Union was the fate of Eastern Europe. The United States was committed to free and democratic elections in Eastern Europe, while the Soviet Union wanted a buffer zone of friendly countries in Eastern Europe to protect it from future attacks from the West.

Even before World War II ended, the Soviet Union had annexed the Baltic states of Estonia, Latvia, and Lithuania, and parts of Czechoslovakia, Finland, Poland, and Romania. Albania established a Communist government in 1944, and Yugoslavia formed one in 1945. In 1946, the Soviet Union organized Communist governments in Bulgaria and Romania and in Hungary and Poland in 1947. Communists took over Czechoslovakia in a coup d'état in 1948.

Another source of East-West tension was control of nuclear weapons. In 1946, the Soviet Union rejected a U.S. proposal for an international agency to control nuclear energy production and research. The Soviets were convinced the United States was trying to preserve its monopoly on nuclear weapons.

A third source of conflict was postwar economic development assistance. The United States refused a Soviet request for massive reconstruction loans. In response, the Soviets called for large reparations from Germany.

In February 1947, Britain told the United States that it could not longer afford to provide aid to Greece and Turkey. The situation seemed urgent. The Greek monarchy was threatened by guerrilla warfare, and the Soviet Union was seeking to control the Dardenelles in Turkey, a water route to the Mediterranean. The U.S. government feared the loss of Greece and

Turkey to communism would open Western Europe and Africa to Soviet influence. The U.S government also worried that if the Soviet Union gained control over the Eastern Mediterranean, it could stop the flow of Middle Eastern oil.

President Truman responded decisively. He asked Congress for $400 million in economic and military aid for Greece and Turkey.

This was an unprecedented amount of foreign aid during peacetime. He also declared that it was the policy of the United States "to support free peoples who are resisting attempted subjugation by armed minorities or by outside pressures."

Truman's message described two ways of life that were engaged in a life-or-death struggle, one free and the other totalitarian. The United States would help free people to keep their free institutions and their territorial integrity against movements that sought to impose totalitarian regimes.

The Truman Doctrine committed the United States to providing aid to countries resisting communist aggression or subversion and provided the first step toward what would become known as the Containment Policy. The end of World War II brought a baby boom to many countries, especially Western ones. There is some disagreement as to the precise beginning and ending dates of the postwar baby boom, but it is most often agreed to begin in the years immediately after the war, ending more than a decade later; birthrates in the United States started to decline in 1957. In areas that had suffered heavy war damage, displacement of people and postwar economic hardship, such as Poland, the boom began some years later.

In the years after the war, couples who could not afford families during the Great Depression made up for lost time; the mood was now optimistic. During the war unemployment ended and the economy greatly expanded; afterwards the country experienced vigorous economic growth until the 1970s. The G.I. Bill enabled record numbers of people to finish high school and attend college. This led to an increase in stock of skills and yielded higher incomes to families.

When the war ended in 1945, millions of veterans returned home and were forced to integrate. To help the integration process, Congress passed the G.I. Bill of Rights. This bill encouraged home ownership and investment in higher education through the distribution of loans at low or no interest rates to veterans.

Returning G.I.'s were getting married, starting families, pursuing higher education and buying their first homes. With veteran's benefits, the twenty-something's found new homes in planned communities on the outskirts of American cities. This group, whose formative years covered the Great Depression, was a generation hardened by poverty and deprived of the security of a home or job.

Now thriving on the American Dream, life was simple, jobs were plentiful and babies were booming. Many Americans believed that lack of postwar government spending would send the United States back into depression. However, consumer demand fueled economic growth. The baby boom triggered a housing boom, consumption boom and a boom in the labor force. Between 1940 and 1960, the nation's GDP jumped more than $300,000 million. The middle class grew and most of America's labor force held white-collar jobs. This increase led to urbanization and increased the demand for ownership in cars and other '50s and '60s inventions.

Economist and demographer Richard Easterlin in his "Twentieth Century American Population Growth" (2000), explains the growth pattern of American population in the twentieth century by examining the fertility rate fluctuations and the decreasing mortality rate.

Easterlin tries to prove the cause of the Baby Boom and Baby Bust by the "relative income" theory, despite the various other theories that these events have been attributed to. The "relative income" theory suggests that couples choose to have children based on a couple's ratio of potential earning power and the desire to get material objects. This ratio depends on the economic stability of the country and how people are raised to value material objects. The "relative income" theory explains the Baby Boom by suggesting that the late 1940s and the 1950s brought low desires to have material objects, because of the Great Depression and World War II, as well as plentiful job opportunities (being a postwar period). These two factors gave rise to a high relative income, which encouraged high fertility.

On June 25, 1950, Communist North Korean forces invaded South Korea, beginning a three-year war. Three days later, the South Korean capital of Seoul fell to the North Koreans.

President Truman immediately ordered U.S. air and sea forces to "give the Korean government troops cover and support." The conflict lasted until July 27, 1953. The United States suffered 54,246 battle deaths and 103,284 wounded.

Tensions had festered since the Korean peninsula had been divided into a Communist North and a nonCommunist South in 1945. With the partition, 10 million Koreans were separated from their families. For three months, the United States could not stop the communist advance. Then, Douglas MacArthur successfully landed two divisions ashore at Inchon, behind enemy lines. The North Koreans fled in disarray across the 38th parallel, the prewar border between North and South Korea.

The initial mandate the United States had received from the United Nations called for the restoration of the original border at the 38th parallel. But the South Korean army had no intention of stopping at the prewar border, and on Sept. 30, 1950, they crossed into the North. The United States pushed an updated mandate through the United Nations, and on Oct. 7, the Eighth Army crossed the border.

By November, U.S. Army and Marine units thought they could end the war in just five more months. China's communist leaders threatened to send combat forces into Korea, but the U.S. commander, Douglas MacArthur, thought they were bluffing.

In mid-October, the first of 300,000 Chinese soldiers slipped into North Korea. When U.S. forces began what they expected to be their final assault in late November, they ran into the Chinese army. There was a danger the U.S. Army might be overrun. The Chinese intervention ended any hope of reunifying Korea by force of arms.

General MacArthur called for the U.S. Joint Chiefs of Staff to unleash American air and naval power against China. But the chairman of the Joint Chiefs of Staff, Army General Omar Bradley, said a clash with China would be "the wrong war, in the wrong place, at the wrong time, and with the wrong enemy." By mid-January 1951, Lt. Gen. Matthew B. Ridgway succeeded in halting an American retreat 50 miles south of the 38th parallel.

A week and a half later, he had the army attacking northward again. By March, the front settled along the 38th parallel and the South Korean capital of Seoul was back in South Korean hands.

American officials told MacArthur that peace negotiations would be sought. In April, President Truman relieved MacArthur of his command after the general, in defiance of Truman's orders, commanded the bombing of Chinese military bases in Manchuria. The president feared that such actions would bring the Soviet Union into the conflict.

The Korean War was filled with lessons for the future. First, it demonstrated the United States was committed to the containment of communism, not only in Western Europe, but throughout the world. Prior to the outbreak of the Korean War, the Truman administration had indicated that Korea stood outside America's sphere of vital national interests. Now, it was unclear whether any nation was outside this sphere.

Second, the Korean War proved how difficult it was to achieve victory even under the best circumstances imaginable. In Korea, the United States faced a rather weak rival and had strong support from its allies. The United States possessed an almost total monopoly of sophisticated weaponry, and yet, the war dragged on for almost four years.

Third, the Korean War showed the difficulty of fighting a limited war. Limited wars are, by definition, fought for limited objectives. They are often unpopular at home because it is difficult to explain precisely what the country is fighting for. The military often complains that it is fighting with one armed tied behind its back. But if one tries to escalate a limited war, a major power, like China, might intervene.

Finally, in Korea U.S. policymakers assumed that they could make the South Korean government do what they wanted. In reality, the situation was often reversed. The South Korean government played a pivotal role in defining military strategy and shaping the peace negotiations. In the end, the United States was only able to extricate itself from the war by making a long-term commitment to the South Korean government in terms of money, men, and material.

In March 1953, Joseph Stalin, who had ruled the Soviet Union since 1928, died at the age of 73. His feared minister of internal affairs, Lavrenti Pavlovich Beria, was subsequently shot for treason. Nikita Khrushchev then became first secretary of the Communist Party. Stalin's death led to a temporary thaw in Cold War tensions. In 1955, Austria regained its sovereignty and became an independent, neutral nation after the withdrawal of Soviet troops from the country.

The next year, Khrushchev denounced Stalin and his policies at the 20th Communist Party conference. After a summit between President Eisenhower and the new Soviet Premier Nikita Khrushchev in Geneva, the Soviets announced plans to reduce its armed forces by more than 600,000 troops. In early 1956, Khrushchev called for "peaceful coexistence" between the East and West.

Beginning with George Washington, presidents have used their farewell address to look back on their experience in office and to offer the public practical advice. In his farewell address, President Dwight D. Eisenhower said that a high level of military spending and the establishment of a large arms industry in peacetime were something "new in the American experience." In the most famous words of his presidency, Eisenhower warned that the country "must guard against the acquisition of unwarranted influence...by the military-industrial complex." President Eisenhower believed that the United States had "to maintain balance" between defense spending and the needs of a healthy economy. During his second term, Congress, the press, and the armed services had pressured Eisenhower to increase defense spending. But even after the Soviet Union launched Sputnik, the first satellite to orbit the earth, he refused to let defense spending unbalance the federal budget. Eisenhower worried that presidents who did not have his military experience would be poor judges of the country's defense needs.

In his speech, Eisenhower warned that the United States faced a "hostile ideology—global in scope, atheistic in character, ruthless in purpose," and must bear "without complaint the burdens of a long and complex struggle." He also feared that the arms industry, military officers, and members of Congress with military installations and defense plants in their districts, would lead the country to build unnecessary weapons. He worried that the "military-industrial complex" would skew national priorities and dictates the direction of American foreign policy.

The election of a new president, John F. Kennedy, was accompanied by intensified Cold War tensions. During the 1960 presidential campaign, Kennedy spoke of a "missile gap" and claimed the Soviet Union had achieved an advantage in long-range missiles. In response to Soviet Premier Khrushchev's pledge to support wars of liberation, Kennedy called for the training of counter-insurgency forces that could combat guerrilla warfare.

In 1959, rebel leader Fidel Castro toppled Cuban dictator Fugencio Batista. In Washington, Castro told U.S. officials that "The [Cuban] movement is not a Communist movement.... We have no intent of expropriating U.S. property, and any property we take we'll pay for." The next year, the Soviet Union agreed to provide Cuba with $100 million in credit and to buy five million tons of Cuban sugar.

After President Eisenhower declared the United States would not allow a regime "dominated by international Communism" to exist in the Western hemisphere, Havana nationalized all banks and large commercial industrial enterprises in Cuba. The United responded by imposing a trade embargo.

In April 1961, a U.S.-sponsored invasion of Cuba led by anti-Castro Cuban émigrés turned into a rout. The members of the invasion force, who had been trained by the CIA in Florida, Louisiana, and Guatemala, were defeated in just three days. On Christmas 1962, the United States traded $53 million worth of medical supplies and foodstuff for 1,113 captured invaders and 922 of their relatives.

In October 1962, the Soviet Union and the United States went eyeball-to-eyeball and were on the brink of nuclear war. Surveillance photographs taken by a U-2 spy plane over Cuba revealed the Soviet Union was installing intermediate-range ballistic missiles. Once operational, in about 10 days, the missiles would need only five minutes to reach Washington, D.C.

President Kennedy decided to impose a naval blockade. Soviet freighters were steaming toward Cuba. The president realized that if the ships were boarded and their cargoes seized, the Soviet Union might regard this as an act of war. Soviet Premier Khrushchev sent a signal that he might be willing to negotiate. In exchange for the Soviets agreeing to remove the missiles, the United States publicly pledged not to invade Cuba and secretly agreed to remove its aging missiles from Turkey.

After the Cuban Missile Crisis, Cold War tensions eased. In July 1963, the United States, the Soviet Union, and Britain approved a treaty to halt the testing of nuclear weapons in the atmosphere, in outer space, and under water.

The following month, the United States and Soviet Union established a hotline providing a direct communication link between the White House and the Kremlin.

In August 1948, Whittaker Chambers, a Time magazine editor and a former Communist, told the House Un-American Activities Committee that Alger Hiss, a former State Department official and president of the Carnegie Endowment for International Peace, supplied Soviet agents with classified U.S. documents.

A federal grand jury indicted Hiss for perjury after Chambers produced a microfilm he had kept hidden in a pumpkin on his Maryland farm. The microfilm contained photographs of the documents Hiss allegedly passed to Chambers.

Hiss's first trial ended in a hung jury, but in 1950, he was found guilty and sentenced to five years in prison. The Hiss case was offered as proof there had been Communists in high government positions.

In May 1950, at the moment that Senator Joseph McCarthy was beginning his crusade against communist subversion, the U.S. Senate created a special committee to investigate another "enemy within": organized crime. Crime statistics suggested the nation was amid an unprecedented wave of violence. Criminologists attributed a surge in burglary, murder, and prostitution to such factors as the wartime disruption of families, shortages of goods, and a continuing public demand for illicit gambling. But journalists and citizen crime commissions identified another villain, organized crime.

For 15 months, a committee headed by Tennessee Democrat Estes Kefauver held hearings in 14 major cities. Television made the committee's hearings among the most influential in American history. As many as 20 to 30 million Americans watched spellbound as crime bosses, bookies, pimps, and hit-men appeared on their television screens. Americans listened intently as the committee's chairman told them that "there is a secret international government-within-a-government" that controlled gambling, vice, and narcotics trafficking, all of which were protected by corrupt police officers, judges, and politicians.

The Cold War was a struggle for the hearts and minds of people across the globe. By the early 1960s, a third of the world's population lived under Communism and another third lived in nonaligned countries.

Public service advertisements on television showed Soviet Premier Nikita Khrushchev warning Americans that their grandchildren will live under Communism. During the Cold War, the Soviet Union exploited the glaring inconsistency between American ideals of liberty and equality and the harsh reality of racial discrimination. During the late 1940s and 1950s, there were strenuous efforts to bring American realities in line with the country's founding ideals. In May 1948, the Supreme Court ruled that restrictive covenants prohibiting the sale of homes to blacks and Jews are not legally enforceable. Two months later, President Truman issued Executive Order 9981; ending segregation in the U.S. armed forces.

The 1947-1948 baseball season opened with a new Brooklyn Dodger at second base: Jackie Robinson, the first African-American in the major leagues. For the first time in the 20th century, professional baseball—the national pastime—was integrated.

In 1946, when the football Rams moved from Cleveland to Los Angeles, they signed two black football stars from UCLA, Kenny Washington and Woody Strode. In 1950, the Boston Celtics of the National Basketball League signed Chuck Cooper, and the New York Knicks signed Nat

"Sweetwater" Clifton. In the wake of the defeat of the Nazis and their abhorrent racial policies, American professional sports were integrated.

Some 150,000 Americans have served in the Peace Corps since it was formed in 1961. Peace Corps volunteers live and work for two years in communities in the developing world. They must learn the languages of the people they serve. They have worked in 132 nations.

In its early years, as many as 15,000 volunteers worked in schools, clinics, and in agricultural and environmental projects. The Peace Corps was a product of the Cold War. A week before the 1960 presidential election, John F. Kennedy observed that the Soviet Union had "hundreds of men and women, scientists, physicists, teachers, engineers, doctors, and nurses...prepared to spend their lives abroad in the service of world communism."

The United States had no equivalent. Kennedy feared the United States was in danger of losing the battle for the hearts and minds of the world's peoples. He believed that a "peace corps" was the answer. "I am convinced," he said, "that our men and women, dedicated to freedom, are able to be missionaries, not only for freedom and peace, but to join in a worldwide struggle against poverty and disease and ignorance."

When John F. Kennedy proposed creating the Peace Corps during the 1960 presidential campaign, the Wall Street Journal asked: "What person can really believe that Africa aflame with violence will have its fires quenched because some Harvard boy or Vassar girl lives in a mud hut and speaks Swahili?" But today, many believe that the Peace Corps volunteers are this country's best ambassadors.

On the morning of March 7, 1949, builder William J. Levitt opened a sales office for a new development of inexpensive single-family homes in a potato field in the center of Long Island's Nassau County. In bitter-cold weather, more than a thousand young couples crowded outside the sales office, waiting for a chance to buy a four-room, 25-by-32-foot house for

$6,999--government financed, no money down. Some had camped out in tents for as long as four days.

To build houses rapidly and inexpensively, Levitt used the method made famous by Henry Ford: the production line. Levitt broke down the construction of a home into 26 separate steps. Teams of construction workers leveled the land, paved streets, poured concrete slabs, planted trees every 28 feet, and installed plumbing and electrical wiring. A hundred houses were built at a time.

Construction was governed by clockwork. By 8 a.m., trucks unloaded prefabricated siding at each house site; at 9:30 a.m., toilets arrived; at 10 a.m., sinks, tubs and Sheetrock ™ were delivered; at 11 a.m., flooring was sent. To speed construction and trim costs, painters used spray guns instead of brushes, and carpenters used power saws. Interior partitions, roof trusses, and door and window units were cut to the required shape before they left the factory.

To give young couples a chance to buy an affordable house, Levitt cut costs by eliminating basements and giving all houses in his development the same floor plan. Interior and exterior painting was limited to a single two-tone color scheme.

Critics derided the monotony and uniformity of this new suburban development. A popular song "Little Boxes" described suburban homes as "all made out of ticky-tacky and they all looked just the same." Nevertheless, newlyweds caught in the postwar housing shortage flocked to Levittown by the thousands. When the first phase of construction was completed, 17,500 families had moved in. A second massive development, near Philadelphia, housed 70,000 people.

One of the most profound social changes of the post-war era was the rapid growth of suburbs. In the ten years following 1948, some 13 million homes were built in the United States; 11 million (85 percent) were built in the suburbs. By 1960 as many Americans lived in the suburbs as in central cities, and the suburban way of life was shaping the patterns and rhythms of American life. Suburbs, which only began to emerge as fringe communities around central cities in the late 1940s, became the country's main hometown.

In 1940, most Americans lived on farms, small towns with fewer than 2,500 inhabitants, or in big cities. But by 2000, four Americans in five live in suburbs.

The federal government had a great deal to do with the spread of the population into the suburbs, as it made mortgage money available at low interest rates through the Veterans Administration and the Federal Home Loan Mortgage Administration. This combined with an abundance of cheap energy for automobile transportation and state and federal policies that encouraged highway construction propelled many middle-class Americans into the suburbs.

In 1947, the United States had, by far, the world's most productive and prosperous economy. With six percent of the world's population, the U.S. had produced 50 percent of the world's manufactured goods, 57 percent of its steel, 62 percent of its oil, and over 80 percent of its cars. The average American made 15 times as much as the average European. Yet, many Americans looked to the future with anxiety. Many Americans feared that the end of heavy wartime spending would bring a return of the economic depression.

Post-war labor strife and inflation contributed to a sense of foreboding. Americans had saved $44 billion during World War II, and pent-up demand caused inflation to soar. By 1948, prices were 48 percent higher than they were in 1945.

Adding to this anxiety was a wave of labor strikes. In January 1946, the automobile, electrical appliance, meatpacking, and steel workers all went on strike.

Congress responded to the labor strife by enacting the Taft-Hartley Act of 1947, over President Truman's veto. Opposed by organized labor, the act restricted union activities, such as mass picketing and boycotts, and allowed states to pass "right to work" laws making it illegal to require workers to join unions. It also allowed the attorney general to seek court orders delaying for 80 days any strike endangering public health or safety.

The federal government would take aggressive steps in the post-war period to stimulate economic growth and to ensure the country would not return to high levels of unemployment. By encouraging the growth of suburbs and of the Sunbelt, these policies transformed the country's face. In 1950, California was the size of Pennsylvania. Florida ranked 21st in size. Now it is ranked 4th. One of the central developments of the second half of the 20th century was the shift in political and economic power from the older industrial cities of the Northeast and Midwest to the South and West. Since 1964, every elected U.S. president has been born or has claimed residence in the Sunbelt.

At the end of World War II, the South was the nation's poorest region, with per capita income barely one-half of the national average. Air conditioning, lower taxes and wages, desegregation, and weaker unions contributed to the postwar growth of the South. So, too, did government spending.

During World War II, the federal government invested almost $9 billion in the South, mainly in defense plants, shipyards, oil refineries, and chemical plants. As recently as 1980, nearly half of the nation's soldiers were stationed in the South, and the Defense Department spent nearly 40 percent of its budget in the region.

The West also prospered as a result of an infusion of federal dollars. Government spending in the West began to increase steeply during the 1930s, as the Roosevelt administration financed major dam, power, and irrigation projects. World War II accelerated the West's growth.

During the war years, the federal government spent $70 billion in the western states, over half in California. Southern California's defense and aerospace industries created more than 250,000 new jobs during the war.

In 1956, President Dwight Eisenhower authorized the largest public works project in the history of the world. The president had been impressed by Hitler's autobahns and believed that a national system of highways was necessary to move troops and military equipment and to provide evacuation routes during national emergencies.

Presently, there are 46,300 miles of interstate highways, which initially cost $129 billion to build. The federal government paid 90 percent of the system's construction costs. Unlike older highways, the interstate had no intersections or traffic signs. To ensure that traffic would not have to stop, engineers had to build more than 55,000 bridges or overpasses.

The Interstate Highway System changed the nation's landscape. Instead of taking trains or buses, workers commuted by cars. Suburbs flourished, and so did suburban sprawl. Shopping centers appeared, like the Detroit shopping center, Northland, that opened with a hundred stores in 1954.

At the same time, highways slashed through the hearts of the nation's cities, cutting through lower-economic class neighborhoods, dividing communities, and facilitating white-flight to the suburbs.

During the Eisenhower era, Americans achieved a level of prosperity they had never known before. While other parts of the world struggled to rebuild from the devastation of World War II, the United States saw their standard of living surpass previous generations.

Eisenhower himself deserves a good deal of credit for this economic growth. He found the right combination of low taxes, balanced budgets, and public spending that allowed the economy to hum along at a steady clip. He also benefitted from steady growth in spending on new homes and consumer goods as citizens turned away from older notions of thrift and began to buy on credit.

The economy overall grew by 37% during the 1950s. At the end of the decade, the median American family had 30% more purchasing power than at the beginning. Inflation, which had wreaked havoc on the economy immediately after World War II, was minimal, in part because of Eisenhower's persistent efforts to balance the federal budget. Except for a mild recession in 1954 and a more serious one in 1958, unemployment remained low, bottoming at less than 4.5% in the middle of the decade. Many factors came together to produce the Fifties boom. The G.I. Bill, which gave military veterans affordable access to a college education, added a productive pool of highly-educated employees to the work force at a time American businesses were willing to pay handsomely for engineering and management skills.

Cheap oil from domestic wells helped keep the engines of industry running. Fat dumb and happy could describe the 1950's pretty well. War had finally paid its dividend and the people were swallowing it up.

Advances in science and technology spurred productivity. At the same time, potential competitors in Europe and Asia were still recovering from being bombed into smithereens during World War II.

Eisenhower's Middle Way steered a balanced course economically. Some Republicans called for rolling back the New Deal, but the president realized that many of Franklin D. Roosevelt's liberal social programs were both popular and effective. Instead of getting rid of Social Security, for example, Ike actually expanded it to cover another ten million people who had been left out of the original program. Instead of turning away from big public works projects, he instead invested federal money in the Interstate Highway System, one of the largest public spending projects in the country's history.

The main economic goal that Eisenhower pursued through both his terms in office was to achieve a balanced federal budget. The government ran a small deficit in 1954 and 1955, and then registered a surplus for each of the next two years. As the nation went into a recession in 1958 and 1959,

Eisenhower allowed the federal deficit to grow in order to stimulate the economy. By 1960, he managed to return to a surplus.

To achieve a balanced federal budget was a balancing act in itself. Democrats were clamoring for increases in defense spending in order to counter the Soviet threat. Congressional representatives from both parties pushed for tax cuts. Eisenhower used his credentials as an experienced military leader to reassure the nation that the defense budget did not need to be increased as much as some wanted. Though he favored low taxes himself, he dug in his heels and fought tax cuts whenever they threatened to plunge the government into debt.

One of the factors that fueled the prosperity of the Fifties was the increase in consumer spending. Americans enjoyed a standard of living that was inconceivable to the rest of the world. The time was ripe for Americans to change their spending patterns. The adults of the Fifties had grown up in conditions of economic deprivation, first due to the general poverty of the Great Depression and then due to the rationing of consumer goods World War II. During the Thirties, with unemployment sky-high and the economy in shambles, most people could simply not afford much beyond the basics. During the war, much of the nation's productive capacity shifted to armaments. Everything from sugar to gasoline to tires to nylon stockings was rationed. When consumer goods became available again, people wanted to spend. By the 1950s, though they made up just 6% of the world's population, Americans consumed a third of all the world's goods and services.

The difference between a production society, which focused on meeting basic needs, and a consumption society, which emphasized customers' wants, was like the difference between a 1908 Ford Model T and a 1959 Ford Galaxy. The Model T, available only in black, was a utilitarian piece of machinery intended for basic transportation.

The Galaxy, decked out in shiny chrome, was a way to show off and to enjoy a sense of luxury, not just to move from place to place. Within a year or two, it would be obsolete as fashion changed. Blessed with abundant resources, America could afford to turn part of its productive capacity to creating glitz and fashionable waste. An older generation was careful to save and reuse; Americans in the Fifties began to use and throw away.

Though Eisenhower tried mightily to balance the federal budget, consumers did not follow suit when it came to their own family budgets. Americans had traditionally been thrifty by nature, but in the Fifties they were willing to "buy now, pay later," as automobile advertisements urged. The Federal Housing Administration and the Veteran's Administration both offered low-interest loans to allow families to buy new homes.

The very first credit card, the Diner's Club card appeared in 1950. That particular card was limited to paying for meals at a limited number of restaurants, but it was quickly followed by other cards, touching off a dramatic growth in borrowing. Private debt more than doubled from $104.8 billion to $263.3 billion during the Fifties. People borrowed to buy houses, cars, appliances, and even swimming pools. Buying on credit stimulated the economy, helping many to enjoy the good things in life even as it kept industry busy and unemployment low. Too much debt, as we've seen lately, can be a dangerous thing, but during the Fifties, borrowing mostly helped fuel the robust economy.

The prosperity of the Eisenhower years did not touch all Americans, however. Even as the nation prospered and the middle class did well, something like 25% of citizens lived in poverty (then defined as an annual income under $3,000 for a family of four). Much of this poverty was said to be "invisible;" it affected blacks in urban neighborhoods and whites in depressed rural areas like the Appalachian Mountains.

Middle-class folks enjoying their new swimming pools in the suburbs could go through their lives without ever seeing the misery in other sectors of American society.

Poverty amid plenty was another paradox of the Fifties, but most was able to ignore it. In the final assessment, President Eisenhower successfully guided the United States to become an economic superpower, giving the majority of its citizens a better life and a sense of security.

In keeping with the split personality of the decade, there were really two separate religious revivals. The first was the type of public religion typified by Eisenhower's stance. This was a reaction to the "godless" Communism of America's enemies. The president said, "Our government makes no sense unless it is founded on a deeply felt religious faith—and I don't care what it is." Eisenhower was worried about citizens "deadened in mind and soul by a materialistic philosophy of life."

In 1954, he signed a bill to add "one nation under God" to the Pledge of Allegiance. Two years later, Congress made "In God We Trust" the national motto of the United States.

A rapidly growing population of young people and extensive coverage by the mass media made the problem seem far graver than it was. Young people adopted the fashions of gangs—the slang, leather jackets, and ducktail hair styles (just as many teens in more recent years have adopted the fashions of "gangsta" culture). But, then as now, most of these stylistically rebellious teens did not commit crimes or get in trouble with the police. But the youth movement of the Fifties did not overturn society, as some grown-up experts feared it would. Youth rebellion was aimed at parents and the confines of daily life, not at society as a whole.

The only youthful rebels of the era who you might truly call revolutionary were the

African Americans who participated in serious protests against wider injustices in society. Most white teenagers did not concern themselves with social problems and some educators referred to them as a "silent generation." Like many in the Fifties, they were restless. But as they grew up, they tended to adapt to the norms of the wider society.

Chapter 5 - Ever Expanding Government

The Great Society

The Great Society was a set of domestic programs proposed or enacted in the United States on the initiative of President Lyndon B. Johnson. Two main goals of the Great Society social reforms were to eliminate poverty and racial injustice. New major spending programs that addressed education, medical care, urban problems, and transportation were launched during this period. The Great Society in scope and sweep resembled the New Deal domestic agenda of Franklin D. Roosevelt, but differed sharply in types of programs enacted.

Some Great Society proposals were stalled initiatives from John F. Kennedy's New Frontier. Johnson's success depended on his skills of persuasion, coupled with the Democratic landslide in the 1964 election that brought in many new liberals to Congress. Antiwar Democrats complained that spending on the Vietnam War choked off the Great Society. While some of the programs have been cancelled or had their funding reduced, many of them, including Medicare, Medicaid, the Older Americans Act and federal education funding, continue to the present. The Great Society's programs expanded under the administrations of Richard Nixon and Gerald Ford.

Unlike the New Deal, which was a response to a severe financial and economic calamity, the Great Society initiatives came just as the United States' post-World War II prosperity was starting to fade. But before the coming decline was being felt by the middle and upper classes. This time rather than changing America in the name of social justice because of crisis, it was now being changed as a matter of government policy.

President Kennedy proposed a tax cut lowering the top marginal rate by 20%, from 91% to 71%, which was enacted in February 1964 (three months after Kennedy's assassination) by Lyndon Johnson.

Gross National Product rose 10% in the first year of the tax cut, and economic growth averaged a rate of 4.5% from 1961 to 1968. Disposable personal income rose 15% in 1966 alone.

Federal revenues increased dramatically from $94 billion in 1961 to $150 billion in 1967. As the Baby Boom generation aged, two and a half times more Americans would enter the labor force between 1965 and 1980 than had between 1950 and 1965.

Racial segregation persisted throughout the South. The Civil Rights Movement was gathering momentum, and in 1964 urban riots began within black neighborhoods in New York City and Los Angeles; by 1968 hundreds of cities had major riots that caused a severe conservative political backlash. Foreign affairs were quiet except for the Vietnam War, which intensified from limited involvement in 1963 to a large-scale military operation in 1968 that soon overshadowed the Great Society.

Although conservatives gained seats in the 1966 midterm elections, and despite the attention given to foreign affairs, Johnson was still able to secure the passage of a wide range of reforms during his last two years in office. During the last summer and autumn of his administration, laws were passed to extend the Food Stamp Program. Additionally to expand consumer protection, to improve safety standards, to train health professionals, to help handicapped Americans, and to further urban programs. By now almost the entire Democrat party and almost half of the Republicans as well were gaining the momentum toward a true ruling class desirous of ever expanding power.

In 1968, a new Housing Act was passed which banned racial discrimination in housing and subsidized the construction or rehabilitation of low-income housing units.

That same year, a new program for federally-funded job retraining for the hardcore unemployed in fifty cities was introduced. Together with the strongest Federal gun control bill relating to the transportation of guns across State lines in American history until that point. By the end of the Johnson Administration, 226 out of 252 major legislative requests (over a four-year period) had been met, Federal Aid to the poor had risen from $9.9 billion in 1960 to $30 billion by 1968, and one million Americans had been retrained under previously nonexistent Federal programs.

President Kennedy had employed several task forces composed of scholars and experts to craft New Frontier legislation and to deal with foreign affairs. The reliance on experts appealed to Johnson, in part because the task forces would work in secret and outside the existing governmental bureaucracy and directly for the White House staff. Almost immediately after the Ann Arbor speech, 14 separate task forces began studying nearly all major aspects of United States society under the guidance of presidential assistants Bill Moyers and Richard N. Goodwin. The average task force had nine members and was composed of governmental experts and academicians. Only one of the task forces on the 1965 legislative program addressed foreign affairs and foreign economic policy; the rest were charged with domestic policy.

After task force reports were submitted to the White House, Moyers began a second round of review. The recommendations were circulated among the agencies concerned and were evaluated by new committees composed mostly of government officials. Experts on relations with Congress were also drawn into the deliberations to get the best advice on persuading the Congress to pass the legislation.

The task force approach, combined with Johnson's electoral victory in 1964 and his talents in securing congressional approval, were widely credited with the success of the legislation agenda in 1965. Critics later cited the task forces as a factor in a perceived elitist approach to Great Society programs.

Also, because many of the initiatives did not originate from outside lobbying, some programs had no political constituencies that would support their continued funding.

Except for of the Civil Rights Act of 1964, the Great Society agenda was not a widely discussed issue during the 1964 presidential election campaigns. Johnson won the election with 61% of the vote, the largest percentage since the popular vote first became widespread in 1824, and he carried all but six states.

Democrats gained enough seats to control more than two-thirds of each chamber in the Eighty-ninth Congress with a 68-32 margin in the Senate and a 295-140 margin in the House of Representatives.

The political realignment allowed House leaders to alter rules that had allowed Southern Democrats to kill New Frontier and civil rights legislation in committee, which aided efforts to pass Great Society legislation. In 1965, the first session of the Eighty-ninth Congress created the core of the Great Society. The Johnson Administration sent eighty-seven bills to Congress, and Johnson signed eighty-four, or 96%.

Historian Alan Brinkley has suggested the most important domestic achievement of the Great Society may have been its success in the civil rights movement into law. Four civil rights acts were passed, including three laws in the first two years of Johnson's presidency. The Civil Rights Act of 1964 forbade job discrimination and the segregation of public accommodations. The Voting Rights Act of 1965 assured minority registration and voting. It suspended use of literacy or other voter-qualification tests that had sometimes served to keep African-Americans off voting lists and provided for federal court lawsuits to stop discriminatory poll taxes. It also reinforced the Civil Rights Act of 1964 by sanctioning the appointment of federal voting examiners in areas that did not meet voter-participation requirements. The Immigration and Nationality Services Act of 1965 abolished the national-origin quotas in immigration law. The Civil Rights Act of 1968 banned housing discrimination and extended constitutional protections to Native Americans on reservations.

The most ambitious and controversial part of the Great Society was its initiative to end poverty. The Kennedy Administration had considered a federal effort against poverty. Johnson, who, as a teacher had observed extreme poverty in Texas among Mexican-Americans, launched an "unconditional war on poverty" in the first months of his presidency with the goal of eliminating hunger and deprivation from American life. The centerpiece of the War on Poverty was the Economic Opportunity Act of 1964, which created an Office of Economic Opportunity (OEO) to oversee various community-based antipoverty programs. The OEO reflected a fragile consensus among policymakers the best way to deal with poverty was not simply to raise the incomes of the poor. It was also to help them better themselves through education, job training, and community development. Central to its mission was the idea of "community action", the participation of the poor in framing and managing the programs designed to help them.

The War on Poverty began with a $1 billion appropriation in 1964 and spent another $2 billion in the following two years. It spawned dozens of programs, among them the Job Corps, whose purpose was to help disadvantaged youth develop marketable skills. The Neighborhood Youth Corps, established to give poor urban youths work experience and to encourage them to stay in school. Volunteers in Service to America (VISTA), a domestic version of the Peace Corps, which placed concerned citizens with community-based agencies to work towards empowerment of the poor. The Model Cities Program for urban redevelopment; Upward Bound, which assisted poor high school students entering college. Legal services for the poor; the Food Stamps program; the Community Action Program, which started local Community Action Agencies charged with helping the poor become self-sufficient; and Project Head Start, which offered preschool education for poor children.

The most extensive educational ingredient of the Great Society was the Elementary and Secondary Education Act of 1965, designed by Commissioner of Education Francis Keppel. It was signed into law on April 11, 1965, less than three months after it was introduced. It ended a long-standing political taboo by providing significant federal aid to public education. Initially allotting more than $1 billion to help schools purchase materials and start special education programs to schools with a high concentration of low-income children. The Act established Head Start, which had originally been started by the Office of Economic Opportunity as an eight-week summer program, as a permanent program. The Higher Education Act of 1965 increased federal money given to universities, created scholarships and low-interest loans for students, and established a national Teacher Corps to provide teachers to poverty-stricken areas of the United States.

The Social Security Act of 1965 authorized Medicare and provided federal funding for many of the medical costs of older Americans.

The legislation overcame the bitter resistance, particularly from the American Medical Association, to the idea of publicly funded health care or "socialized medicine" by making its benefits available to everyone over sixty-five, regardless of need, and by linking payments to the existing private insurance system.

In 1966 welfare recipients of all ages received medical care through the Medicaid program. Medicaid was created on July 30, 1965 under Title XIX of the Social Security Act of 1965. Each state administers its own Medicaid program while the federal Centers for Medicare and Medicaid Services (CMS) monitors the state-run programs and establishes requirements for service delivery, quality, funding, and eligibility standards.

The most sweeping reorganization of the federal government since the National Security Act of 1947 was the consolidation of transportation agencies into a cabinet-level Department of Transportation. The department was authorized by Congress on October 15, 1966 and began operations on April 1, 1967. The Urban Mass Transportation Act of 1964 provided $375 million for large-scale urban public or private rail projects in the form of matching funds to cities and states and created the Urban Mass Transit Administration now the Federal Transit Administration. The National Traffic and Motor Vehicle Safety Act of 1966 and the Highway Safety Act of 1966 were enacted, largely as a result of Ralph Nader's book Unsafe at Any Speed.

In 1964, Johnson named Assistant Secretary of Labor Esther Peterson to be the first presidential assistant for consumer affairs. The Cigarette Labeling Act of 1965 required packages to carry warning labels. The Motor Vehicle Safety Act of 1966 set standards through creation of the National Highway Traffic Safety Administration. The Fair Packaging and Labeling Act require products identify manufacturer, address, clearly mark quantity and servings.

The statute also authorizes permits HEW and FTC to establish and define voluntary standard sizes. The nanny state was not only on the move but it was in full swing.

Joseph A. Califano, Jr. has suggested that Great Society's main contribution to the environment was an extension of protections beyond those aimed at to conserve untouched resources. Discussing his administration's environmental policies, Lyndon Johnson suggested that "the air we breathe, our water, our soil and wildlife, are being blighted by poisons and chemicals which are the by-products of technology and industry. The society that receives the rewards of technology, must, as a cooperating whole, take responsibility for [their] control. To deal with these new problems will require a new conservation.

We must not only protect the countryside and save it from destruction; we must restore what has been destroyed and salvage the beauty and charm of our cities. Our conservation must be not just the classic conservation of protection and development, but a creative conservation of restoration and innovation." At the behest of Secretary of the Interior Stewart Udall, the Great Society included several new environmental laws to protect air and water. Environmental legislation enacted included: Clear Air, Water Quality and Clean Water Restoration Acts and Amendments. Wilderness Act of 1964, Endangered Species Preservation Act, Solid Waste Disposal Act of 1965, Motor Vehicle Air Pollution Control Act of 1965 and the National Historic Preservation Act of 1966.

Libertarian economist Thomas Sowell argues that the Great Society programs only contributed to the destruction of African American families, saying "the black family. Those families had survived centuries of slavery and discrimination, began rapidly disintegrating in the liberal welfare state that subsidized unwed pregnancy and changed welfare from an emergency rescue to a way of life." Professor William L. Anderson also criticized the War on Poverty, noting the increase of dependency on the government as being harmful to the lower classes.

Lyndon B. Johnson (LBJ), as he took over the presidency after the death of Kennedy, initially did not consider Vietnam a priority and was more concerned with his "Great Society" and progressive social programs. Presidential aide Jack Valenti recalls, "Vietnam at the time was no bigger than a man's fist on the horizon. We hardly discussed it because it was not worth discussing." On 24 November 1963, Johnson said, "the battle against communism... must be joined... with strength and determination."

The military revolutionary council, meeting in lieu of a strong South Vietnamese leader, was made up of 12 members headed by General Duong Van Minh—whom Stanley Karnow, a journalist on the ground, later recalled as "a model of lethargy." Lodge, frustrated by the end of the year, cabled home about Minh: "Will he be strong enough to get on top of things?" His regime was overthrown in January 1964 by General Nguyen Khanh. However, there was persistent instability in the military as several coups—not all successful—occurred in a short space of time. On 2 August 1964, the USS Maddox, on intelligence mission along North Vietnam's coast, allegedly fired upon and damaged several torpedo boats that had been stalking it in the Gulf of Tonkin.

A second attack was reported two days later on the USS Turner Joy and Maddox in the same area. The circumstances of the attack were murky. Lyndon Johnson commented to Undersecretary of State George Ball that "those sailors out there may have been shooting at flying fish." The second attack led to retaliatory air strikes, prompted Congress to approve the Gulf of Tonkin Resolution, and gave the president power to conduct military operations in Southeast Asia without declaring war. In the same month, Johnson pledged that he was not "... committing American boys to fighting a war that I think ought to be fought by the boys of Asia to help protect their own land."

An undated NSA publication declassified in 2005, however, revealed that there was no attack on 4 August. It had already been called into question long before this. "Gulf of Tonkin incident", writes Louise Gerdes "is an oft-cited example of the way in which Johnson misled the American people to gain support for his foreign policy in Vietnam."

From strength of approximately 5,000 at the start of 1959 the Viet Cong's ranks grew to about 100,000 at the end of 1964. Between 1961 and 1964 the Army's strength rose from about 850,000 to nearly a million men. The numbers for U.S. troops deployed to Vietnam during the same period were quite different; 2,000 in 1961, rising rapidly to 16,500 in 1964.

The National Security Council recommended a three-stage escalation of the bombing of North Vietnam. On 2 March 1965, following an attack on a U.S. Marine barracks at Pleiku, Operation Flaming Dart initiated when

Soviet Premier Alexei Kosygin was at a state visit to North Vietnam, Operation Rolling Thunder and Operation Arc Light commenced.

The bombing campaign, which ultimately lasted three years, was intended to force North Vietnam to cease its support for the National Front for the Liberation of South Vietnam. As well, it was aimed at bolstering the morale of the South Vietnamese. Between March 1965 and November 1968, "Rolling Thunder" deluged the north with a million tons of missiles, rockets and bombs.

Bombing was not restricted to North Vietnam. Other aerial campaigns, such as Operation Commando Hunt, targeted different parts of the NLF and VPA infrastructure. These included the Ho Chi Minh trail, which ran through Laos and Cambodia. The objective of forcing North Vietnam to stop its support for the NLF, however, was never reached.

The plan was approved by Johnson and marked a profound departure from the previous administration's insistence that the government of South Vietnam was responsible for defeating the guerrillas. Westmoreland predicted victory by the end of 1967. Johnson did not, however, communicate this change in strategy to the media. Instead he emphasized continuity. The change in U.S. policy depended on matching the North Vietnamese and the NLF in a contest of attrition and morale.

The opponents were locked in a cycle of escalation. The idea that the government of South Vietnam could manage its own affairs was shelved.

Washington encouraged its SEATO allies to contribute troops. Australia, New Zealand, the Republic of Korea, Thailand, and the Philippines all agreed to send troops. Major allies, however, notably NATO nations Canada and the United Kingdom, declined Washington's troop requests.

The Johnson administration employed a "policy of minimum candor" in its dealings with the media. Military information officers sought to manage media coverage by stressing stories that portrayed progress in the war. Overtime, this policy damaged the public trust in official pronouncements. As the media's coverage of the war and that of the Pentagon diverged, a so-called credibility gap developed.

On 10 May 1968, despite low expectations, peace talks began between the United States and the Democratic Republic of Vietnam. Negotiations stagnated for five months, until Johnson gave orders to halt the bombing of North Vietnam. The Democratic candidate, Vice President Hubert Humphrey, was running against Republican former vice president Richard Nixon.

As historian Robert Dallek writes, "Lyndon Johnson's escalation of the war in Vietnam divided Americans into warring camps... cost 30,000 American lives by the time he left office, and destroyed Johnson's presidency..."

His refusal to send more U.S. troops to Vietnam was seen as Johnson's admission that the war was lost. It can be seen that the refusal was a tacit admission that the war could not be won by escalation, at least not at a cost acceptable to the American people. As Secretary of Defense Robert McNamara noted, "the dangerous illusion of victory by the United States was therefore dead."

Protests against the brutality and stupidity of the war in Vietnam started slowly, beginning in Berkeley, California in 1965. By 1968, there were massive anti-Vietnam war marches, protests, sit-ins and strikes in major cities and on college campuses across the country. A turning point was in on May 4, 1970, when four peaceful student demonstrators at Kent State University in Ohio were killed by Ohio National Guardsmen during a noon-time campus anti-war rally. Nine other students were injured by being shot by Ohio National Guardsmen as well.

After that, things got very nasty across the country as thousands of students took to the streets, outraged at the shedding of blood in America by government agents. Anti-war protests became increasingly violent in tone; some college campuses became virtual war zones, with arson and bombings as well as low-level vandalism, such as spray-painting and window-breaking.

The draft was used by the United States government to force young adult men into uniform to fight the raging war on Vietnam. However, among many college age men and among some young working men, there was a growing resistance to the draft and in particular to serving in the Vietnam War Theater of operations. Resistance at first was scattered, but as the war heated up and as anti-war protests grew more organized in the middle of the 1960s, a formal anti-draft movement called, The Resistance, made its appearance. There were mass anti-draft rallies on the campuses of many of the more elite colleges and Universities including Stanford University, University of California at Berkeley, UCLA, Harvard University, Columbia University and University of Michigan. Draft cards, which were official documents issued by the Selective Service System, an agency of the U. S. government, were burned en masse at these public rallies.

Part and parcel with the growing anti-Vietnam war protests in the 1960s was a growing general disillusionment with American middle class material progress, with the "keeping up with the Jones mentality" and the general emptiness of American life. As alienated kids protested, grew their hair and smoked their pot, they began to reorder their lives and some of them "dropped out" of school and traditional careers to pursue different styles of living. These kids and young adults became known as "hippies." Of course, no one really knew what a "hippie" really was, so you just smiled when someone asked you if you were a "hippie."

The Great Society is the direct descendant of those other pretentiously named policies of twentieth-century America: the Square Deal, the New Freedom, the New Era, the New Deal, the Fair Deal, and the New Frontier. All of these assorted Deals created a basic and fundamental shift in American life.

A shift from a relatively laissez-faire economy and minimal state to a society in which the state is unquestionably king. In the previous century, the government could safely have been ignored by almost everyone; now we have become a country in which the government is the great and unending source of power and privilege.

Every act of the state is necessarily an occasion for inflicting burdens and assigning subsidies and privileges. By seizing revenue by means of coercion and assigning rewards as it disburses the funds, the state creates ruling and ruled classes; for one example, classes of what Calhoun discerned as net "taxpayers" and "tax-consumers," those who live off taxation. And since by its nature can only be supported out of the surplus of production above subsistence, the ruling class does constitute a minority of the citizenry. Promoting this ideology among the masses has always been a prime function of intellectuals, a function that has created the basis for co-opting a corps of intellectuals into a secure and permanent place in the state apparatus. In former centuries, these intellectuals formed a priestly caste that was able to wrap a cloak of mystery and divinity about the actions of the state for the public.

In wartime various states find themselves in danger from one another, every state has found war a fertile field for spreading the myth among its subjects that they are the ones in deadly danger, from which their state is protecting them.

In this way states have been able to dragoon their subjects into fighting and dying to save them under the pretext that the subjects were being saved from the dread Foreign Enemy. In the United States, the process of statization began in earnest under cover of the Civil War conscription, military rule, income tax, excise taxes, high tariffs, national banking and credit expansion for favored businesses, paper money, land grants to railroads, and reached full flower as a result of World Wars I and II, to finally culminate in the Great Society.

The indispensable intellectual role of engineering popular consent for state rule is played, for the Great Society, by the liberal intelligentsia, who provide the rationale of "general welfare," "humanity," and the "common good" just as the conservative intellectuals work the other side of the Great Society street by offering the rationale of "national security" and "national interest".

The liberals, in short, push the "welfare" part of our omnipresent welfare-warfare state, while the conservatives stress the warfare side of the pie. This analysis of the role of the liberal intellectuals puts into more sophisticated perspective the seeming "sellout" of these intellectuals as compared to their role during the 1930s. In the thirties, the proponents of the New Deal were concerned with condemning as "reactionaries" those big businessmen who clung to older individualist ideals and failed to understand or adhere to the new monopoly system of the corporate state.

The cruelest myth fostered by the liberals is that the Great Society functions as a great boon and benefit to the poor; in reality, when we cut through the frothy appearances to the cold reality underneath, the poor are the major victims of the welfare state. The poor are the ones to be conscripted to fight and die in the Great Society's imperial wars. The poor are cruelly victimized by an income tax that left and right alike misconstrue as an egalitarian program to soak the rich; actually, various tricks and exemptions insure that it is the poor and the middle classes who are hit the hardest.

The poor are victimized too by a welfare state of which the cardinal tenet is perpetual if controlled inflation. The inflation and the heavy government spending favor the businesses of the military-industrial complex, while the poor and the retired, those on fixed pensions or Social Security, are hit the hardest. Liberals have often scoffed at the anti-inflationist's' stress on the "widows and orphans" as major victims of inflation, but these remain major victims nevertheless.

Farm programs that supposedly aid poor farmers actually serve the large wealthy farmers at the expense of sharecropper and consumer alike; and commissions that regulate industry serve to cartelize it. The mass of workers is forced by governmental measures into trade unions that tame and integrate the labor force into the toils of the accelerating corporate state, there to be subjected to arbitrary wage "guidelines" and ultimate compulsory arbitration.

The role of the liberal intellectual and of liberal rhetoric is even starker in foreign economic policy. Ostensibly designed to "help the underdeveloped countries," foreign aid has served as a gigantic subsidy by the American taxpayer of American export firms, a similar subsidy to American foreign investment through guarantees and subsidized government loans, an engine of inflation for the recipient country, and a form of massive subsidy to the friends and clients of our government in the recipient country.

The symbiosis between liberal intellectuals and despotic statism at home and abroad is, furthermore, no accident. For at the heart of this mentality is an enormous desire to do good to the mass of other people, and since people don't usually wish to be done good to. The liberal welfarist inevitably ends by reaching for the big stick with which to push the ungrateful masses around. So, the liberal doctrine itself provides a powerful stimulant for the intellectuals to seek state power and ally themselves with the other rulers of the corporate state.

The chaotic events of the 60's, including war and social change, seemed intended to continue in the 70's. Major trends included a growing disillusionment of government, advances in civil rights, increased influence of the women's movement, a heightened concern for the environment, and increased space exploration. Many of the "radical" ideas of the 60's gained wider acceptance in the new decade, and were mainstreamed into American life and culture.

Amid war, social realignment and presidential impeachment proceedings, American culture flourished. Indeed, the events of the times were reflected in and became the inspiration for much of the music, literature, entertainment, and even fashion of the decade.

Although the explanations for the increase in divorce vary, many experts believe that because the courts accepted mental cruelty as grounds for divorce. Courts tended to award custody of children to their mothers, divorce and remarriage became more acceptable to and for women.

The role of women in society was profoundly altered with growing feminism across the world and with the presence and rise of a significant number of women as heads of state. Outside of monarchies and heads of government in a number of countries across the world during the 1970s, many being the first women to hold such positions. Non-monarch women heads of state and heads of government in this period included Isabel Martínez de Perón as the first woman President in Argentina and the first woman non-monarch head of state in the Western hemisphere in 1974.

Elisabeth Domitien becomes the first woman Prime Minister of the Central African Republic, Indira Gandhi continuing as Prime Minister of India until 1977 (and taking office again in 1980),

Prime Minister Golda Meir of Israel and acting Chairman Soong Ching-ling of the People's Republic of China continuing their leadership from the sixties, Lidia Gueiler Tejada becoming the interim President of Bolivia beginning from 1979 to 1980. Maria de Lourdes Pintasilgo becoming the first woman Prime Minister of Portugal in 1979, and Margaret Thatcher becoming the first woman Prime Minister of the United Kingdom in 1979. Both Indira Gandhi and Margaret Thatcher would remain important political figures in the following decade in the 1980s.

In the Western world, social progressive values that began in the 1960s, such as increasing political awareness and political and economic liberty of women, continued to grow.

The hippie culture, which started in the latter half of the 1960s, waned by the early 1970s and faded towards the middle part of the decade, which involved opposition to the Vietnam War, opposition to nuclear weapons, the advocacy of world peace, and hostility to the authority of government and big business. The environmentalist movement began to increase dramatically in this period. Industrialized countries, except Japan, experienced an economic recession due to an oil crisis caused by oil embargoes by the Organization of Arab Petroleum Exporting Countries. The crisis saw the first instance of stagflation which began a political and economic trend of the replacement of Keynesian economic theory with neoliberal economic theory, in with the first neoliberal governments being created in Chile, where a military coup led by Augusto Pinochet took place in 1973, and in the United Kingdom with the 1979 elections resulting in the victory of its Conservative Party under Margaret Thatcher in 1979.

Novelist Tom Wolfe coined the term Me decade in his article "The "Me" Decade and the Third Great Awakening," published by New York magazine in August 1976 referring to the 1970s. The term describes a general new attitude of Americans towards atomized individualism in clear contrast with the 1960s.

Wolfe attributes disappearance of the "proletariat" with the appearance of the "lower middle class," citing the economic boom of Post-War America. It afforded the average American a sort of self determination and individuation that ran alongside economic prosperity. The nature of the "chivalric tradition" and the philosophy behind "the finishing school" are inherently dedicated to the building and forming of personal character and conduct.

The attitude of the counter-culture of the 1960s and The New Left promoted a recovery of the self in the wave, of what was deemed, a flawed, corrupt, and almost fascistic, America.

131

This philosophy left the 1970s with the promise that the use LSD or acid unveiled the true and the real self. Wolfe describes the revelatory experience of hallucinogens as attenuating the ecstatic religious experience, transforming the religious climate in American. Chronicling the First and Second Great Awakenings, Wolfe comes to describe the "Me decade as the "Third Great Awakening."

Inflation and Stagflation

The Feminist Movement in the United States which began in the 1960s carried over to the 1970s, and took a prominent role within society. The fiftieth anniversary of the passage of the Nineteenth Amendment to the United States Constitution which legalized female suffrage in 1970 was commemorated by the Women's Strike for Equality and other protests.

With the anthology Sisterhood is Powerful and other works, such as Sexual Politics, being published at the start of the decade, feminism started to reach a larger audience than ever before. In addition, the Supreme Court's 1973 decision of Roe v. Wade that constitutionalized the right to an abortion brought the women's rights movement into the national political spotlight. Gloria Steinem, Betty Friedan, Betty Ford, Shirley Chisholm, Bella Abzug, Robin Morgan, Kate Millet, Elizabeth Holtzman, among many others, led the movement for women's equality.

Doors of opportunity were more numerous and much further open than before as women gained unheard of success in business, politics, education, science, the law, and even the home. Though most aims of the movement were successful, however, there were some significant failures. Most notably the failure to ratify the Equal Rights Amendment to the U.S. Constitution with only three more states needed to ratify it efforts to ratify ERA. Also, the wage gap failed to close, but it did become smaller there is also action still taken to ensure pay equality to this day.

The original feminist movement largely ended in 1982 with the failure of the Equal Rights Amendment. With new conservative leadership in Washington, D.C. American women created a brief, but powerful, third-wave in the early 1990s. Sexual harassment inspired by the Anita Hill–Clarence Thomas Senate Judiciary Committee hearings of 1991 and violence against women. The results of the movement included a new awareness of such issues amongst women, and unprecedented numbers of women elected to public office, particularly the United States Senate.

The seventies were seen as the "woman's turn", though many feminists incorporated civil rights ideals into their movement. A fearless feminist who had inherited the leadership position of the civil rights movement from her husband, Coretta Scott King, as leader of the black movement, called for an end to all discrimination, helping the Woman's Liberation movement and other movements as well. At the National Women's Conference in 1977 a minority women's resolution, promoted by King and others, passed to ensure racial equality in the movement's goals.

After which, in one of the most emotional moments of the Conference, women of all races joined hands and sung "We Shall Overcome".

Similarly, the gay movement made a huge step forward in the 1970s with the election of political figures such as Harvey Milk to public office and the advocating of anti-gay discrimination legislation passed and not passed during the decade. Many celebrities, including Freddie Mercury and Andy Warhol, also "came out" during this decade, bringing gay culture further into the limelight.

The economies of much of the developing world continued to make steady progress in the early 1970s, because of the Green Revolution. They might have thrived and become stable in the way that Europe recovered after World War II through the Marshall Plan; however, their economic growth was slowed by the oil crisis but boomed immediately after. Developing nations that were rich in oil experienced economic growth.

Others, not so endowed, saw the economic strain of oil price hikes lead to economic decline. Particularly in Africa where many moderately democratic states became dictatorial regimes. Many Middle Eastern democracies turned into regimes with pseudo-democratic governments. Several Asian countries also saw the rise of dictators, including Indonesia, Philippines, and South Korea.

People were influenced by the rapid pace of societal change and the hope for a more egalitarian society in cultures that were long colonized and have an even longer history of hierarchical social structure. Other common global situations of the 1970s world include: increasingly flexible and varied gender roles for women in industrialized societies. More women could enter the workforce. However, the gender role of men remained as that of a breadwinner. The period also saw the socioeconomic affect of an ever-increasing number of women entering the nonagrarian economic workforce. The Iranian revolution also affected global attitudes to and among those of the Muslim faith toward the end of the 1970s.

The global experience of the cultural transition of the 1970s and an experience of a global zeitgeist revealed the interdependence of economies since World War II, in a world increasingly polarized between the United States and the Soviet Union.

The 1970s were perhaps the worst decade of most industrialized countries' economic performance since the Great Depression. Although there was no severe economic depression as witnessed in the 1930s, economic growth rates were lower than previous decades. As a result, the 1970s adversely distinguished itself from the prosperous postwar period between 1945 and 1973. The oil shocks of 1973 and 1979 added to the existing ailments and conjured high inflation throughout much of the world for the rest of the decade. U.S. manufacturing industries began to decline as a result, with the US running its last trade surplus (as of 2009) in 1975. In contrast, Japan's economy continued to expand and prosper during the decade, boosted by growing exports.

The average annual inflation rate from 1900 to 1970 was about 2.5%. From 1970, however, the average rate hit about 6%, topping out at 13.3% by 1979. This period is also known for "stagflation", in which inflation and unemployment steadily increased, therefore leading to double-digit interest rates that rose to unprecedented levels (above 12% per year).

The prime rate hit 21.5 in December 1980, the highest in history. By the time of 1980, when U.S. President Jimmy Carter was running for reelection against Ronald Reagan, the misery index (the sum of the unemployment rate and the inflation rate) had reached an all-time high of 21.98%.

The economic problems of the 1970s would result in a sluggish cynicism replacing the optimistic attitudes of the 1950s and 1960s. Faith in government was at an all-time low in the aftermath of Vietnam and Watergate, as exemplified by the low voter turnout in the 1976 United States presidential election.

In Eastern Europe, Soviet-style command economies began showing signs of stagnation, in which successes were persistently dogged by setbacks. The oil shock increased East European, particularly Soviet, exports, but a growing inability to increase agricultural output caused growing concern to the governments of the COMECON block, and a growing dependence on food imported from democratic nations.

On the other hand, export-driven economic development in Asia, especially by the Four Asian Tigers (Hong Kong, South Korea, Singapore, and Taiwan), resulted in rapid economic transformation and industrialization. Their abundance of cheap labor, combined with educational and other policy reforms, set the foundation for development in the region during the 1970s and beyond.

Economically, the 1970s were marked by the energy crisis which peaked in 1973 and 1979 (see 1973 oil crisis and 1979 oil crisis). After the first oil shock in 1973, gasoline was rationed in many countries.

Europe particularly depended on the Middle East for oil; the U.S. was also affected even though it had its own oil reserves. Many European countries introduced car-free days and weekends. In the U.S., customers with a license plate ending in an odd number were only allowed to buy gasoline on odd-numbered days, while even-numbered plate-holders could only buy gasoline on even-numbered days. The realization that oil reserves were not endless and technological development was not sustainable without potentially harming the environment ended the belief in limitless progress that had existed since the 19th century. As a result, ecological awareness rose substantially. This had a huge affect on the economy then.

The 1970s was an era of fuel price increases, rising insurance rates, safety concerns, and emissions controls. The 1973 oil crisis caused a move towards smaller, fuel-efficient vehicles. Attempts were made to produce electric cars, but they were largely unsuccessful. In the United States, imported cars became a significant factor for the first time, and several domestic-built subcompact models entered the market.

American-made cars such as the "quirky" AMC Gremlin, the jelly bean shaped AMC Pacer, and Pontiac Firebird's powerful Trans Am "sum up" the decade. Muscle cars and convertible models faded from favor during the early-1970s.

It was believed the 1976 Cadillac Eldorado would be the last American-built convertible, ending the open body style that once dominated the auto industry.

The Japanese automobile industry flourished during the 1970s compared to other major auto industries. Japanese vehicles became internationally renowned for their affordability, reliability, and fuel-efficiency, which was very important to many customers because of the oil embargo.

Japanese car manufacturing was prominent in its computerized robotic manufacturing techniques and lean manufacturing, and this contributed to high-efficiency and low production costs.

The Honda Civic was introduced in 1973, and sold at record numbers because of its high fuel-efficiency. Other popular compact cars included the Toyota Corolla and the Datsun Sunny, as well as other cars from those companies and others such as Subaru, Mitsubishi, and Mazda

In October 1973, the members of Organization of Arab Petroleum Exporting Countries or the OPEC (consisting of the Arab members of OPEC, plus Egypt and Syria) proclaimed an oil embargo "in response to the U.S. decision to re-supply the Israeli military" during the Yom Kippur war. The war lasted until March 1974. OPEC declared it would limit or stop oil shipments to the United States and other countries if they supported Israel in the conflict. With the US actions seen as initiating the oil embargo, the long-term possibility of embargo-related high oil prices, disrupted supply and recession, created a strong rift within NATO. Both European countries and Japan sought to disassociate themselves from the US Middle East policy. Arab oil producers had also linked the end of the embargo with successful US efforts to create peace in the Middle East, which complicated the situation.

To address these developments, the Nixon Administration began parallel negotiations with both Arab oil producers to end the embargo, and with Egypt, Syria, and Israel to arrange an Israeli pull back from the Sinai and the Golan Heights. After the fighting stopped, by January 18, 1974, Secretary of State Henry Kissinger had negotiated an Israeli troop withdrawal from parts of the Sinai.

The promise of a negotiated settlement between Israel and Syria was sufficient to convince Arab oil producers to lift the embargo in March 1974. By May, Israel agreed to withdraw from the Golan Heights.

Independently, the OPEC members agreed to use their leverage over the world price-setting mechanism for oil to stabilize their real incomes by raising world oil prices.

This action followed several years of steep income declines after the recent failure of negotiations with the major Western oil companies earlier in the month.

For the most part, industrialized economies relied on crude oil and OPEC was their major supplier. Because of the dramatic inflation experienced during this period, a popular economic theory has been that these price increases were to blame, as being suppressive of economic activity. However, the causality stated by this theory is often questioned.

The targeted countries responded with a wide variety of new, and mostly permanent, initiatives to contain their further dependency. The 1973 "oil price shock", along with the 1973–1974 stock market crash, has been regarded as the first event since the Great Depression to have a persistent economic effect.

A crisis emerged in the United States in 1979 during the wake of the Iranian Revolution. Amid massive protests, the Shah of Iran, Mohammad Reza Pahlavi, fled his country in early 1979, allowing the Ayatollah Khomeini to gain control. The protests shattered the Iranian oil sector. While the new regime resumed oil exports, it was inconsistent and at a lower volume, forcing prices to go up. Saudi Arabia and other OPEC nations, under the presidency of Dr. Mana Alotaiba increased production to offset the decline, and the overall loss in production was about 4 percent. However, a widespread panic resulted, driving the price far higher than would be expected under normal circumstances.

In 1980, following the Iraqi invasion of Iran, oil production in Iran nearly stopped, and Iraq's oil production was severely cut as well. After 1980, oil prices began a decline as production in Iran/Iraq stabilized and returned to normal.

The decade of the 1970s was a period of limited economic growth due in part to the energy crises of that decade. Though the mid decade was the worst period for the United States the economy was generally weak until the 1980s. The period marked the end of the general post-World War II economic boom. It differed from many previous recessions as being a stagflation, where high unemployment coincided with high inflation.

Other causes that contributed to the recession included the Vietnam War, which turned out costly for the United States of America and the fall of the Bretton Woods system.

The emergence of newly industrialized countries rose competition in the metal industry, triggering a steel crisis, where industrial core areas in North America and Europe were forced to re-structure. The 1973-1974 stock market crash made the recession evident.

According to the National Bureau of Economic Research, the recession in the United States lasted from November 1973 to March 1975. Although the economy was expanding from 1975 to the first recession of the early 1980s, which began in January 1980, inflation remained extremely high for the rest of the decade.

Since Israel's declaration of independence in 1948 this state has found itself in nearly continual conflict with the Arab world and some other predominantly Muslim countries. The animosity between the Arabs and the Israelis became a global issue during the 1970s. The Yom Kippur War of 1973, with the supplying of Israel by its Western allies while some Arab states received Soviet supplies, made this one of the most internationally threatening confrontations of the period.

The large oil discoveries in the Middle East and southwestern Asia, and the peaking of production in some of the more industrialized areas of the world gave some Muslim countries unique leverage in the world, beginning in the 1960s. The 1973 and 1979 crises, in particular, were demonstrations of the new power that these countries had found. The United States and other countries were forced to become more involved in the conflicts between these states and Israel leading to peace initiatives such as the Camp David Accords.

A challenge OPEC faced in the 1970s was the United States' unilaterally pulling out of the Bretton Woods Accord and taking the U.S. off the established Gold Exchange Standard in 1971. With that standard, only the value of the U.S. dollar was pegged to the price of gold and all other currencies were pegged to the U.S. dollar. The change resulted in instability in world currencies and depreciation of the value of the U.S. dollar, as well as other currencies, and decreasing real revenues for OPEC whose producers still priced oil in dollars.

OPEC was slow to adjust to the situation but finally made the decision to price oil against gold. Frustrated negotiations between OPEC and the major oil companies to revise the oil price agreement as well as the ongoing Middle East conflicts continued to stall OPEC's efforts at stabilization through this era.

As the 1960s the United States had made two successful manned lunar landings. Many Americans lost interest afterward, feeling that since the country had accomplished President John F. Kennedy's goal of landing on the moon by the end of the 1960s, there was no need for further missions. There was also a growing sentiment that the billions of dollars spent on the space program should be put to other uses. The moon landings continued through 1972, but the near loss of the Apollo 13 astronauts in April 1970 served to further anti-NASA feelings. Many of the ambitious projects NASA had planned for the 1970s were canceled amid heavy budget cutbacks, and instead it would devote most of the decade to the development of the space shuttle.

Meanwhile, the Soviets, having failed completely in their attempt at manned lunar landings, canceled the program in 1972. But by then, they had already started flying space stations. This would have problems of its own, especially the tragic loss of the Soyuz 11 crew in July 1971.

It eventually proved a success, with missions as long as six months being conducted by the end of the decade.

The decade of the 1970s were aligned for perhaps the most failed presidencies in our nation's history. The succession of Richard Nixon, Gerald Ford and Jimmy Carter were a burden to America. They were big government liberal, moderate and even some would call conservative.

Born on January 9, 1913, in Yorba Linda, California, Richard Millhouse Nixon grew up to be a hard-working lawyer. He served in the navy during World War II, and then returned to California to run for Congress as a Republican. After two terms in the House, Nixon won a Senate seat. In Congress, Nixon earned a reputation as a right-wing anti-communist.

Dwight Eisenhower chose Nixon as his running mate in 1952. Eisenhower thought the conservative Nixon would balance the ticket (Eisenhower was a moderate Republican), and would help the Republicans win California. Eisenhower and Nixon won the election. Nixon was Vice President for two terms. He was an active Vice President and often represented the President abroad, traveling to more than 56 countries.

In 1960, Nixon ran against John Kennedy for the White House. It was one of the closest races in history, but Nixon lost. In 1962, Nixon ran for the governorship of California, but lost again. He moved to New York to practice law. For a while, it seemed as if Nixon's political career was over. But during the Kennedy and Johnson years, Nixon kept in touch with Republican leaders. In 1968, they chose him to be their presidential candidate once again. This time, Nixon beat Democrat Hubert Humphrey.

Nixon's biggest problem during the early years of his presidency was the Vietnam War. Nixon slowly but steadily reduced the number of American troops in Southeast Asia, yet he also expanded the fighting to Cambodia and Laos. The widening war drew increased protests at home. But in August 1972, the last American ground troops left Vietnam.

A peace agreement was signed in Paris in January, 1973 that allowed American prisoners of war to return home. Nixon faced a Democratic majority in Congress, and most of his achievements are in foreign policy. Nixon established normal relations with communist China and made his memorable visit.

In May 1972, Nixon and Soviet leader Leonid Brezhnev signed the first Strategic Arms Limitation Talks (SALT) agreement. This agreement helped to slow the arms race and reduced American-Soviet tensions. Running for reelection on these achievements, Nixon easily defeated Democrat George McGovern in 1972.

Nixon's second term was slowly destroyed by the Watergate scandal. On June 17, 1972, five men who worked for Nixon's reelection committee were arrested while trying to burglarize the Democratic National Headquarters at the Watergate Hotel in Washington, D.C.

The investigation that followed gradually revealed a corrupt side to the Nixon administration. The President and his associates regarded political opponents as enemies to be destroyed—whether by legal or illegal means. Nixon may not have authorized many of the "dirty tricks" that were carried out in his name. But it became clear that he was involved in covering up the crimes of his underlings.

While the Watergate investigation was underway, a separate investigation revealed that Vice President Spiro Agnew had taken bribes while governor of Maryland. Agnew resigned in order to escape prosecution, and Nixon replaced him with Gerald Ford, a member of Congress. In July 1974, the House Judiciary Committee voted to impeach Nixon. To avoid impeachment, Nixon resigned on August 9, 1974, and Vice President Ford became President. The new President quickly pardoned Nixon. Nixon called the pardon "the most humiliating day of my life."

No man ever came to the White House in a more unusual way than did Gerald Rudolph Ford. Ford was the first President who was never elected to either the presidency or the vice presidency. Instead, Ford was chosen by President Richard Nixon to replace Vice President Spiro Agnew, who had resigned his office in disgrace. When Nixon himself resigned, Ford was elevated to the highest American political office.

"Jerry" Ford was born in Omaha, Nebraska, but he grew up in Grand Rapids, Michigan. Ford was a handsome and athletic young man who was especially good at football. He coached football and boxing while attending Yale Law School. When the United States entered World War II, Ford joined the navy. For most of the war, Ford was a gunnery officer on an aircraft carrier, and he took part in many of the major battles in the South Pacific.

After the war, Ford returned to Grand Rapids to practice law and to run for Congress. He won his first seat in 1949, and was reelected 11 times. Ford's honesty and sunny disposition made him a popular member of Congress.

His highest goal was to become Speaker of the House. But Ford realized that as a moderate Republican, he had no chance of reaching that goal in a Congress controlled by Democrats. He had decided to retire from Congress in 1976. But in 1973, Nixon chose him as the new Vice President. Ford was easily confirmed by Congress, and on December 6, 1973, he took the oath of office as Vice President. Less than a year later, Nixon's resignation made Ford President. One of Ford's first acts as President was to pardon Nixon for any crimes he might have committed as President. Ford wanted the nation to put the "long national nightmare of Watergate" behind. But many people thought Nixon should have been tried for his crimes, and the pardon cost Ford much popularity and support.

One of the major problems Ford faced was an economy in recession. Whip Inflation Now (WIN), Ford's program of voluntary wage and price controls, was a failure. Nor did his attempts to cut taxes and government spending seem to help. The unhealthy economy hurt Ford politically, and he was defeated by Democrat Jimmy Carter in the presidential race of 1976.

James Earl Carter, Jr. grew up in Plains, Georgia. He attended Annapolis Naval Academy and entered the navy in 1946. There, he joined the submarine service, and later became a nuclear submarine officer. When his father died, Carter resigned from the navy to run the family peanut farm. Carter applied modern agricultural methods on the farm and it eventually made him a millionaire. In 1962, Carter ran for the Georgia state senate, and won his seat after proving that his opponent had committed vote fraud. He won the governorship of Georgia in 1970. Carter proved to be a progressive governor who fought racism and promoted education.

In 1972, Carter began campaigning for the presidency. It seemed impossible at first that an obscure one-term southern governor could win. Carter's surprisingly strong showing in the primaries attracted enormous media attention. Campaigning as a Washington outsider, Carter promised a more honest, open, and responsive government. He defeated President Ford by a narrow margin.

Carter proved to be as hard-working and straightforward as he had promised. But many of the problems he faced had no easy solution. The nation's economic woes were aggravated by oil price increases from the Organization of Petroleum Exporting Countries (OPEC). Between 1978 and 1979 the price of oil rose almost 500 percent. It would take years for the economy to adjust to a new world of expensive energy. To make matters worse for Carter, on November 4, 1979, Iranian militants seized the United States embassy in Iran and took more than 60 hostages. The

Iranians soon released women and African Americans, but 52 hostages were held for more than a year. Carter froze Iranian assets in the United States, mounted an all-out diplomatic effort, and finally authorized a rescue attempt on April 24, 1980. The operation failed when American rescue helicopters malfunctioned and collided in the Iranian desert. Carter resisted pressure for a stronger military response, which probably would have led to the deaths of some or all of the hostages. Iran finally agreed to release the hostages in exchange for their frozen assets.

One notable triumph of his presidency was Carter's key role in negotiating a peace treaty between the Middle Eastern nations of Egypt and Israel. But the hostage crisis was a humiliating experience for many Americans, and Carter suffered for it at the polls. In 1980, Carter lost his reelection bid to Republican Ronald Reagan.

The seventies were a true trifecta of failure. Nixon's tarnished presidency filled was with poor economic decisions and illegal activity. Just when we thought it couldn't get worse along came Gerald Ford and corrected the record as he presided over a failing economy and more regulation.

But then when we really thought that it couldn't get worse, wrong again here's Jimmy! As president Jimmy Carter presided over one of the worst economies in our history. He was the third strike in a really bad at bat for the American presidency.

Chapter 6 - Trying to Correct Course

The Reagan Revolution

During the 1980s, hostile takeovers, leveraged buyouts, and mega-mergers spawned a new breed of billionaire. Donald Trump, Leona Helmsley and Ivan Boesky iconed the meteoric rise and fall of the rich and famous. If you've got it, flaunt it and you can have it all! Were watchwords. Forbes' list of 400 richest people became more important than its 500 largest companies. Binge buying and credit became a way of life and 'Shop Til you Drop' was the watchword. Labels were everything, even or especially for our children. Video games, aerobics, minivans, camcorders, and talk shows became part of our lives. The decade began with double-digit inflation, Reagan declared a war on drugs, Kermit didn't find it easy to be green, hospital costs rose, we lost many, many of our finest talents to AIDS which before the decade ended spread to black and Hispanic women, and unemployment rose. On the bright side, the US Constitution had its 200th birthday, Gone with the Wind turned 50, ET phoned home, and in 1989 Americans gave $115,000,000,000 to charity. And, internationally, at the very end of the decade the Berlin Wall was removed - making great changes for the decade to come!

Science and technology made terrific strides in the eighties. Large numbers of Americans began using personal computers in their homes, offices, and schools. Columbia, America's first reusable spacecraft was launched in 1981. A sad day in our history was January 28, 1986, when space shuttle Challenger exploded 74 seconds after liftoff at Cape Canaveral, Florida killing all seven astronauts, including school teacher Christa McAuliffe. Research money allowed for studies and new treatments for heart, cancer, and other diseases. Major advances in genetics research led to the 1988 funding of the Human Genome Project.

During this decade Wayne Williams was arrested in Atlanta for the murders of 23 black children, Sandra Day O'Connor became the first woman Supreme Court Justice, 52 hostages were released from their 444 days of captivity in Iran, the Vietnam Veterans Memorial inscribed with 57,939 names of American soldiers killed or missing in Vietnam was dedicated, income climbed more than 20 percent, Ivan Boesky of Drexel Burnham Lambert made headlines with insider trading scandals, Geraldine Ferraro was the first woman presidential candidate, Jesse Jackson was the first black candidate, the stock market tripled in 7 years yet survived the 1987 crash, and televangelist Jim Bakker was sentenced to 45 years for selling bogus lifetime vacations.

The sexual revolution encountered a major adversary when Rock Hudson died of AIDS in 1985. Prisons overflowed and violent crime rates which, in 1980, had tripled since 1960, continued to climb with the appearance of crack in 1985. From 1985 to 1990 the use of cocaine addiction was up 35 percent, though the number of users had declined. Nancy Reagan's Just Say No campaign had great influence.

Toward the end of the decade, President Bush called for a kinder, gentler nation and volunteerism and contributions reached an all time high. Families changed drastically during these years. The 80s continued the trends of the 60s and 70s - more divorces, more unmarrieds living together, more single parent families. The two-earner family was even more common than in previous decades, more women earned college and advanced degrees, married, and had fewer children. 1980 study by UCLA and American Council on Education indicated that college freshmen were more interested in status, power, and money than at any time during the past 15 years. Business Management was the most popular major.

American education came under fire during the 1980s. Liberals cried out against budget cuts and rising student costs. School districts offered teachers exams and exit exams became a part of graduating for Education majors.

Conservatives like E.D.Hirsch, Jr. and William Bennett advocated a return to the classics for college students and back to the basic skills for public school students.

An attempt was made to improve the teacher quality by raising salaries slightly. Columbia University, the last all male Ivy League school, began accepting women in 1983. President Reagan endorsed a constitutional amendment to permit school prayer. It was defeated.

Americans enjoyed many fundamental changes in their standard of living in the 1980s. One major transformation was the new, expanded role of television. Cable Television although available in the 1970s, became standard for most American households. This change ushered in a whole host of new programming.

Sports-minded Americans could watch the ESPN network 24 hours a day. Stations catered to the children of the baby boomers with youth-centered daily programming, and to the boomers themselves by broadcasting reruns of classic sitcoms at night. Americans could catch up with the news at any time by watching CNN.

MTV, or Music Television, brought a revolution to the recording industry. MTV broadcast music video interpretations of popular songs. Beginning in 1981 with the prophetic Buggles tune "Video Killed the Radio Star," MTV redefined popular music.

Stars like Madonna and Michael Jackson were much more able to convey an image as well as music. Madonna's " Material Girl" message typified the values of an increasingly materialistic decade.

Perhaps the product that introduced the greatest change in American lifestyles of the 1980s was the Personal Computer. Introduced by Apple in 1977, the personal computer allowed management of personal finances, quick word-processing, and desktop publishing from the home. Businesses could manage payroll, mailing lists, and inventories from one small machine. Gone were the ledgers of the past. The Silicon Valley of

California, which was the home to many of the firms that produced the processors that made these computers run, became the symbolic heart of the American technological economy.

"Greed is good," declared the lead character of the movie Wall Street. With the growing economy, many middle-class Americans rushed to invest in the bullish stock market and to flaunt their newly acquired wealth. Young Urban Professionals, or Yuppiess, replaced the socially conscious hippie of the previous generation of youth. Yuppies sought executive track jobs in large corporations and spent their money on upscale consumer products like Ray-Ban sunglasses, Polo apparel, and Mercedes and BMW automobiles. The health and fitness industry exploded as many yuppies engaged in regular fitness routines.

The hedonism of the 1970s was being re-evaluated. Many drugs, which were considered recreational in the '70s, were revealed as addictive, deadly substances. As reports of celebrities entering rehabilitation centers and the horrors of drug-ridden inner cities became widely known, First lady Nancy Reagan's message to "Just Say No" to drugs became more powerful. Regardless, newer and more dangerous substances like crack cocaine exacerbated the nations drug problem.

The sexual revolution was rocked by the spread of Acquired Immune Deficiency Syndrome, or AIDS. This deadly disease was most commonly communicated by sexual contact and the sharing of intravenous needles. With the risks of promiscuous behavior rising to a mortal level, monogamy and "safe sex" with condoms were practiced more regularly.

On February 6, 1911, Ronald Wilson Reagan was born in Tampico, Illinois. He attended high school in nearby Dixon and then worked his way through Eureka College. There, he studied economics and sociology, played on the football team, and acted in school plays. Upon graduation, he became a radio sports announcer.

A screen test in 1937 won him a contract in Hollywood. During the next two decades he appeared in 53 films.

As president of the Screen Actors Guild, Reagan became embroiled in disputes over the issue of Communism in the film industry; his political views shifted from liberal to conservative. He toured the country as a television host, becoming a spokesman for conservatism. In 1966 he was elected Governor of California by a margin of a million votes; he was re-elected in 1970.

Ronald Reagan won the Republican Presidential nomination in 1980 and chose as his running mate former Texas Congressman and United Nations Ambassador George Bush. Voters troubled by inflation and by the year-long confinement of Americans in Iran swept the Republican ticket into office. Reagan won 489 electoral votes to 49 for President Jimmy Carter.

On January 20, 1981, Reagan took office. Only 69 days later he was shot by a would-be assassin, but quickly recovered and returned to duty. His grace and wit during the dangerous incident caused his popularity to soar.

Dealing skillfully with Congress, Reagan obtained legislation to stimulate economic growth, curb inflation, increase employment, and strengthen national defense. He embarked upon a course of cutting taxes and Government expenditures, refusing to deviate from it when the strengthening of defense forces led to a large deficit.

The central theme of Reagan's national agenda, however, was his belief that the federal government had become too big and intrusive. In the early 1980s, while he was cutting taxes, Reagan was also slashing social programs. Reagan also undertook a campaign throughout his tenure to reduce or eliminate government regulations affecting the consumer, the workplace, and the environment. At the same time, however, he feared that the United States had neglected its military in the wake of the Vietnam War, so he successfully pushed for big increases in defense spending.

The combination of tax cuts and higher military spending overwhelmed more modest reductions in spending on domestic programs. As a result, the federal budget deficit swelled even beyond the levels it had reached during the recession of the early 1980s. From $74,000 million in 1980, the federal budget deficit rose to $221,000 million in 1986. It fell back to $150,000 million in 1987, but then started growing again. Some economists worried that heavy spending and borrowing by the federal government would re-ignite inflation, but the Federal Reserve remained vigilant about controlling price increases, moving quickly to raise interest rates any time it seemed a threat.

Under Chairman Paul Volcker and his successor, Alan Greenspan, the Federal Reserve retained the central role of economic traffic cop, eclipsing Congress and the president in guiding the nation's economy.

A renewal of national self-confidence by 1984 helped Reagan and Bush win a second term with an unprecedented number of electoral votes. Their victory turned away Democratic challengers Walter F. Mondale and Geraldine Ferraro.

In 1986 Reagan obtained an overhaul of the income tax code, which eliminated many deductions and exempted millions of people with low incomes.

At the end of his administration, the Nation was enjoying its longest recorded period of peacetime prosperity without recession or depression. The revision of the tax code led to an extraordinary investment in american business.

In foreign policy, Reagan sought to achieve "peace through strength." During his two terms he increased defense spending 35 percent, but sought to improve relations with the Soviet Union. In dramatic meetings with Soviet leader Mikhail Gorbachev, he negotiated a treaty that would eliminate intermediate-range nuclear missiles. Reagan declared war against international terrorism, sending American bombers against Libya after evidence came out that Libya was involved in an attack on American soldiers in a West Berlin nightclub.

By ordering naval escorts in the Persian Gulf, he maintained the free flow of oil during the Iran-Iraq war. In keeping with the Reagan Doctrine, he gave support to anti-Communist insurgencies in Central America, Asia, and Africa.

Overall, the Reagan years saw a restoration of prosperity, and the goal of peace through strength seemed to be within grasp. At the end of his two terms in office, Ronald Reagan viewed with satisfaction the achievements of his innovative program known as the Reagan Revolution, which aimed to reinvigorate the American people and reduce their reliance upon Government. He felt he had fulfilled his campaign pledge of 1980 to restore "the great, confident roar of American progress and growth and optimism."

During Jimmy Carter's last year in office (1980), inflation averaged 12.5%, compared to 4.4% during Reagan's last year in office (1988). Over those eight years, the unemployment rate declined from 7.1% to 5.5%, hitting annual rate highs of 9.7% (1982) and 9.6% (1983) and averaging 7.5% during Reagan's administration.

Reagan implemented policies based on supply-side economics and advocated a classical liberal and laissez-faire philosophy, seeking to stimulate the economy with large, across-the-board tax cuts.

Citing the economic theories of Arthur Laffer, Reagan promoted the proposed tax cuts as potentially stimulating the economy enough to expand the tax base, offsetting the revenue loss due to reduced rates of taxation, a theory that entered political discussion as the Laffer curve. Reaganomics was the subject of debate with supporters pointing to improvements in certain key economic indicators as evidence of success, and critics pointing to large increases in federal budget deficits and the national debt. His policy of "peace through strength" resulted in a record peacetime defense buildup including a 40% real increase in defense spending between 1981 and 1985.

During Reagan's presidency, federal income tax rates were lowered significantly with the signing of the bipartisan Economic Recovery Tax Act of 1981 which lowered the top marginal tax bracket from 70% to 50% and the lowest bracket from 14% to 11%, however other tax increases signed by Reagan ensured that tax revenues over his two terms were 18.2% of GDP as compared to 18.1% over the past 40 years. Then, in 1982 the Job Training Partnership Act of 1982 was signed into law, initiating one of the nation's first public/private partnerships and a major part of the president's job creation program. Reagan's Assistant Secretary of Labor and Chief of Staff, Al Angrisani, was a primary architect of the bill. The Tax Reform Act of 1986, another bipartisan effort championed by Reagan, reduced the top rate further to 28% while raising the bottom bracket from 11% to 15% and reducing the quantity of brackets to 4. Conversely,

Congress passed and Reagan signed into law tax increases of some nature in every year from 1981 to 1987 to continue funding such government programs as TEFRA, Social Security, and the Deficit Reduction Act of 1984. Despite the fact that TEFRA was the "largest peacetime tax increase in American history," Reagan is better known for his tax cuts and lower-taxes philosophy. Real gross domestic product (GDP) growth recovered strongly after the early 1980s recession ended in 1982, and grew during his eight years in office at an annual rate of 3.85% per year.

Unemployment peaked at 10.8% monthly rate in December 1982, higher than any time since the Great Depression, then dropped during the rest of Reagan's presidency. Sixteen million new jobs were created, while inflation significantly decreased.

The net effect of all Reagan-era tax bills was a 1% decrease in government revenues when compared to Treasury Department revenue estimates from the Administration's first post-enactment January budgets. However, federal Income Tax receipts increased from 1980 to 1989, rising from $308.7Bn to $549.0Bn.

During the Reagan Administration, federal receipts grew at an average rate of 8.2% (2.5% attributed to higher Social Security receipts), and federal outlays grew at an annual rate of 7.1%. Reagan's policies proposed that economic growth would occur when marginal tax rates were low enough to spur investment, which would then lead to increased economic growth, higher employment and wages.

Critics labeled this "trickle-down economics", the belief that tax policies that benefit the wealthy will create a "trickle-down" effect to the poor. Questions arose whether Reagan's policies benefited the wealthy more than those living in poverty, and many poor and minority citizens viewed Reagan as indifferent to their struggles.

Following his less-government intervention views, Reagan cut the budgets of non-military programs including Medicaid, food stamps, federal education programs and the EPA.

While he protected entitlement programs, such as Social Security and Medicare, his administration attempted to purge many people with disabilities from the Social Security disability rolls.

The administration's stance toward the Savings and Loan industry contributed to the Savings and loan crisis. It is also suggested, by a minority of Reaganomics critics, that the policies partially influenced the stock market crash of 1987, but there is no consensus regarding a single source for the crash. In order to cover newly spawned federal budget deficits, the United States borrowed heavily both domestically and abroad, raising the national debt from $997 billion to $2.85 trillion. Reagan described the new debt as the "greatest disappointment" of his presidency.

He reappointed Paul Volcker as Chairman of the Federal Reserve, and in 1987 he appointed monetarist Alan Greenspan to succeed him. Reagan ended the price controls on domestic oil which had contributed to energy crises in the early 1970s. The price of oil subsequently dropped, and the 1980s did not see the fuel shortages that the 1970s had. Reagan also fulfilled a 1980 campaign promise to repeal the Windfall profit tax in 1988, which had previously increased dependence on foreign oil. Some economists, such as Nobel Prize winners Milton Friedman and Robert A. Mundell, argue that Reagan's tax policies invigorated America's economy and contributed to the economic boom of the 1990s.

Reagan escalated the Cold War, accelerating a reversal from the policy of détente which began in 1979 following the Soviet invasion of Afghanistan.

Reagan ordered a massive buildup of the United States Armed Forces and implemented new policies towards the Soviet Union: reviving the B-1 bomber program that had been canceled by the Carter administration, and producing the MX "Peacekeeper" missile. In response to Soviet deployment of the SS-20, Reagan oversaw NATO's deployment of the Pershing II missile in West Germany.

Under a policy that came to be known as the Reagan Doctrine, Reagan and his administration also provided overt and covert aid to anti-communist resistance movements in an effort to "rollback" Soviet-backed communist governments in Africa, Asia and Latin America. Reagan deployed the CIA's Special Activities Division to Afghanistan and Pakistan. They were instrumental in training, equipping and leading Mujaheddin forces against the Soviet Army. President Reagan's Covert Action program has been given credit for assisting in ending the Soviet occupation of Afghanistan, though the US funded armaments introduced then would later pose a threat to US troops in the 2000s war in Afghanistan. However, in a break from the Carter policy of arming Taiwan under the Taiwan Relations Act.

Reagan also agreed with the communist government in China to reduce the sale of arms to Taiwan.

Reagan, the first American president ever to address the British Parliament, predicts Marxism-Leninism will be left on the "ash-heap of history". Together with the United Kingdom's Prime Minister Margaret Thatcher, Reagan denounced the Soviet Union in ideological terms. In a famous address on June 8, 1982 to the British Parliament in the Royal Gallery of the Palace of Westminster, Reagan said, "the forward march of freedom and democracy will leave Marxism-Leninism on the ash-heap of history." On March 3, 1983, he predicted that communism would collapse, stating, "Communism is another sad, bizarre chapter in human history whose last pages even now are being written." In a speech to the National Association of Evangelicals on March 8, 1983, Reagan called the Soviet Union "an evil empire"

In March 1983, Reagan introduced the Strategic Defense Initiative (SDI), a defense project that would have used ground and space-based systems to protect the United States from attack by strategic nuclear ballistic missiles. Reagan believed that this defense shield could make nuclear war impossible, but disbelief that the technology could ever work led opponents to dub SDI "Star Wars" and argue that the technological objective was unattainable.

The Soviets became concerned about the possible effects SDI would have; leader Yuri Andropov said it would put "the entire world in jeopardy".

For those reasons, David Gergen, former aide to President Reagan, believes that in retrospect, SDI hastened the end of the Cold War.

Critics labeled Reagan's foreign policies as aggressive, imperialistic, and chided them as "warmongering," though they were supported by leading American conservatives who argued that they were necessary to protect U.S. security interests.

A reformer, Mikhail Gorbachev, would later rise to power in the Soviet Union in 1985, implementing new policies for openness and reform that were called glasnost and perestroika.

Midway into his second term, Reagan declared more militant policies in the War on Drugs. He said that "drugs were menacing our society" and promised to fight for drug-free schools and workplaces, expanded drug treatment, stronger law enforcement and drug interdiction efforts, and greater public awareness.

In 1986, Reagan signed a drug enforcement bill that budgeted $1.7 billion to fund the War on Drugs and specified a mandatory minimum penalty for drug offenses. The bill was criticized for promoting significant racial disparities in the prison population and critics also charged that the policies did little to reduce the availability of drugs on the street, while resulting in a great financial burden for America. Defenders of the effort point to success in reducing rates of adolescent drug use. First Lady Nancy Reagan made the War on Drugs her main priority by founding the "Just Say No" drug awareness campaign, which aimed to discourage children and teenagers from engaging in recreational drug use by offering various ways of saying "no". Mrs. Reagan traveled to 65 cities in 33 states, raising awareness about the dangers of drugs including alcohol.

Relations between Libya and the U.S. under President Reagan were continually contentious, beginning with the Gulf of Sidra incident in 1981; by 1982, Gaddafi was considered by the CIA to be, along with USSR leader Leonid Brezhnev and Cuban leader Fidel Castro, part of a group known as the "unholy trinity" and was also labeled as "our international public enemy number one" by a CIA official as well.

These tensions were later revived in early April 1986, when a bomb exploded in a Berlin discothèque, resulting in the injuries of 63 American military personnel and death of one serviceman.

Citing that there was "irrefutable proof" that Libya had directed the terrorist bombing, Reagan authorized the use of force against the country. In the late evening of April 15, 1986, the U.S. launched a series of air strikes on ground targets in Libya. The attack was designed to halt Libyan leader Muammar Gaddafi's ability to export terrorism, offering him "incentives and reasons to alter his criminal behavior". The president addressed the nation from the Oval Office after the attacks had commenced, stating, "When our citizens are attacked or abused anywhere in the world on the direct orders of hostile regimes, we will respond so long as I'm in this office." During his time in office, Reagan referred to Gaddafi as "the mad dog of the Middle East" and considered him to be public enemy number one.

Reagan signed the Immigration Reform and Control Act in 1986. The act made it illegal to knowingly hire or recruit illegal immigrants, required employers to attest to their employees' immigration status, and granted amnesty to approximately 3 million illegal immigrants who entered the United States prior to January 1, 1982, and had lived in the country continuously. Critics argue that the employer sanctions were without teeth and failed to stem illegal immigration.

Upon signing the act at a ceremony held beside the newly refurbished Statue of Liberty, Reagan said, "The legalization provisions in this act will go far to improve the lives of a class of individuals who now must hide in the shadows, without access to many of the benefits of a free and open society. Very soon many of these men and women will be able to step into the sunlight and, ultimately, if they choose, they may become Americans.

By the early 1980s, the USSR had built up a military arsenal and army surpassing that of the United States. Previously, the U.S. had relied on the qualitative superiority of its weapons to essentially frighten the Soviets, but the gap had been narrowed.

After President Reagan's military buildup, the Soviet Union did not further dramatically build up its military; the enormous military expenses, in combination with collectivized agriculture and inefficient planned manufacturing, were a heavy burden for the Soviet economy.

At the same time, the Reagan Administration persuaded Saudi Arabia to increase oil production, which resulted in a drop of oil prices in 1985 to one-third of the previous level; oil was the main source of Soviet export revenues. These factors gradually brought the Soviet economy to a stagnant state during Gorbachev's tenure.

Reagan recognized the change in the direction of the Soviet leadership with Mikhail Gorbachev, and shifted to diplomacy, with a view to encourage the Soviet leader to pursue substantial arms agreements. Reagan's personal mission was to achieve "a world free of nuclear weapons," which he regarded as "totally irrational, totally inhumane, good for nothing but killing, possibly destructive of life on earth and civilization." He was able to start discussions on nuclear disarmament with General Secretary Gorbachev. Gorbachev and Reagan held four summit conferences between 1985 and 1988: the first in Geneva, Switzerland, the second in Reykjavík, Iceland, the third in Washington, D.C., and the fourth in Moscow. Reagan believed that if he could persuade the Soviets to allow for more democracy and free speech, this would lead to reform and the end of Communism.

Speaking at the Berlin Wall on June 12, 1987, Reagan challenged Gorbachev to go further, saying: "General Secretary Gorbachev, if you seek peace, if you seek prosperity for the Soviet Union and Eastern Europe, if you seek liberalization, comes here to this gate! Mr. Gorbachev, open this gate! Mr. Gorbachev, tear down this wall!"

Prior to Gorbachev visiting Washington, D.C., for the third summit in 1987, the Soviet leader announced his intention to pursue significant arms agreements.

The timing of the announcement led Western diplomats to contend that Gorbachev was offering major concessions to the U.S. on the levels of conventional forces, nuclear weapons, and policy in Eastern Europe. He and Reagan signed the Intermediate-Range Nuclear Forces (INF) Treaty at the White House, which eliminated an entire class of nuclear weapons. The two leaders laid the framework for the Strategic Arms Reduction Treaty, or START I;

Reagan insisted that the name of the treaty be changed from Strategic Arms Limitation Talks to Strategic Arms Reduction Talks.

When Reagan visited Moscow for the fourth summit in 1988, he was viewed as a celebrity by the Soviets. A journalist asked the president if he still considered the Soviet Union the evil empire. "No," he replied, "I was talking about another time, another era." At Gorbachev's request, Reagan gave a speech on free markets at the Moscow State University. In his autobiography, An American Life, Reagan expressed his optimism about the new direction that they charted and his warm feelings for Gorbachev.[226] In November of 1989, the Berlin Wall was torn down, the Cold War was officially declared over at a Malta Summit on December 3, 1989and two years later, the Soviet Union collapsed.

The Ronald Reagan Presidential Library was dedicated on November 4, 1991. Supporters have pointed to a more efficient and prosperous economy and a peaceful end to the Cold War. Critics argue that his economic policies caused huge budget deficits, quadrupling the United States national debt, and that the Iran-Contra affair lowered American credibility. As time has passed, he has generally come to be viewed in a more positive light, and ranks highly among presidents in many public opinion polls.

Many conservative and liberal scholars agree that Reagan has been the most influential president since Franklin D. Roosevelt, leaving his imprint on American politics, diplomacy, culture, and economics.

Since he left office, historians have reached a consensus, as summarized by British historian M. J. Heale, who finds that scholars now concur that Reagan rehabilitated conservatism, turned the nation to the right, practiced a pragmatic conservatism that balanced ideology and the constraints of politics, revived faith in the presidency and in American self respect, and contributed to victory in the Cold War.

Ronald Reagan was the most famous American Conservative President but also in some ways also had a Libertarian streak in him. However he was still a man committed too much to policing the world to be too close to a good Libertarian.

In the 1980 presidential contest, the Libertarian Party gained ballot access in all 50 states, Washington, D.C., and Guam, the first time a third party accomplished this since the Socialist Party in 1916. The ticket of Ed Clark and David H. Koch spent several million dollars on this political campaign and earned more than one percent of the popular vote with almost one million votes, the most successful Libertarian presidential campaign to date.

On December 29, 1981, the first widely reported successful election in the continental United States of a Libertarian Party candidate in a partisan race occurred as Richard P. Siano, a Boeing 707 pilot for Trans World Airlines, running against both a Republican and a Democrat, was elected to the office of Kingwood Township Committeeman in western Hunterdon County, New Jersey. His election resulted from the special election held on December 29, 1981 to break a tie vote in the general election between him and the Democratic candidate. He received 63% of the votes cast in the special election. He served a three-year term of office.

In 1983, the party was divided by internal disputes; former party leaders Edward Crane and David H. Koch left, taking a number of their supporters with them. In 1984, the party's presidential nominee, David Bergland, gained access to the ballot in 36 states and earned one-quarter of one percent of the popular vote. In 1987, Doug Anderson became the first Libertarian elected to office in a major city, elected to the Denver Election Commission (later, in 2005, Anderson was elected to the Lakewood, Colorado city council). In 1988, Republican Congressman Ron Paul won the Libertarian nomination for president and was on the ballot in 46 states. Paul later successfully ran for United States House of Representatives from Texas, once again as a Republican, an office in which he still serves. He ran in the Republican primaries in 2008 and currently is sponsoring HR 1207 in the House of Representatives, a bill to audit the Federal Reserve.

The Roaring Nineties

The '90s is often considered the true dawn of the Information Age. Though info-age technologies pre-date the '80s, it wasn't until the late 1980s and the 1990s that they became widely used by the general public. A combination of factors including the mass mobilization of capital markets through neoliberalism, the beginning of the widespread proliferation of new media such as the Internet, and the dissolution of the Soviet Union led to a realignment and reconsolidation of economic and political power across the world, and within countries. The 1990s is often considered the end of Modernity and the dawn of the current postmodern age. Living standards and democratic governance generally improved in many areas of the world, notably East Asia, much of Eastern Europe, Latin America, and South Africa. The economies and living standards of some countries such as South Korea and Ireland improved to such an extent that they were considered 1st World nations by the decades end.

In the Western World, particularly the United States, it is remembered as relatively peaceful and quiet time in international affairs, occurring after the effective end of the Cold War (1945–1991) but before the start of the

War on Terror (2001–Present). New ethnic conflicts emerged in Africa, the Caucasus and the Balkans, and signs of any resolution of tensions in the Middle East remained elusive.

We would not have been able to publish this decade's web site if it weren't for the Internet.   The World Wide Web was born in 1992, changing the way we communicate (email), spend our money (online gambling, stores), and do business (e-commerce). In 1989, 15% of American households had a computer. And by 2000, this figure increased to 51%, with 41.5% online. Internet lingo **like plug-ins, BTW (by the way), GOK (God only knows), IMHO (in my humble opinion), FAQS, SPAM, FTP, ISP, and phrases like "See you online" or "The server's down" or "Bill Gates" became part of our everyday vocabulary.**

In the 1990's the United States played the role of world policeman, sometimes alone but more often in alliances. The decade began with Saddam Hussein's invasion of Kuwait and the resultant Gulf War. In 1993, war was in the African country of Somalia, as television images of starving children led to an attempt to oust the warlord, General Mohamed Farrah Aidid. By September, 1994, the U.S. was once again sending troops to a foreign country to overthrow a military dictatorship, this time in Haiti.

In 1996 about 20,000 American troops were deployed to Bosnia as part of a NATO peace keeping force. In late March 1999, the U.S. joined NATO in air strikes against Yugoslavia in an effort to halt the Yugoslavian government's policy of ethnic cleansing in its province of Kosovo. The decade was to end much as it began with U.S. forces deployed in many countries, and the U.S. playing arbitrator, enforcer, and peace keeper throughout the world.

The 90s have been called the Merger Decade. On the domestic front some big issues were health care, social security reform, and gun control -

debated and unresolved throughout the whole decade. Violence and sex scandals dominated the media starting with the Tailhook affair in which Navy and Marine Corps fliers were accused of sexually abusing 26 women. President Clinton kept the gossip flowing as several women accused him of sexual misconduct. The ten years ended with this president narrowly surviving a trial to remove him from office for perjury and obstruction of justice. President Clinton's escapades were proving to be a hindrance to his Vice President Al Gore's campaign for the oval office and polls were reporting that 70% of the American people were saying that they were "tired of the Clintons".

Violence seemed a part of life. In 1992 South-Central Los Angeles rioted after four white policemen were acquitted of video-taped assault charges for beating a black motorist, Rodney King. 1993 brought terrorism to the American shores as a bomb was detonated in the garage beneath the World Trade Center.

That same month of February saw four agents of the U.S. Bureau of Alcohol, Tobacco, and Firearms killed during an unsuccessful raid on the Branch Davidian cult compound in Waco, Texas led by David Koresh.

Americans were glued to their TV sets in 1995 as the football hero, O.J. Simpson, was tried for the murder of his ex-wife, Nicole, and her male friend, Ron Goldman. This trial pointed out the continued racial division in the country as most blacks applauded the not guilty verdict while most whites thought an obviously guilty man had gotten away with murder. The shock of the bombing of the Alfred P. Murrah Federal Building in Oklahoma City on April 19, 1995, was compounded by the revelation that the perpetrators were not foreign terrorists but were U.S. citizens led by a U.S. Army veteran, Timothy McVeigh. In the months between February 1996 and April 1999 there were at least fourteen incidents of school shootings with the most lethal being on April 20, 1999 when 14 students and 1 teacher were killed and 23 wounded at Columbine High School in Littleton, Colorado.

There was good news, too. The booming economy led to record low unemployment. Minimum wage was increased to $5.15 an hour. The stock market reached an all time high as individuals learned to buy and trade via the internet.

Americans enjoyed the country's affluence by traveling more (up 40% since 1986), by reveling in sporting events such as the Atlanta Summer Olympics -1996, and by "consuming" as never before. America faced the new millennium with an open, diversified society, a functioning democracy, a healthy economy, and the means and will, hopefully, to face and overcome its problems.

About eighty-three and one-half percent of the population in 1999 completed four years of high school as opposed to only forty-one percent in 1960. Education subject guides sprang up on the web. The Elementary and Secondary Education Act, (No Child Left Behind) provided assistance to disadvantaged students or pupils with limited proficiency in English and was intended to improve instruction in areas like drug use prevention, math, and science. ERIC (Educational Resources database) went online. Ritalin became the drug of choice for schools and parents alike as more students were labeled ADD or ADHD. The BIG change was that students could complete their education without coming on campus, through Distance Education Programs. In the classroom, many schools required uniforms.

The Americans with Disabilities Act, effective in July, 1990, began the decade on a positive note by protecting the rights of all Americans with physical or mental disabilities. Introduced first as a policy for the military, in September, 1993, a law called "don't ask, don't tell," directed people to keep their sexuality hidden if they intended to stay in military careers. An important gun control bill (now expired) aimed at protecting all Americans became law in 1994. The Brady Bill provides a five day waiting period when purchasing a gun. In January, 1994, the North American Free Trade Agreement was intended to eliminate barriers to trade between neighboring countries, particularly Mexico and Canada.

In 1994, Republicans won a majority in Congress for the first time in forty years. Part of the reason for the party's success was a ten point plan called the Contract with America which outlined a promise to reshape government by decentralizing federal authority, giving states and local government more control over taxes, and social programs, and by improving the way government did business. Welfare reform began in 1988 with the federal Family Support Act which initiated changes such as directing states to phase in welfare-to-work programs by 1990, giving states control over welfare expenses.

This program continued in 1996, when the controversial Aid to Families with Dependent Children Act was abolished as part of the new block grant called Temporary Assistance to Needy Families (TANF). TANF converts state funding to a fixed level, directs that minor parents of dependent children can only receive TANF funds if they were living at home or in another adult supervised setting, and limits federal aid in a lifetime to five years for families receiving welfare.

In March, 1996, a bill was passed giving the president line item veto authority allowing the president to veto specific parts of a spending bill while approving the rest, thus increasing presidential power. The bill was declared unconstitutional by the Supreme Court in June 1998.

George Bush brought to the White House a dedication to traditional American values and a determination to direct them toward making the United States "a kinder and gentler nation." In his Inaugural Address he pledged in "a moment rich with promise" to use American strength as "a force for good." Coming from a family with a tradition of public service, George Herbert Walker Bush felt the responsibility to make his contribution both in time of war and in peace. Born in Milton, Massachusetts, on June 12, 1924, he became a student leader at Phillips Academy in Andover. On his 18th birthday he enlisted in the armed forces. The youngest pilot in the Navy when he received his wings, he flew 58 combat missions during World War II. On one mission over the Pacific as a torpedo bomber pilot he was shot down by Japanese antiaircraft fire and was rescued from the water by a U. S. submarine. He was awarded the Distinguished Flying Cross for bravery in action.

Like his father, Prescott Bush, who was elected a Senator from Connecticut in 1952, George became interested in public service and politics. He served two terms as a Representative to Congress from Texas. Twice he ran unsuccessfully for the Senate. Then he was appointed to a series of high-level positions: Ambassador to the United Nations, Chairman of the Republican National Committee, Chief of the U. S. Liaison Office in the People's Republic of China, and Director of the Central Intelligence Agency.

In 1980 Bush campaigned for the Republican nomination for President. He lost, but was chosen as a running mate by Ronald Reagan. As Vice President, Bush had responsibility in several domestic areas, including Federal deregulation and anti-drug programs, and visited scores of foreign countries. In 1988 Bush won the Republican nomination for President and, with Senator Dan Quayle of Indiana as his running mate, he defeated Massachusetts Governor Michael Dukakis in the general election.

Bush faced a dramatically changing world, as the Cold War ended after 40 bitter years, the Communist empire broke up, and the Berlin Wall fell. The Soviet Union ceased to exist; and reformist President Mikhail Gorbachev, whom Bush had supported, resigned. While Bush hailed the march of democracy, he insisted on restraint in U. S. policy toward the group of new nations. In other areas of foreign policy, President Bush sent American troops into Panama to overthrow the corrupt regime of General Manuel Noriega, who was threatening the security of the canal and the Americans living there. Noriega was brought to the United States for trial as a drug trafficker.

Bush's greatest test came when Iraqi President Saddam Hussein invaded Kuwait, and then threatened to move into Saudi Arabia. Vowing to free Kuwait, Bush rallied the United Nations, the U. S. people, and Congress and sent 425,000 American troops. They were joined by 118,000 troops from allied nations. After weeks of air and missile bombardment, the 100-hour land battle dubbed Desert Storm routed Iraq's million-man army.

Despite unprecedented popularity from this military and diplomatic triumph, Bush was unable to withstand discontent at home from a faltering economy, rising violence in inner cities, and continued high deficit spending. In 1992 he lost his bid for reelection to Democrat William Clinton.

Bill Clinton was elected governor of Arkansas in 1978, but lost a bid for reelection in 1980. He regained the governorship two years later and served until 1993. During his 12 years in office, Governor Clinton earned national recognition for his progressive programs, especially his efforts to improve the quality of public education.

After a tough primary campaign, Bill Clinton won his party's nomination and went on to defeat Republican President George Bush, and independent candidate Ross Perot in the 1992 presidential race. When President Clinton won reelection in 1996, he became the first Democrat since Franklin D. Roosevelt to win a second term.

Following the early failure of his health care reform initiative, President Clinton pursued a moderate but progressive domestic agenda. During his tenure, the welfare system was reformed, the sale of handguns was restricted, environmental regulations were strengthened, and a massive federal budget deficit was turned into a surplus.

On the international scene, the Clinton Administration expanded international trade, intervened militarily to end "ethnic cleansing" in Bosnia, launched peace and trade initiatives in Africa and the Middle East, and promoted a framework for peace aimed at ending the strife in Northern Ireland.

In 1998, his relationship with a young White House intern resulted in the President's impeachment by the House of Representatives. A trial in the Senate found the President not guilty of the charges brought against him. President Clinton apologized for his conduct and vowed to keep working as hard as he could for the American people. As a result, Bill Clinton left office with historically high approval ratings for the job he had done as the 42nd President of the United States.

Many countries, institutions, companies, and organizations were prosperous during the 1990s. High-income countries such as the United States, Japan, Singapore, Hong Kong, Taiwan, South Korea, and those in Western Europe experienced steady economic growth for much of the decade. However, in the former Soviet Union GDP decreased as their economies restructured to produce goods they needed and some capital flight occurred.

GATT update and creation of the World Trade Organization and other global economic institutions, but opposition by anti-globalization activists showed up in nearly every GATT summit, like the demonstrations in Seattle in December 1999. The anti-globalization protests at the World Trade Organization Ministerial Conference of 1999 in Seattle, Washington began on November 30, 1999. This marks the beginning of a steady increase in anti-globalization protests which occurred in the first decade of the 21st century as well as increasing hostility to neoliberalism.

Decades before the word "dotcom" slipped past our lips as the answer to all of our problems, the internet was created by the U.S. military, who vastly underestimated how much people would want to be online. Commercially the internet started to catch on in 1995 with an estimated 18 million users. The rise in usage meant an untapped market—an international market.

Soon, speculators were barely able to control their excitement over the "new economy."

Companies underwent a similar phenomenon to the one that gripped Seventeenth century England and America in the early eighties: investors wanted big ideas more than a solid business plan. Buzzwords like networking, new paradigm, information technologies, internet, consumer-driven navigation, tailored web experience, and many more examples of empty double-speak filled the media and investors with a rabid hunger for more. The IPOs of internet companies emerged with great frequency, sweeping the nation. Investors were blindly grabbing new issues without looking at a business plan to find out, how long the company would take before making a profit, if ever.

Obviously, there was a problem. The first shots through this bubble came from the companies themselves: many reported huge losses and some folded outright within months of their offering. Siliconaires were moving out of $4 million estates and back to the room above their parents' garage. In the year 1999, there were 457 IPOs, most of which were internet and technology related. Of those 457 IPOs, 117 doubled in price on the first day of trading. In 2001 the number of IPOs dwindled to 76, and none of them doubled on the first day of trading.

Many argue that the dotcom boom and bust was a case of too much too fast. Companies that couldn't decide on their corporate creed were given millions of dollars and told to grow to Microsoft size by tomorrow.

The fundamentals of the Dot-com bubble were horrible, most new public companies weren't profitable and some had no intention of ever making a profit. IPOs were going sky high while the business model itself showed no realistic way to turn a profit. These big warnings are known as red flags, and they were everywhere during the dot-com bubble.

The educated investors and professionals in the stock market saw these red flags and knew that a crash was coming, and that's why they were successful during the Dot-com bubble. The rest were left to fight to sell their rapidly devaluing stocks.

If you are investing in the stock market for the long term, don't invest when prices are overvalued and fundamentals are poor. The combination of these two problems are practically begging for an eventual stock market crash if things don't turn around. You want to invest when you see nothing but green flags, not red.

The stock market rallied during the dot-com bubble for good reason: everyone and their grandma were excited about Internet based companies. The overall investor's belief was optimistic and this fueled a multi-year rally that had seemingly endless momentum. But as we just learned, the fundamentals were garbage and when the momentum died, the party was over and the stock market crashed.

If trading/short-term investing is your thing, then get your profit and get out. Don't get caught up in how much higher your stocks can go, just sell them when you believe it's time to get out. When the reality of overbought stocks comes into realization, you want to be the guy with all of your stock sold, not the guy caught off guard while panicking about what you should do.

The optimism for the Dot-com bubble was supported by the belief that internet business was somehow going to instantly take off and going to retail stores would be a thing of the past. Huge issues such as customers having to pay heavy shipping fees were regarded as not important, and the stock market rallied while believing that we'd all be buying our groceries online and ordering our pizza from a .com site. The problem was that none of this was actually occurring, and it was really just wishful thinking since most companies had no realistic business model to get these society changing ideas off the ground.

The proliferation of special interest spending in the federal budget in recent years has created much waste and corruption. Politicians have helped special interests while helping themselves. But the main problem has not been that politicians have their hands in the cookie jar; it is that the cookie jar has grown so large. There are 1,696 subsidy programs in the federal budget, which dispense hundreds of billions of dollars annually to state governments, businesses, nonprofit groups, and individuals. The number of subsidy programs is rising rapidly, with a 44 percent increase since 1990.

The Clinton years featured the biggest reduction in government spending relative GDP since the end of World War II, with federal spending relative to GDP dropping from 22.1% in fiscal year 1992 to 18.4% in fiscal year 2000.

This decline was mostly the result of lower military spending after the end of the Cold War and before the beginning of the "War on terror" and lower interest payments due to the surpluses, but even excluding military and interest spending, federal spending fell from 14.1% of GDP to 13.1%.

Also, while the taxation of regular income rose for top earners, the capital gains tax was actually reduced. The boom in the 1990s was of course partly the result of the unsound tech stock-bubble, but to the extent it was sound, it was because it featured the biggest reduction in the burden of federal spending since the end of World War II. By contrast, growth has been weak after first Bush Jr. and then Obama started to dramatically increase the burden of federal spending.

Republicans were denounced for twin government shutdowns in 1995 and 1996 when Newt Gingrich was House speaker. But Gingrich says the shutdown led to the first discretionary spending cut since 1969. In his words: "Ultimately, standing firm led to the first four balanced budgets in our lifetime."

Gingrich says the choice today doesn't have to be between tax increases and draconian spending cuts. He says reining in waste and abuse and streamlining government management could help save money.

Chapter 7 -   The Bubble Starts to Burst

The 9/11 Effect

The 2000 census enumerates a population of 281,421,906, increasing 13.2% since 1990. As regions, the South and West continued to pick up the majority of the increase in population, moving the geographic center of U.S. population to Phelps County, Missouri.

George W. Bush, son of the former President, and Vice President Al Gore hold a virtual dead-heat for the presidency, with a disputed vote in Florida holding off the naming of the winner of the President Election until the Supreme Court of the United States voted in favor of Bush on December 12. This ruling gave Florida to the Bush camp by a 527 vote majority, and a victory in the Electoral College, 271-266, despite gaining less popular votes than Gore.

January 6, 2001 - Certification of the Electoral College victory of the 2000 United States Presidential election in the U.S. Senate confirms George W. Bush as the victor, with Dick Cheney as his Vice-President.Early on, the Bush administration withdrew from a number of international treaty processes, notably the Kyoto Protocol on global warming. A series of terrorist attacks occurred eight months into Bush's first term as president on September 11, 2001. In response, Bush announced a global War on Terror, ordered an invasion of Afghanistan that same year and an invasion of Iraq in 2003. In addition to national security issues, Bush promoted policies on the economy, health care, education, and social security reform. He signed into law broad tax cuts, the No Child Left Behind Act, the Partial-Birth Abortion Ban Act, and Medicare prescription drug benefits for seniors. His tenure saw national debates on immigration, Social Security, electronic surveillance, waterboarding and other "enhanced interrogation techniques".

In 2004, Bush commanded broad support in the Republican Party and did not encounter a primary challenge. He appointed Ken Mehlman as campaign manager, with a political strategy devised by Karl Rove.

Bush and the Republican platform included a strong commitment to the wars in Iraq and Afghanistan, support for the USA PATRIOT Act, a renewed shift in policy for constitutional amendments banning abortion and same-sex marriage, reforming Social Security to create private investment accounts, creation of an ownership society, and opposing mandatory carbon emissions controls.

Bush also called for the implementation of a guest worker program for immigrants, which was criticized by conservatives. The Bush campaign advertised across the U.S. against Democratic candidates, including Bush's emerging opponent, Massachusetts Senator John Kerry.

Kerry and other Democrats attacked Bush on the Iraq War, and accused him of failing to stimulate the economy and job growth. The Bush campaign portrayed Kerry as a staunch liberal who would raise taxes and increase the size of government. The Bush campaign continuously criticized Kerry's seemingly contradictory statements on the war in Iraq, and argued that Kerry lacked the decisiveness and vision necessary for success in the War on Terror.

In the election, Bush carried 31 of 50 states, receiving a total of 286 electoral votes. He won an outright majority of the popular vote (50.7% to his opponent's 48.3%).The previous President to win an outright majority of the popular vote was Bush's father in the 1988 election. Additionally, it was the first time since Herbert Hoover's election in 1928 that a Republican president was elected alongside re-elected Republican majorities in both Houses of Congress. Bush's 2.5% margin of victory was the narrowest ever for a victorious incumbent President, breaking Woodrow Wilson's 3.1% margin of victory against Charles Evans Hughes in the election of 1916.

In a conventional war, there is a well defined enemy. There is a reasonably well defined cause over which the war is being fought. A conventional war ends when one side surrenders, or is rendered incapable of continuing the struggle, or when both sides agree to stop fighting. In a war on terror the situation is much different. There is nobody who can surrender on behalf of all terrorists. There are no war aims other than the complete and permanent elimination of terrorism, an obviously unattainable goal.

An unending war implies a permanent loss of liberty, as well as a serious on-going financial burden. We see today, as a result of the current wars being waged, ostensibly to combat terrorism, serious losses of privacy as email and telephone communications are now subject to ever-increasing surveillance by security agencies.

Terrorism is generally defined as the calculated use of violence, or the threat of violence, against civilians in order to attain goals that are political or religious or ideological in nature. Sadly, it has a long history, encompassing virtually every segment of humanity all over the world.

A serious effort to thwart all plausible terrorist attacks would involve measures that would alter our lives drastically. It would require a good deal more than requiring people to take off shoes at airports. As with respect to more commonplace crimes, there are sensible things that could be done to make things harder for terrorists.

Locking the flight deck doors of airliners and supplementing air marshals with a program to encourage law enforcement officers to carry side arms on flights, and maybe a few other simple measures, might be the best we can do to discourage airline hijacking. More generally, the kind of international cooperation employed to combat other types of criminals ought to be effective against terrorist organizations. The most effective defense would be to reduce sharply the number of people supporting and joining them.

With every war we fight we lose more liberty to the federal government. I say this not as an indictment for some kind of conspiracy but rather as a factual statement involving the very nature of war. War drives fear in the citizenry and fear drives the government to institute programs for our welfare and safety. In reality with programs like the Patriot Act we surrender the very thing that makes our country unique in the world and that is our liberty.

In a February 28, 2001, message to the Congress, Bush estimated that there would be a $5.6 trillion surplus over the next ten years. Facing opposition in Congress, Bush held town hall-style public meetings across the U.S. in 2001 to increase public support for his plan for a $1.35 trillion tax cut program—one of the largest tax cuts in U.S. history. Bush argued that unspent government funds should be returned to taxpayers, saying "the surplus is not the government's money. The surplus is the people's money." With reports of the threat of recession from Federal Reserve Chairman Alan Greenspan, Bush argued that such a tax cut would stimulate the economy and create jobs. Others, including the Treasury Secretary at the time Paul O'Neill, were opposed to some of the tax cuts on the basis that they would contribute to budget deficits and undermine Social Security. O'Neill disputes the claim made in Bush's book "Decision Points" that he never openly disagreed with him on planned tax cuts. By 2003, the economy showed signs of improvement, though job growth remained stagnant. Another tax cut program was passed that year.

The September 11 terrorist attacks were a major turning point in Bush's presidency. That evening, he addressed the nation from the Oval Office, promising a strong response to the attacks but emphasizing the need for the nation to come together and comfort the families of the victims. On September 14, he visited Ground Zero, meeting with Mayor Rudy Giuliani, firefighters, police officers, and volunteers. Bush addressed the gathering via a megaphone while standing on a heap of rubble, to much applause: I can hear you. The rest of the world hears you. And the people who knocked these buildings down will hear all of us soon.

In a September 20 speech, Bush condemned Osama bin Laden and Al-Qaeda, and issued an ultimatum to the Taliban regime in Afghanistan, where bin Laden was operating, to "hand over the terrorists, or ... share in their fate".

After September 11, Bush announced a global War on Terror. The Afghan Taliban regime was not forthcoming with Osama bin Laden, so Bush ordered the invasion of Afghanistan to overthrow the Taliban regime.

In his January 29, 2002 State of the Union Address, he asserted that an "axis of evil" consisting of North Korea, Iran, and Iraq was "arming to threaten the peace of the world" and "pose[d] a grave and growing danger". The Bush Administration proceeded to assert a right and intention to engage in preemptive war, also called preventive war, in response to perceived threats. This would form a basis for what became known as the Bush Doctrine.

The broader "War on Terror", allegations of an "axis of evil", and, in particular, the doctrine of preemptive war, began to weaken the unprecedented levels of international and domestic support for Bush and United States action against al-Qaeda following the September 11 attacks.

Some national leaders alleged abuse by U.S. troops and called for the U.S. to shut down the Guantanamo Bay detention camp and other such facilities. Dissent from, and criticism of, Bush's leadership in the War on Terror increased as the war in Iraq expanded. In 2006, a National Intelligence Estimate expressed the combined opinion of the United States' own intelligence agencies, concluding that the Iraq War had become the "cause célèbre for jihadists" and that the jihad movement was growing.

On October 7, 2001, U.S. and British forces initiated bombing campaigns that led to the arrival on November 13 of Northern Alliance troops in

Kabul. The main goals of the war were to defeat the Taliban, drive al-Qaeda out of Afghanistan, and capture key al-Qaeda leaders. In December 2001, the Pentagon reported that the Taliban had been defeated but cautioned that the war would go on to continue weakening Taliban and al-Qaeda leaders. Later that month the UN had installed the Afghan Interim Authority chaired by Hamid Karzai.

Efforts to kill or capture al-Qaeda leader Osama bin Laden failed as he escaped a battle in December 2001 in the mountainous region of Tora Bora, which the Bush Administration later acknowledged to have resulted from a failure to commit enough U.S. ground troops. It was not until May 2011, two years after Bush left office, that Bin Laden was killed by U.S. forces. Bin Laden's successor, Ayman al-Zawahiri, as well as the leader of the Taliban, Mohammed Omar, remain at large.

Despite the initial success in driving the Taliban from power in Kabul, by early 2003 the Taliban was regrouping, amassing new funds and recruits. In 2006, the Taliban insurgency appeared larger, fiercer and better organized than expected, with large-scale allied offensives such as Operation Mountain Thrust attaining limited success. As a result, Bush commissioned 3,500 additional troops to the country in March 2007.

Beginning with his January 29, 2002 State of the Union address, Bush began publicly focusing attention on Iraq, which he labeled as part of an "axis of evil" allied with terrorists and posing "a grave and growing danger" to U.S. interests through possession of weapons of mass destruction.

The war effort was joined by more than 20 other nations (most notably the United Kingdom), designated the "coalition of the willing". The invasion of Iraq commenced on March 20, 2003, and the Iraqi military was quickly defeated. The capital, Baghdad, fell on April 9, 2003. On May 1, Bush declared the end of major combat operations in Iraq. The initial success of U.S. operations increased his popularity, but the U.S. and allied forces faced a growing insurgency led by sectarian groups; Bush's "Mission Accomplished" speech was later criticized as premature.

From 2004 until 2007, the situation in Iraq deteriorated further, with some observers arguing that there was a full scale civil war in Iraq. Bush's policies met with criticism, including demands domestically to set a timetable to withdraw troops from Iraq. The 2006 report of the bipartisan Iraq Study Group, led by James Baker, concluded that the situation in Iraq was "grave and deteriorating". While Bush admitted that there were strategic mistakes made in regards to the stability of Iraq, he maintained he would not change the overall Iraq strategy.

In January 2005, free, democratic elections were held in Iraq for the first time in 50 years. According to Iraqi National Security Advisor Mowaffak al-Rubaie, "This is the greatest day in the history of this country."[243] Bush praised the event as well, saying that the Iraqis "have taken rightful control of their country's destiny". This led to the election of Jalal Talabani as President and Nouri al-Maliki as Prime Minister of Iraq.

A referendum to approve a constitution in Iraq was held in October 2005, supported by the majority Shiites and many Kurds.

On January 10, 2007, Bush addressed the nation regarding the situation in Iraq. In this speech, he announced a surge of 21,500 more troops for Iraq, as well as a job program for Iraqis, more reconstruction proposals, and $1.2 billion for these programs. On May 1, 2007, Bush used his veto for only the second time in his presidency, rejecting a congressional bill setting a deadline for the withdrawal of U.S. troops. Five years after the invasion, Bush called the debate over the conflict "understandable" but insisted that a continued U.S. presence there was crucial.

In March 2008, Bush praised the Iraqi government's "bold decision" to launch the Battle of Basra against the Mahdi Army, calling it "a defining moment in the history of a free Iraq". He said he would carefully weigh recommendations from his commanding General David Petraeus and

Ambassador Ryan Crocker about how to proceed after the end of the military buildup in the summer of 2008. He also praised the Iraqis' legislative achievements, including a pension law, a revised de-Baathification law, a new budget, an amnesty law, and a provincial powers measure that, he said, set the stage for the Iraqi elections.

On July 31, 2008, Bush announced that with the end of July, American troop deaths had reached their lowest number—thirteen—since the war began in 2003. Due to increased stability in Iraq, Bush announced the withdrawal of additional American forces. This reflected an emerging consensus between the White House and the Pentagon that the war has "turned a corner". He also described what he saw as the success of the 2007 troop surge

Under the Bush Administration, real GDP grew at an average annual rate of 2.5%, considerably below the average for business cycles from 1949 to 2000. Bush entered office with the Dow Jones Industrial Average at 10,587, and the average peaked in October 2007 at over 14,000. When Bush left office, the average was at 7,949, one of the lowest levels of his presidency.[101] Unemployment originally rose from 4.2% in January 2001 to 6.3% in June 2003, but subsequently dropped to 4.5% as of July 2007. Adjusted for inflation, median household income dropped by $1,175 between 2000 and 2007, while Professor Ken Homa of Georgetown University has noted that "after-tax median household income increased by 2%"The poverty rate increased from 11.3% in 2000 to 12.3% in 2006 after peaking at 12.7% in 2004. By October 2008, due to increases in domestic and foreign spending, the national debt had risen to $11.3 trillion, an increase of over 100% from the start of the year 2000 when the debt was $5.6 trillion. Most debt was accumulated as a result of what became known as the "Bush tax cuts" and increased national security spending.

By the end of Bush's presidency, unemployment climbed to 7.2%. The perception of Bush's effect on the economy is significantly affected by partisanship.

In December 2007, the United States entered the longest post–World War II recession, which included a housing market correction, a subprime mortgage crisis, soaring oil prices, and a declining dollar value. In February, 63,000 jobs were lost, a five-year record.

To aid with the situation, Bush signed a $170 billion economic stimulus package which was intended to improve the economic situation by sending tax rebate checks to many Americans and providing tax breaks for struggling businesses.

The Bush administration pushed for significantly increased regulation of Fannie Mae and Freddie Mac in 2003, and after two years, the regulations passed the House but died in the Senate. Many Republican senators, as well as influential members of the Bush Administration, feared that the agency created by these regulations would merely be mimicking the private sector's risky practices. In September 2008, the crisis became much more serious beginning with the government takeover of Fannie Mae and Freddie Mac followed by the collapse of Lehman Brothers and a federal bailout of American International Group for $85 billion.

Many economists and world governments determined that the situation became the worst financial crisis since the Great Depression. Additional regulation over the housing market would have been beneficial, according to former Federal Reserve Chairman Alan Greenspan. Bush, meanwhile, proposed a financial rescue plan to buy back a large portion of the U.S. mortgage market. Vince Reinhardt, a former Federal Reserve economist now at the American Enterprise Institute, said "it would have helped for the Bush administration to empower the folks at Treasury and the Federal Reserve and the comptroller of the currency and the FDIC to look at these issues more closely", and additionally, that it would have helped "for Congress to have held hearings".

In November 2008, over 500,000 jobs were lost, which marked the largest loss of jobs in the United States in 34 years. The Bureau of Labor Statistics reported that in the last four months of 2008, 1.9 million jobs were lost. By the end of 2008, the U.S. had lost a total of 2.6 million jobs.

Bush undertook a number of educational priorities, such as increasing the funding for the National Science Foundation and National Institutes of Health in his first years of office, and creating education programs to strengthen the grounding in science and mathematics for American high school students. Funding for the NIH was cut in 2006, the first such cut in 36 years, due to rising inflation.

One of the administration's early major initiatives was the No Child Left behind Act, which aimed to measure and closes the gap between rich and poor student performance, provide options to parents with students in low-performing schools, and target more federal funding to low-income schools.

This landmark education initiative passed with broad bipartisan support, including that of Senator Ted Kennedy of Massachusetts. It was signed into law by Bush in early 2002. Many contend that the initiative has been successful, as cited by the fact that students in the U.S. have performed significantly better on state reading and math tests since Bush signed "No Child Left Behind" into law.

After being re-elected, Bush signed into law a Medicare drug benefit program that, according to Jan Crawford Greenburg, resulted in "the greatest expansion in America's welfare state in forty years;" the bill's costs approached $7 trillion. In 2007, Bush opposed and vetoed State Children's Health Insurance Program (SCHIP) legislation, which was added by the Democrats onto a war funding bill and passed by Congress. The SCHIP legislation would have significantly expanded federally funded health care benefits and plans to children of some low-income families from about six million to ten million children. It was to be funded by an increase in the cigarette tax. Bush viewed the legislation as a move toward socialized health care, and asserted that the program could benefit families making as much as $83,000 per year who did not need the help.

Following Republican efforts to pass the Medicare Act of 2003, Bush signed the bill, which included major changes to the Medicare program by providing beneficiaries with some assistance in paying for prescription drugs, while relying on private insurance for the delivery of benefits. The retired persons lobby group AARP worked with the Bush Administration on the program and gave their endorsement. Bush said the law, estimated to cost $400 billion over the first ten years, would give the elderly "better choices and more control over their health care".

Bush began his second term by outlining a major initiative to reform Social Security, which was facing record deficit projections beginning in 2005. Bush made it the centerpiece of his domestic agenda despite opposition from some in the U.S. Congress. In his 2005 State of the Union Address, Bush discussed the potential impending bankruptcy of the program and outlined his new program, which included partial privatization of the system, personal Social Security accounts, and options to permit Americans to divert a portion of their Social Security tax (FICA) into secured investments. Democrats opposed the proposal to partially privatize the system.

Bush embarked on a 60-day national tour, campaigning vigorously for his initiative in media events, known as the "Conversations on Social Security", in an attempt to gain support from the general public. Despite the energetic campaign, public support for the proposal declined and the House Republican leadership decided not to put Social Security reform on the priority list for the remainder of their 2005 legislative agenda. The proposal's legislative prospects were further diminished by the political fallout from the Hurricane Katrina in the fall of 2005.

After the Democrats gained control of both houses of the Congress as a result of the 2006 midterm elections, the prospects of any further congressional action on the Bush proposal were dead for the remainder of his term in office.

In 2006, Bush urged Congress to allow more than 12 million illegal immigrants to work in the United States with the creation of a "temporary guest-worker program". Bush did not support amnesty for illegal immigrants, but argued that the lack of legal status denies the protections of U.S. laws to millions of people who face dangers of poverty and exploitation, and penalizes employers despite a demand for immigrant labor. Nearly 8 million immigrants came to the United States from 2000 to 2005, more than in any other five-year period in the nation's history. Almost half entered illegally.

Bush also urged Congress to provide additional funds for border security and committed to deploying 6,000 National Guard troops to the Mexico – United States border. In May–June 2007, Bush strongly supported the Comprehensive Immigration Reform Act of 2007, which was written by a bipartisan group of Senators with the active participation of the Bush administration. The bill envisioned a legalization program for undocumented immigrants, with an eventual path to citizenship; establishing a guest worker program; a series of border and work site enforcement measures; a reform of the green card application process and the introduction of a point-based "merit" system for green cards; elimination of "chain migration" and of the Diversity Immigrant Visa; and other measures. Bush contended that the proposed bill did not amount to amnesty.

A heated public debate followed, which resulted in a substantial rift within the Republican Party, the majority of conservatives opposed it because of its legalization or amnesty provisions. The bill was eventually defeated in the Senate on June 28, 2007, when a cloture motion failed on a 46–53 vote. Bush expressed disappointment upon the defeat of one of his signature domestic initiatives. The Bush administration later proposed a series of immigration enforcement measures that do not require a change in law.

During his Presidential campaign, Bush's foreign policy platform included support for a stronger economic and political relationship with Latin America, especially Mexico, and a reduction of involvement in "nation-building" and other small-scale military engagements. The administration pursued a national missile defense.

Bush was an advocate of China's entry into the World Trade Organization. He said open trade was a force for freedom in China.

After the September 11 attacks, Bush launched the War on Terror, in which the United States military and an international coalition invaded Afghanistan. In 2003, Bush launched the invasion of Iraq, which he described as being part of the War on Terrorism.

Those invasions led to the toppling of the Taliban regime in Afghanistan and the removal of Saddam Hussein from power in Iraq as well as the deaths of many Iraqis, with surveys indicating between four hundred thousand to over one million dead, excluding the tens of thousands of civilians in Afghanistan.

Bush began his second term with an emphasis on improving strained relations with European nations. He appointed long-time adviser Karen Hughes to oversee a global public relations campaign. Bush lauded the pro-democracy struggles in Georgia and Ukraine.

In March 2006, a visit to India led to renewed ties between the two countries, reversing decades of U.S. policy. The visit focused particularly on areas of nuclear energy and counter-terrorism cooperation, discussions that would lead eventually to the U.S.-India Civil Nuclear Agreement. This is in stark contrast to the stance taken by his predecessor, Clinton, whose approach and response to India after the 1998 nuclear tests was that of sanctions and hectoring. The relationship between India and the United States was one that dramatically improved during Bush's tenure.

Midway through Bush's second term, it was questioned whether Bush was retreating from his freedom and democracy agenda, highlighted in policy changes toward some oil-rich former Soviet republics in central Asia.

In an address before both Houses of Congress on September 20, 2001, Bush thanked the nations of the world for their support following the September 11 attacks. He specifically thanked British Prime Minister Tony Blair for traveling to the Washington to show "unity of purpose with America", and said "America has no truer friend than Great Britain."

Bush withdrew U.S. support for several international agreements, including the Anti-Ballistic Missile Treaty (ABM) with Russia. Bush emphasized a careful approach to the conflict between Israel and the Palestinians; he denounced Palestine Liberation Organization leader Yasser Arafat for his support of violence, but sponsored dialogues between Prime Minister Ariel Sharon and Palestinian National Authority President Mahmoud Abbas. Bush supported Sharon's unilateral disengagement plan, and lauded the democratic elections held in Palestine after Arafat's death.

Bush also expressed U.S. support for the defense of Taiwan following the stand-off in April 2001 with the People's Republic of China over the Hainan Island incident, when an EP-3E Aries II surveillance aircraft collided with a People's Liberation Army Air Force jet, leading to the detention of U.S. personnel. In 2003–2004, Bush authorized U.S. military intervention in Haiti and Liberia to protect U.S. interests. Bush condemned the militia attacks Darfur and denounced the killings in Sudan as genocide.

Bush said that an international peacekeeping presence was critical in Darfur, but opposed referring the situation to the International Criminal Court. From October to December, the gross domestic product—which measures the total output of goods and services within U.S. borders—shrank at a higher annual rate than previously estimated at 6.3 percent, and profits dropped 16.5 percent from the prior quarter, the most since 1953, Bloomberg News reported.

The government last month estimated the fall in fourth-quarter GDP at 6.2 percent. Facing rising unemployment, falling home values and shrinking investment portfolios, businesses and consumers are curtailing purchases and leading companies to slash production and jobs.

The economy grew 1.1 percent for all of 2008, the same as previously estimated, as exports and government tax rebates in the first six months helped offset the slump in consumer spending that followed. Consumer spending, which accounts for about 70 percent of the economy, fell at a 4.3 percent pace last quarter, marking the first back-to-back decreases in excess of 3 percent since record-keeping began in 1947, Bloomberg News reported.

A government program created for the establishment and management of a Treasury fund, in an attempt to curb the ongoing financial crisis of 2007-2008. The TARP gives the U.S. Treasury purchasing power of $700 billion to buy up mortgage backed securities (MBS) from institutions across the country, in an attempt to create liquidity and un-seize the money markets. The fund was created by a bill that was made law on October 3, 2008 with the passage of H.R. 1424 enacting the Emergency Economic Stabilization Act of 2008.

The Treasury will be given $250 billion immediately, and the President must certify additional funds as they are needed. The additional funds will be distributed as $100 billion, and then as the final $350 billion is given, Congress has the right to not approve the additional amounts.

Global credit markets came to a near stand still in September 2008, as several major financial institutions, such as Lehman Brothers, Fannie Mae,

Freddie Mac and American International Group, went under. In a few surprising moves, heavyweights Goldman Sachs and Morgan Stanley even changed their charter to become commercial banks, in an attempt to stabilize their capital situation. The bailout will attempt to increase the liquidity of the secondary mortgage markets by purchasing the illiquid MBS, and through that, reducing the potential losses that could be felt by the institutions who currently own them.

In October of 2008, revisions to the program were announced by Treasury Secretary Paulson and President Bush; allowing for the first $250 billion to be used to buy equity stakes in nine major U.S. banks, and many smaller banks. This program demands that companies involved lose some tax benefits, and in many cases incur limits on executive compensation.

The Obama Evolution

Barack Hussein Obama II born August 4, 1961 is the 44th President of the United States. He is the first African American to hold the office. Obama previously served as a United States Senator from Illinois, from January 2005 until he resigned following his victory in the 2008 presidential election.

A native of Honolulu, Hawaii, Obama is a graduate of Columbia University and Harvard Law School, where he was the president of the Harvard Law Review. He was a community organizer in Chicago before earning his law degree. He worked as a civil rights attorney in Chicago and taught constitutional law at the University Of Chicago Law School from 1992 to 2004. He served three terms representing the 13th district in the Illinois Senate from 1997 to 2004.

Following an unsuccessful bid against the Democratic incumbent for a seat in the United States House of Representatives in 2000, Obama ran for United States Senate in 2004. Several events brought him to national attention during the campaign, including his victory in the March 2004

189

Democratic primary and his keynote address at the Democratic National Convention in July 2004.

He won election to the U.S. Senate in Illinois in November 2004. His presidential campaign began in February 2007, and after a close campaign in the 2008 Democratic Party presidential primaries against Hillary Rodham Clinton, he won his party's nomination. In the 2008 presidential election, he defeated Republican nominee John McCain, and was inaugurated as president on January 20, 2009. In October 2009, Obama was named the 2009 Nobel Peace Prize laureate.

As president, Obama signed economic stimulus legislation in the form of the American Recovery and Reinvestment Act in February 2009 and the Tax Relief, Unemployment Insurance Reauthorization, and Job Creation Act in December 2010. Other domestic policy initiatives include the Patient Protection and Affordable Care Act, the Dodd–Frank Wall Street Reform and Consumer Protection Act and the Don't Ask, Don't Tell Repeal Act.

In foreign policy, he gradually withdrew combat troops from Iraq, increased troop levels in Afghanistan, signed the New START arms control treaty with Russia, ordered enforcement of the United Nations-sanctioned no-fly zone over Libya. And issued a direct order to a small group of American military forces to kill al-Qaeda leader Osama bin Laden in Pakistan. In April 2011, Obama declared his intention to seek re-election in the 2012 presidential election.

Of his early childhood, Obama recalled, "That my father looked nothing like the people around me—that he was black as pitch, my mother white as milk—barely registered in my mind." He described his struggles as a young adult to reconcile social perceptions of his multiracial heritage. Reflecting later on his formative years in Honolulu, Obama wrote: "The opportunity that Hawaii offered—to experience a variety of cultures in a climate of mutual respect—became an integral part of my world view, and a basis for the values that I hold most dear." Obama has also written and talked about using alcohol, marijuana and cocaine during his teenage years to "push questions of who I was out of my mind." At the 2008 Civil Forum on the Presidency, Obama identified his high-school drug use as a great moral failure.

Following high school, Obama moved to Los Angeles in 1979 to attend Occidental College. In February 1981, he made his first public speech, calling for Occidental's disinvestment from South Africa due to its policy of apartheid. In mid-1981, Obama traveled to Indonesia to visit his mother and sister Maya, and visited the families of college friends in Pakistan and India for three weeks.

Later in 1981, he transferred to Columbia University in New York City, where he majored in political science with a specialty in international relations and graduated with a Bachelor of Arts in 1983. He worked for a year at the Business International Corporation, then at the New York Public Interest Research Group. Two years after graduating, Obama was hired in Chicago as director of the Developing Communities Project (DCP), a church-based community organization originally comprising eight Catholic parishes in Greater Roseland (Roseland, West Pullman and Riverdale) on Chicago's far South Side. He worked there as a community organizer from June 1985 to May 1988.

During his three years as the DCP's director, its staff grew from one to thirteen. He helped set up a job training program, a college preparatory tutoring program, and a tenants' rights organization in Altgeld Gardens. Obama also worked as a consultant and instructor for the Gamaliel Foundation, a community organizing institute. In mid-1988, he traveled for the first time in Europe for three weeks and then for five weeks in Kenya, where he met many of his paternal relatives for the first time. He returned in August 2006 for a visit to his father's birthplace, a village in rural western Kenya.

In late 1988, Obama entered Harvard Law School. He was selected as an editor of the Harvard Law Review at the end of his first year, and president of the journal in his second year. During his summers, he returned to Chicago, where he worked as a summer associate at the law firms of Sidley Austin in 1989 and Hopkins & Sutter in 1990. After graduating with a Juris Doctor Magna cum laude from Harvard in 1991, he returned to Chicago. Obama's election as the first black president of the Harvard Law Review gained national media attention and led to a publishing contract and advance for a book about race relations, which evolved into a personal memoir. The manuscript was published in mid-1995 as Dreams from My Father.

On February 10, 2007, Obama announced his candidacy for President of the United States in front of the Old State Capitol building in Springfield, Illinois. The choice of the announcement site was viewed as symbolic because it was also where Abraham Lincoln delivered his historic "House Divided" speech in 1858. Obama emphasized the issues of rapidly ending the Iraq War, increasing energy independence, and providing universal health care, in a campaign that projected themes of "hope" and "change".

A large number of candidates entered the Democratic Party presidential primaries. The field narrowed to a duel between Obama and Senator Hillary Rodham Clinton after early contests, with the race remaining close throughout the primary process but with Obama gaining a steady lead in pledged delegates due to better long-range planning, superior fundraising, dominant organizing in caucus states, and better exploitation of delegate allocation rules. Clinton ended her campaign and endorsed him on June 7, 2008.

Obama announced on August 23 that he had selected Delaware Senator Joe Biden as his vice presidential running mate, from a field speculated to include Senator Evan Bayh and Virginia Governor Tim Kaine.

At the Democratic National Convention in Denver, Colorado, Hillary Clinton called for her delegates and supporters to endorse Obama, and she and Bill Clinton gave convention speeches in support of Obama. Obama delivered his acceptance speech, not at the convention center where the Democratic National Convention was held, but at Invesco Field at Mile High to a crowd of over 75,000and presented his policy goals; the speech was viewed by over 38 million people worldwide. During both the primary process and the general election, Obama's campaign set numerous fundraising records, particularly in the quantity of small donations.

Senator John McCain was nominated as the Republican candidate and the two engaged in three presidential debates in September and October 2008. On November 4, Obama won the presidency with 365 electoral votes to 173 received by McCain. Obama won 52.9% of the popular vote to McCain's 45.7%. He became the first African American to be elected president. Obama delivered his victory speech before hundreds of thousands of supporters in Chicago's Grant Park.

The inauguration of Barack Obama as President, and Joe Biden as Vice President, took place on January 20, 2009. In his first few days in office Obama issued executive orders and presidential memoranda directing the U.S. military to develop plans to withdraw troops from Iraq. He ordered the closing of the Guantanamo Bay detention camp "as soon as practicable and no later than" January 2010, but during his first two years in office he has been unable to persuade Congress to appropriate funds required to accomplish the shutdown. He also reversed George W. Bush's ban on federal funding to foreign establishments that allow abortions.

The first bill signed into law by Obama was the Lilly Ledbetter Fair Pay Act of 2009, relaxing the statute of limitations for equal-pay lawsuits. Five days later, he signed the reauthorization of the State Children's Health Insurance Program (SCHIP) to cover an additional 4 million children currently uninsured.

In March 2009, Obama reversed a Bush-era policy which had limited funding of embryonic stem cell research. Obama stated that he believed "sound science and moral values...are not inconsistent" and pledged to develop "strict guidelines" on the research.

Obama appointed two women to serve on the Supreme Court in the first two years of his Presidency. Sonia Sotomayor, nominated by Obama on May 26, 2009, to replace retiring Associate Justice David Souter, was confirmed on August 6, 2009, becoming the first Hispanic to be a Supreme Court Justice. Elena Kagan, nominated by Obama on May 10, 2010, to replace retiring Associate Justice John Paul Stevens, was confirmed on August 5, 2010, bringing the number of women sitting simultaneously on the Court to three, for the first time in American history.

On September 30, 2009, the Obama administration proposed new regulations on power plants, factories and oil refineries in an attempt to limit greenhouse gas emissions and to curb global warming. On October 8, 2009, Obama signed the Hate Crimes Prevention Act, a measure that expands the 1969 United States federal hate-crime law to include crimes motivated by a victim's actual or perceived gender, sexual orientation, gender identity, or disability.

On March 30, 2010, Obama signed the Health Care and Education Reconciliation Act, a reconciliation bill which ends the process of the federal government giving subsidies to private banks to give out federally insured loans, increases the Pell Grant scholarship award, and makes changes to the Patient Protection and Affordable Care Act.

In a major space policy speech in April 2010, Obama announced a planned change in direction at NASA, the U.S. space agency. He ended plans for a return of human spaceflight to the moon and ended development of the Ares I rocket, Ares V rocket and Constellation program. He is focusing funding on Earth science projects and a new rocket type, as well as research and development for an eventual manned mission to Mars. Missions to the International Space Station are expected to continue until 2020.

On December 22, 2010, Obama signed the Don't Ask, Don't Tell Repeal Act of 2010, a bill that provides for repeal of the Don't ask, don't tell policy of 1993 that has prevented gay and lesbian people from serving openly in the United States Armed Forces. Repealing "Don't ask, don't tell" had been a key campaign promise that Obama had made during the 2008 presidential campaign.

On January 25, 2011, in his 2011 State of the Union Address, President Obama focused strongly on the themes of education and innovation, stressing the importance of innovation economics in working to make the United States more competitive globally. Among other plans and goals, Obama spoke of a enacting a five-year freeze in domestic spending, eliminating tax breaks for oil companies and tax cuts for the wealthiest 2 percent of Americans, banning congressional earmarks, and reducing healthcare costs. Looking to the future, Obama promised that by 2015, the United States would have 1 million electric vehicles on the road and by 2035; clean-energy sources would be providing 80 percent of U.S. electricity.

On February 17, 2009, Obama signed the American Recovery and Reinvestment Act of 2009, a $787 billion economic stimulus package aimed at helping the economy recover from the deepening worldwide recession. The act includes increased federal spending for health care, infrastructure, education, various tax breaks and incentives, and direct assistance to individuals, which is being distributed over the course of several years.

In March, Obama's Treasury Secretary, Timothy Geithner, took further steps to manage the financial crisis, including introducing the Public-

Private Investment Program for Legacy Assets, which contains provisions for buying up to $2 trillion in depreciated real estate assets.

Obama intervened in the troubled automotive industry in March 2009, renewing loans for General Motors and Chrysler to continue operations while reorganizing. Over the following months the White House set terms for both firms' bankruptcies, including the sale of Chrysler to Italian automaker Fiat and a reorganization of GM giving the U.S. government a 60% equity stake in the company, with the Canadian government shouldering a 12% stake. In June 2009, dissatisfied with the pace of economic stimulus, Obama called on his cabinet to accelerate the investment. He signed into law the Car Allowance Rebate System, known colloquially as "Cash for Clunkers", that had mixed results. Although spending and loan guarantees from the Federal Reserve and the Treasury Department authorized by the Bush and Obama administrations totaled about $11.5 trillion, only $3 trillion had actually been spent by the end of November 2009.

However, Obama and the Congressional Budget Office predict that the 2010 budget deficit will be $1.5 trillion or 10.6% of the nation's gross domestic product (GDP) compared to the 2009 deficit of $1.4 trillion or 9.9% of GDP.For 2011, the administration predicted the deficit will slightly shrink to $1.34 trillion, While the 10-year deficit will increase to $8.53 trillion or 80% of GDP. The most recent increase in the U.S. debt ceiling to $14.3 trillion was signed into law on February 12, 2010.

On February 17, 2009, Obama signed the American Recovery and Reinvestment Act of 2009, a $787 billion economic stimulus package aimed at helping the economy recover from the deepening worldwide recession. The act includes increased federal spending for health care, infrastructure, education, various tax breaks and incentives, and direct assistance to individuals, which is being distributed over the course of several years.

In March, Obama's Treasury Secretary, Timothy Geithner, took further steps to manage the financial crisis, including introducing the Public-Private Investment Program for Legacy Assets, which contains provisions for buying up to S2 trillion in depreciated real estate assets.

The unemployment rate rose in 2009, reaching a peak in October at 10.1% and averaging 10.0% in the fourth quarter. Following a decrease to 9.7% in the first quarter of 2010, the unemployment rate fell to 9.6% in the second quarter, where it stayed the rest of the year. Between February and December 2010, employment rose by 0.8%, which was less than the average of 1.9%, experienced during comparable periods in the past four employment recoveries. GDP growth returned in the third quarter of 2009, expanding at a 1.6% pace, followed by a 5.0% increase in the fourth quarter. Growth continued in 2010, posting an increase of 3.7% in the first quarter, with lesser gains throughout the rest of the year.

In July 2010, the Federal Reserve expressed that although economic activity continued to increase, its pace had slowed and it's Chairman, Ben Bernanke, stated that the economic outlook was "unusually uncertain." Overall, the economy expanded at a rate of 2.9% in 2010.

The Congressional Budget Office and a broad range of economists credit Obama's stimulus plan for economic growth. The CBO released a report stating that the stimulus bill increased employment by 1–2.1 million, while conceding that "It is impossible to determine how many of the reported jobs would have existed in the absence of the stimulus package." Although an April 2010 survey of members of the National Association for Business Economics showed an increase in job creation for the first time in two years, 73% of the 68 respondents believed that the stimulus bill has had no impact on employment. The country's recovery was anemic and the President received much of the blame along with Congress as well.

Within a month of the 2010 midterm elections, Obama announced a compromise deal with the Congressional Republican leadership that included a temporary, two-year extension of the 2001 and 2003 income tax rates, a one-year payroll tax reduction, continuation of unemployment benefits, and a new rate and exemption amount for estate taxes.

The compromise overcome opposition from some in both parties, and the resulting $858 billion Tax Relief, Unemployment Insurance Reauthorization, and Job Creation Act of 2010 passed with bipartisan majorities in both houses of Congress before Obama signed it on December 17, 2010.

Obama called for Congress to pass legislation reforming health care in the United States, a key campaign promise and a top legislative goal. He proposed an expansion of health insurance coverage to cover the uninsured, to cap premium increases, and to allow people to retain their coverage when they leave or change jobs. His proposal was to spend $900 billion over 10 years and include a government insurance plan, also known as the public option, to compete with the corporate insurance sector as a main component to lowering costs and improving quality of health care.

It would also make it illegal for insurers to drop sick people or deny them coverage for pre-existing conditions, and require every American carry health coverage. The plan also includes medical spending cuts and taxes on insurance companies that offer expensive plans.

On July 14, 2009, House Democratic leaders introduced a 1,017-page plan for overhauling the U.S. health care system, which Obama wanted Congress to approve by the end of 2009. After much public debate during the Congressional summer recess of 2009, Obama delivered a speech to a joint session of Congress on September 9 where he addressed concerns over his administration's proposals. In March 2009, Obama lifted a ban on stem cell research.

On November 7, 2009, a health care bill featuring the public option was passed in the House.

On December 24, 2009, the Senate passed its own bill—without a public option—on a party-line vote of 60–39. On March 21, 2010, the health care bill passed by the Senate in December was passed in the House by a vote of 219 to 212. Obama signed the bill into law on March 23, 2010.

On March 19, Obama continued his outreach to the Muslim world, releasing a New Year's video message to the people and government of Iran. This attempt at outreach was rebuffed by the Iranian leadership. In April, Obama gave a speech in Ankara, Turkey, which was well received by many Arab governments. On June 4, 2009, Obama delivered a speech at Cairo University in Egypt calling for "a new beginning" in relations between the Islamic world and the United States and promoting Middle East peace.

On June 26, 2009, in response to the Iranian government's actions towards protesters following Iran's 2009 presidential election, Obama said: "The violence perpetrated against them is outrageous. We see it and we condemn it." On July 7, while in Moscow, he responded to a Vice President Biden comment on a possible Israeli military strike on Iran by saying: "We have said directly to the Israelis that it is important to try and resolve this in an international setting in a way that does not create major conflict in the Middle East."

On September 24, 2009, Obama became the first sitting U.S. president to preside over a meeting of the United Nations Security Council. His international appeal had great acceptance from much of the world's leadership.

In March 2010, Obama took a public stance against plans by the government of Israeli Prime Minister Benjamin Netanyahu to continue building Jewish housing projects in predominantly Arab neighborhoods of East Jerusalem. During the same month, an agreement was reached with the administration of Russian President Dmitry Medvedev to replace the 1991 Strategic Arms Reduction Treaty with a new pact reducing the number of long-range nuclear weapons in the arsenals of both countries by about one-third.

The New START treaty was signed by Obama and Medvedev in April 2010, and was ratified by the U.S. Senate in December 2010.

During his presidential transition, President-elect Obama announced that he would retain the incumbent Defense Secretary, Robert Gates, in his Cabinet. President Obama ended using most of the apparatus that President Bush had used in his terms in office.

On February 27, 2009, Obama declared that combat operations would end in Iraq within 18 months. His remarks were made to a group of Marines preparing for deployment to Afghanistan. Obama said, "Let me say this as plainly as I can: By August 31, 2010, our combat mission in Iraq will end." The Obama administration scheduled the withdrawal of combat troops to be completed by August 2010, decreasing troop's levels from 142,000 while leaving a transitional force of 35,000 to 50,000 in Iraq until the end of 2011. On August 19, 2010, the last United States combat brigade exited Iraq. The plan is to transition the mission of the remaining troops from combat operations to counter-terrorism and the training, equipping, and advising of Iraqi security forces. On August 31, 2010, Obama announced that the United States combat mission in Iraq was over.

At this time Obama moved to bolster U.S. troop strength in Afghanistan. He announced an increase to U.S. troop levels of 17,000 in February 2009 to "stabilize a deteriorating situation in Afghanistan"; an area he said had not received the "strategic attention, direction and resources it urgently requires".

He replaced the military commander in Afghanistan, General David D. McKiernan, with former Special Forces commander Lt. Gen. Stanley A. McChrystal in May 2009, indicating that McChrystal's Special Forces experience would facilitate the use of counterinsurgency tactics in the war.

On December 1, 2009, Obama announced the deployment of an additional 30,000 military personnel to Afghanistan. He also proposed to begin troop withdrawals 18 months from that date. McChrystal was replaced by David Petraeus in June 2010 after McChrystal's staff criticized White House personnel in a magazine article.

During the initial years of the Obama administration, the U.S. increased military cooperation with Israel, including a record number of U.S. troops participating in military exercises in the country, increased military aid, and the re-establishment of the U.S.-Israeli Joint Political Military Group and the Defense Policy Advisory Group.

It was reported high-ranking defense officials from both countries had been making an unusual number of trips between the two countries, including Ehud Barak. Part of the military aid increase in 2010 was to fund Israel's missile defense shield.

In 2011, Obama's Ambassador to the United Nations vetoed a resolution condemning Israeli settlements, with the U.S. the only nation on the Security Council doing so. Like previous American presidential administrations, Obama supports the two-state solution to the Arab-Israeli conflict based on the 1967 borders with land swaps. His announcement was met with negative reaction on both sides in the conflict.

In March 2011, as forces loyal to Muammar Gaddafi advanced on rebels across Libya, formal calls for a no-fly zone came in from around the world, including Europe, the Arab League, and a resolution passed unanimously by the U.S. Senate. In response to the unanimous passage of United Nations Security Council Resolution 1973 on March 17, Gaddafi who had previously vowed to "show no mercy" to the citizens of Benghazi announced an immediate cessation of military activities. Yet reports came in that his forces continued shelling Misrata. The next day, on Obama's orders, the U.S. military took a lead role in air strikes to destroy the Libyan government's air defense capabilities in order to protect civilians and enforce a no-fly-zone, including the use of Tomahawk missiles, B-2s, and fighter jets. Six days later, on March 25, by unanimous vote of all 28 members of NATO, that organization took over leadership of the effort. Some congressmen questioned whether Obama had the constitutional authority to order military action in addition to questions about its cost, structure and aftermath.

Starting with information received in July 2010, intelligence developed by the CIA over the next several months determined what they believed to be the location of Osama bin Laden in a large compound in Abbottabad, Pakistan, a suburban area 35 miles from Islamabad. CIA head Leon Panetta reported this intelligence to President Obama in March 2011. Meeting with his national security advisers over the course of the next six weeks, Obama rejected a plan to bomb the compound, and authorized a "surgical raid" to be conducted by United States Navy SEALs. The operation took place on May 1, 2011, resulting in the death of bin Laden and the seizure of papers and computer drives and disks from the compound. Bin Laden's body was identified through DNA testing, and buried at sea several hours later. Within minutes of the President's announcement from Washington, DC, late in the evening on May 1, there were spontaneous celebrations around the country as crowds gathered outside the White House, and at New York City's Ground Zero and Times Square. Reaction to the announcement was positive across party lines, including from former Presidents Bill Clinton and George W. Bush and from many countries around the world.

Obama called the November 2, 2010 election, where the Democratic Party lost 63 seats in, and control of, the House of Representatives, "humbling" and a "shellacking". He said that the results came because not enough Americans had felt the effects of the economic recovery. According to the Gallup Organization, Obama began his presidency with a 68% approval rating before gradually declining for the rest of the year, and eventually bottoming out at 41% in August 2010.

In December 2008, Time magazine named Barack Obama as its Person of the Year for his historic candidacy and election, which it described as "the steady march of seemingly impossible accomplishments".

On October 9, 2009, the Norwegian Nobel Committee announced that Obama had won the 2009 Nobel Peace Prize "for his extraordinary efforts to strengthen international diplomacy and cooperation between peoples". Obama accepted this award in Oslo, Norway on December 10, 2009, with "deep gratitude and great humility." The award drew a mixture of praise and criticism from world leaders and media figures. Obama is the fourth U.S. president to be awarded the Nobel Peace Prize and the third to become a Nobel laureate while in office. He was also the only U.S. President to do absolutely nothing to deserve the award.

The Tea Party movement is an American populist political movement that is generally recognized as conservative and libertarian, and has sponsored protests and supported political candidates since 2009.

It endorses reduced government spending, opposition to taxation in varying degrees, reduction of the national debt and federal budget deficit, and adherence to conservative interpretation of the United States Constitution.

The name "Tea Party" is a reference to the Boston Tea Party, a protest by colonists who objected to a British tax on tea in 1773 and demonstrated by dumping British tea taken from docked ships into the harbor. Some commentators have referred to the Tea in "Tea Party" as the acronym "Taxed Enough Already".

The Tea Party movement has caucuses in the House of Representatives and the Senate of the United States. The Tea Party movement has no central leadership but is composed of a loose affiliation of national and local groups that determine their own platforms and agendas. The Tea Party movement has been cited as an example of grassroots political activity, although it has also been cited as an example of astro turfing.

The Tea Party's most noted national figures include Republican politicians such as Sarah Palin, Dick Armey, and Ron Paul, with Paul described as the "intellectual grandfather" of the movement. As of 2011, the Tea Party movement is not a national political party, but has endorsed Republican candidates. Polls show that most Tea Partiers consider themselves to be Republicans.

Commentators, including Gallup editor-in-chief Frank Newport, have suggested that the movement is not a new political group but simply a rebranding of traditional Republican candidates and policies. An October 2010 Washington Post canvass of local Tea Party organizers found 87% saying "dissatisfaction with mainstream Republican Party leaders" was "an important factor in the support the group has received so far".

On February 19, 2009, in a broadcast from the floor of the Chicago Mercantile Exchange, CNBC Business News editor Rick Santelli criticized the government plan to refinance mortgages, which had just been announced the day before. He said that those plans were "promoting bad behavior" by "subsidizing losers' mortgages".

He suggested holding a tea party for traders to gather and dump the derivatives in the Chicago River on July 1. A number of the floor traders around him cheered on his proposal, to the amusement of the hosts in the studio. Santelli's "rant" became a viral video after being featured on the Drudge Report.

In response to Santelli, websites such as ChicagoTeaParty.com (registered in August 2008 by Chicago radio producer Zack Christenson) were live within 12 hours. About 10 hours after Santelli's remarks, reTeaParty.com was bought to coordinate Tea Parties scheduled for Independence Day and, as of March 4, was reported to be receiving 11,000 visitors a day. According to The New Yorker writer Ben McGrath and New York Times reporter Kate Zernike, this is where the movement was first inspired to coalesce under the collective banner of "Tea Party". By the next day, guests on Fox News had already begun to mention this new "Tea Party".

As reported by The Huffington Post, a facebook page was developed on February 20 calling for Tea Party protests across the country. Soon, the "Nationwide Chicago Tea Party" protest was coordinated across over 40 different cities for February 27, 2009, thus establishing the first national modern Tea Party protest. The movement has been supported nationally by at least 12 prominent individuals and their associated organizations.

Beginning in 2009, the Gadsden flag has become a favorite among the Tea Party movement nationwide, serving as an alternative to the stars and stripes for Tea Party protesters who feel patriotism for their country and are upset at the government. It was also seen being displayed by members of Congress at Tea Party rallies. Some lawmakers have dubbed it a political symbol due to the Tea Party connection, and the political nature of Tea Party supporters.

The Second Revolution flag gained national attention on January 19, 2010. It is a version of the Betsy Ross American flag, with a Roman Numeral II in the center of the circle of 13 stars, symbolizing the second Revolution in America. The Second Revolution flag has been called synonymous with Tea Party causes and events. Several polls have been conducted on the demographics of the movement.

One Gallup poll found that other than gender, income and politics, self-described Tea Party members were demographically similar to the population as a whole.

When surveying supporters or participants of the Tea Party movement, polls have shown that they are to a very great extent more likely to be registered Republican, have a favorable opinion of the Republican Party and an unfavorable opinion of the Democratic Party. In an August 2010 article for Foreign Policy magazine, Ron Paul outlined foreign policy views the Tea Party movement should emphasize: "I see tremendous opportunities for movements like the Tea Party to prosper by capitalizing on the Democrats' broken promises to overturn the George W. Bush administration's civil liberties abuses and end the disastrous wars in Iraq and Afghanistan.

A return to the traditional U.S. foreign policy of active private engagement but government non interventionism is the only alternative that can restore our moral and fiscal health."

Walter Russell Mead analyzes the foreign policy views of the Tea Party movement in a 2011 essay published in Foreign Affairs. Mead says that Jacksonian populists, such as the Tea Party, combine a belief in American exceptionalism and its role in the world with skepticism of American's "ability to create a liberal world order". When necessary, they favor total war and unconditional surrender over "limited wars for limited goals". Mead identifies two main trends, one somewhat personified by Ron Paul and the other by Sarah Palin. "Paulites" have a Jeffersonian, "neo-isolationist" approach that seeks to avoid foreign military involvement. "Palinites", while seeking to avoid being drawn into unnecessary conflicts, favor a more aggressive response to maintaining America's primacy in international relations. Mead says that both groups share distaste for "liberal internationalism".

Sarah Palin headlined four "Liberty at the Ballot Box" bus tours, to raise money for candidates and the Tea Party Express. One of the tours visited 30 towns and covered 3,000 miles. Following the formation of the Tea Party Caucus, Michele Bachmann raised $10 million for a political action committee, Michele PAC, and sent funds to the campaigns of Sharron Angle, Christine O'Donnell, Rand Paul, and Marco Rubio. In September 2010, the Tea Party Patriots announced it had received a $1,000,000 USD donation from an anonymous donor.

In 2010 Tea Party-endorsed candidates upset established Republicans in several primaries, such as Alaska, Colorado, Delaware, Florida, Nevada,

New York, South Carolina and Utah, giving a new momentum to the conservative cause in the 2010 elections. In the 2010 midterm elections, The New York Times has identified 138 candidates for Congress with significant Tea Party support, and reported that all of them were running as Republicans—of whom 129 are running for the House and 9 for the Senate.

A USA Today/Gallup poll conducted in March 2010, found that 28% of those surveyed considered themselves supporters of the Tea Party movement, 26% were opponents, and 46% were neither.

These figures have remained stable through January 2011, as has public opinion of the movement. In the USA Today/Gallup poll conducted in January 2011, approximately 70% of adults, including approximately 9 out of 10 Republicans, feel Republican leaders in Congress should give consideration to Tea Party movement ideas. The Center for American Progress, a progressive group, used this poll to assert that the Tea Party movement holds views that differ from those the general public. The Tea Party differed on views related to Roe v. Wade, income taxes, and Obama. An NBC News/Wall Street Journal poll later the same month found 27% considered themselves Tea Party supporters. In that poll, 42% said the Tea Party has been good for the U.S. political system; 18% called it a bad thing. Those with an unfavorable view of the Tea Party outnumbered those with a favorable view 36–30%. In comparison, the Democratic Party was viewed unfavorably by a 42–37% margin and the Republican Party by 43–31%.

Occupy Wall Street (OWS) is an ongoing series of demonstrations beginning September 17, 2011, in New York City's Zuccotti Park in the Wall Street financial district. The protests have focused on social and economic inequality, high unemployment, greed, as well as corruption, and the undue influence of corporations—particularly that of the financial services sector—on government.

The protesters' slogan We are the 99% refers to the growing difference in wealth in the U.S. between the wealthiest 1% and the rest of the population.

The Congressional Budget Office said that between 1979 and 2007 the incomes of the top 1% of Americans grew by an average of 275%. During the same time period, the 60% of Americans in the middle of the income scale saw their income rise by 40%. Since 1979 the average pre-tax income for the bottom 90% of households has decreased by $900, while that of the top 1% increased by over $700,000, as federal taxation became less progressive. From 1992-2007 the top 400 income earners in the U.S. saw their income increase 392% and their average tax rate reduced by 37%.

In 2009, the average income of the top 1% was $960,000 with a minimum income of $343,927. A 2010 poll found that an overwhelming majority of Americans across the political spectrum, including the wealthiest, want more equitable distribution of wealth.

The protesters vary in political outlook; some are liberals, political independents, anarchists, with others identifying as socialists, libertarians, or environmentalists. Early on the protesters were mostly young due to their pronounced use of social networks through which they promoted the protests. As the protest grew, older protesters also became involved. Various religious faiths have been represented at the protest including Muslims, Jews, and Christians. On October 10 the Associated Press reported that "there's a diversity of age, gender and race" at the protest. Some news organizations have compared the protest to a left-leaning version of the Tea Party protests.

The group has been frequently criticized for its lack of specific policy demands. The General Assembly has already adopted a "Declaration of the Occupation of New York City," which includes a list of grievances against corporations, and many protesters believe that the general statement is enough.

However, in early October other protesters, strongly in favor of a need for demands, had formed a *Demands Working Group* to identify and present a formal statement of specific actions they would ask local and federal governments to adopt. The Demands group published its list of demands in the New York Times in mid-October.

Various sources report that OWS has received as much as $500,000 in donations as of October 27, 2011. According to *The Wall Street Journal*, "A few weeks ago, the Alliance for Global Justice, a Washington-based nonprofit, agreed to sponsor Occupy Wall Street and lend it its tax-exempt status, so donors could write off contributions. That means the Alliance for Global Justice's board has final say on spending, though it says it's not involved in decisions and will only step in if the protesters want to spend money on something that might violate their tax-exempt status."

An October CBS News/New York Times polls found 43% of Americans agree with Occupy Wall Street while 27% disagree. An October Rasmussen poll found an almost even split, shows that 33 percent of Americans have a favorable view, while 27 percent are unfavorable and 40 percent have no opinion. An October United Technologies/National Journal Congressional poll found that 59 percent of Americans agree with the movement while 31 percent disagree.

A November 3 poll done by Quinnipiac University found that just 30 percent of American voters have a favorable view of the protests, while 39 percent do not.

The same poll found that among independent voters, 29 percent have a favorable view opposed to 42 percent who have an unfavorable view. However, an ORC International poll released the same time found an increase in recognition and support of "Occupy Wall Street" from early October. 36% said they agreed with the overall positions of Occupy Wall Street, while 19% say they disagreed.

During a hearing before the Joint Economic Committee October 4, 2011, Federal Reserve Chairman Ben Bernanke said, "[P]eople are quite unhappy with the state of the economy and what's happening. They blame, with some justification, the problems in the financial sector for getting us into this mess, and they're dissatisfied with the policy response here in Washington. And at some level, I can't blame them. Certainly, 9 percent unemployment and very slow growth is not a good situation." Dallas Federal Reserve President Richard W. Fisher said that he was "somewhat sympathetic" to the views of the protesters, and added, "We have too many people out of work. We have a very uneven distribution of income.

We have a very frustrated people, and I can understand their frustration." Federal Reserve Chairman Ben Bernanke commented about protester's blame of the Fed saying: ""The concerns about the Fed are based on misconceptions, A very simplistic interpretation of that [criticism] was that we were doing that because we wanted to preserve banker salaries. That was obviously not the case." Bernanke has stated that policies aimed at boosting the economy will continue.

Whether you agree or disagree with the Occupy Wallstreet movement it must be agreed they are having an impact for good or bad.

The OWS movement has spread around the nation and is to some degree having a great affect on the discourse in poltics today. The OWS movement is less organized than the Tea Party movement, but no less entusiastic in its fervor.

Chapter 8 - Reformation

Crony Capitalism

We must have severe punishment for those who manipulate the system. Insiders who betray the public trust must be dealt harshly as they take property protected by our constitution. This punishment of those who bribe and are bribed in the ruling class must be a major emphasis of reforming the system. If we are ever to achieve real liberty then we must go after it aggressively with a vengeance.

Mill wrote that he believed his work *On Liberty* to be about "the importance, to man and society, of a large variety in types of character, and of giving full freedom to human nature to expand itself in innumerable and conflicting directions." This celebration of individuality and contempt for conformity runs throughout *On Liberty*. He argues the only time coercion is acceptable is when a person's behavior harms other people—, society should treat diversity with respect.

The people with power exercise it over those without power. In particular, a majority may consciously try to oppress a minority. Mill writes that this idea of a tyranny of the majority has come to be accepted by major thinkers. Mill argues that society can also tyrannize without using political means. Rather, the power of public opinion can be more constricting to individuality and dissent than any law could be. There must also be protection for people against the popular public opinions, and the tendency of society to impose its values on others. Real freedom means pursuing one's own good in one's own way, as long as it does not prevent others from doing the same. These ideas directly contradict society's increasing tendency to demand conformity, and unless moral conviction turns against this tendency, the demand for conformity will only increase.

Mills states that his essay can be broken down into two basic principles. First, people aren't accountable to society for actions that only concern themselves. Second, the individual is accountable for actions that hurt others, and society can punish a person socially or legally as is considered necessary for such actions. Mill remarks that sometimes when an action causes harm to others, such as when a person succeeds in a competitive job market, the general social good is positive, and there is no right to punish people for the harm caused.

David Cay Johnston's *Free Lunch* a well documented and detailed account of how fewer than 1% of Americans are getting rich of the backs of the other 99%.

A forerunner to the Occupy Wallstreet movement that it isn't just individuals who are reaping millions of dollars from taxpayers, it's also corporations.

Some of the items presented in detail in the book include how the New York Yankees destroyed a public park for a new stadium, had it paid by the citizens and gave payback to politicians who helped.

The two major hunting and fishing chains that got millions and millions in tax subsidies to build stores based on false and unsustainable promises. They continue to try to rob the treasuries of communities across the country with more false promises. Or Warren Buffet's Geico Insurance company who built a call center in Buffalo using tax subsidies and sold it to the public through a newspaper owned by the same company.

These are just several examples of the material detailed in the book. As well as showing who is taking, and how, the author details who is fighting back and how they are trying to in an era when the courts and politicians are held by corporate interests. *Free Lunch* is a great read that explains well this bizarre state of affairs of Corporate welfare.

Johnston explains what the invisible hand of Adam Smith means to us all. Smith postulated that a free market economy creates competition that serves the common good but, does not work if government provides them subsidies, or allows them to collude to keep prices high. He also stated there would be enterprises that would work to seek bounties only, the equivalent of modern corporate welfare.

Abuse of eminent domain runs rampant in America which is supposed to mean setting aside land for the common good such as a new highway or airport. Now it is used to support developers who wish to profit at the expense of the homeowner. Billions are flowing into the pockets of the wealthy few who have privileged access to government. Special tax breaks not only do companies such as Wal-Mart, Cabela, or Bass Pro insist on property tax breaks that annihilate the local economy rather than improve it, but they might even insist on keeping the sales tax. Communities may not see a return on their investment for decades if at all.

Government intervention in the form of legislation that benefits large companies at the expense of the citizen such as "free market" energy.

Banks who enrich themselves through a legal form of loan sharking by stealing from kids in college. They take student loans and are finding out that what they thought was a loan at six percent suddenly became eighteen percent guaranteeing that they will pay far more than they borrowed for years to come, and the lender is guaranteed no risk. The government is guaranteeing the loans to the banks making the loans. No risk and huge rewards smells disgustingly like crony capitalism.

Our government is also lavishing subsidies onto for-profit health care companies that consistently look for ways to deny claims. No subsidies go to nonprofit health systems even though studies show they offer superior care. Adam Smith said: "What improves the circumstances of the greater part can never be regarded as an inconveniency to the whole".

Lobbyists use their time with legislators, to explain the issues of the organizations which they represent. Many of these lobbyists are employed by lobbying firms or by law firms, which keep clients outside lobbying, other lobbyists are employed directly by advocacy groups, trade associations, companies, and state and local governments. Lobbying are also performed at the state level, and lobbyists try to influence legislation in the state legislatures in each of the 50 states.

At the local municipal level, some lobbying occur with city council members and county commissioners, especially in the larger cities and more populous counties.

Many local areas are requiring legislative agents register as lobbyists to represent the interests of clients to local city council members such as in the swing state of Ohio cities such as Columbus and Cincinnati. Local lobbyists can be asked to represent various organizations including charitable nonprofits such as 501C(3) tax-exempt corporations. Many lobbyists represent nonprofits pro-bono for issues in which they are personally interested. For the public good clients offer to meet and socialize with local legislators on neutral territory like fund-raisers and awards ceremonies.

The capacity of individuals and groups to petition their government is protected by our constitution. However when lobbying crosses the line to bribery then it becomes a coercive affect and therefore no longer deserves protection of the constitution. Instead at that point it becomes a criminal activity, one that we should be vigilant in guarding.

In Washington, representatives often see lobbyists as essential in helping them to deal with their legislative workloads, and well settled regulations exist to ensure good practice and help produce greater awareness of what a lobbyist's role is. There are some 30,000 lobbyists in the U.S. today compared with 6,000 ten years ago and 3,000 twenty years ago.

The explosion in lobbyists in America is leading to the siphoning of billions to the big business and union interests.

Prior to the 1980s lawmakers rarely became lobbyists as the profession was generally considered 'tainted' and 'unworthy' for once-elected officials such as themselves. In addition lobbying firms and trade groups were leery of hiring former members of Congress because they were reputed to be lazy as lobbyists and unwilling to ask former colleagues for favors. New higher salaries, increasing demand and a greater turnover in Congress and a change in the control of the House all contributed to a change in attitude about the appropriateness of former elected officials becoming lobbyists from that time onwards. The route between these roles became known as the revolving door.

While the Congress has done much to quell criticisms against the leverage of domestic lobbying firms by updating domestic lobbying legislation such as the revision of the Lobbyist Disclosure Act in 1997, its inaction in correcting loopholes in legislation regulating foreign lobbying has spawned a culture of foreign lobbying scandals in Congress. A Harvard Law Review article in 1986 noted that companies such as Burger King, Dr Pepper, and Baskin-Robbins, while bearing façades of Americana as they are mainly operated in America, were, in fact, subsidiaries of foreign corporations. Today, all three of the named companies are again American-owned, having been sold or spun off by their foreign owners in the first decade of the 21st century. Foreign-funded lobbying efforts include the Israel, Saudi Arabia, Turkish, Egypt, Pakistan, Iran and China lobbies.

An upsurge of lobbying by U.S. subsidiaries of foreign-owned companies against Democratic proposals limiting the former's spending on political campaigns was spurred in early 2010. The proposed bill would ban "spending by any U.S. subsidiary of a foreign company or any U.S. corporation that has foreign debt, one or more non-U.S. director or any foreign ownership".

$40 million for a National Bio and Agro- defense facility in Kansas, $8 million for expanding Anchorage's port, $1 million for arthropod damage control, $ 2.5. million to improve pedestrian and bicycling paths in Illinois. Then there is $ 15 million to lessen emission – caused pollution in California, $1 million for AFL – CIO training programs. These are some programs that cross party lines and represent a small drop in the bucket of the tens of billions of lobbyist backed earmarks passed by Congress every year.

More than half the major fundraisers for the presidential campaigns come from just three segments of the U.S. economy. Lawyers and law firms, representing both corporate and consumer interests; the financial sector; and real estate, according to a study by the Campaign Finance Institute. There is a widespread problem of potential government contractors attempting to buy lucrative government contracts through campaign donations known as "pay-to-play." Some advocates for state and federal legislation to curtail pay-to-play abuses. Only a few states, have implemented some form of pay-to-play restriction, though the ranks appear to be growing in light of new contracting scandals.

The Federal Reserve System is the central banking system of the United States. It was created on December 23, 1913 with the enactment of the Federal Reserve Act, largely in response to a series of financial panics, particularly a severe panic in 1907.

Over time, the roles and responsibilities of the Federal Reserve System have expanded and its structure has evolved. Events such as the Great Depression were major factors leading to changes in the system. Its duties today, are to conduct the nation's monetary policy, supervise and regulate banking institutions, maintain the stability of the financial system and provide financial services to depository institutions, the U.S. government, and foreign official institutions. The task of the Federal Reserve System is to maintain employment, keep prices stable, and keep interest rates at a moderate level by regulating monetary policy. Components of the Federal Reserve System also supervise banks, provide financial services, and conduct research on the United States economy and the economies in the surrounding region.

The first ever audit of the Federal Reserve was completed in July of 2011, led by Ron Paul and Allen Grayson and their call for an audit. What was revealed in the audit was startling: $16,000,000,000,000.00 had been secretly given out to US banks and corporations and foreign banks everywhere from France to Scotland.

From the period between December 2007 and June 2010, the Federal Reserve had secretly bailed out many of the world's banks, corporations, and governments. The Federal Reserve likes to refer to these secret bailouts as an all-inclusive loan program, but virtually none of the money has been returned and it was loaned out at 0% interest. Why the Federal Reserve had never been public about this or even informed the United States Congress about the $16 trillion dollar bailout is obvious, the American public would have been outraged to find out that the Federal Reserve bailed out foreign banks while Americans were struggling to find jobs.

As a traditional conservative who tends to be anti welfare as it exists today it will be hard for me to ever criticize welfare recipients when we see what our government has done for the bankers.

To place $16 trillion into perspective, remember that GDP of the United States is only $14.12 trillion. The entire national debt of the United States government spanning its 235+ year history is "only" $ 15 trillion. The budget that is being debated so heavily in Congress and the Senate is "only" $3.5 trillion. Take all the outrage and debate over the $1.5 trillion deficit into consideration, and swallow this Red pill: There was no debate about whether $16,000,000,000,000 would be given to failing banks and failing corporations around the world.

In late 2008, the TARP Bailout bill was passed and loans of $800 billion were given to failing banks and companies. That was a flagrant lie because of that Goldman Sachs alone received 814 billion dollars. As is turns out, the Federal Reserve gave $2.5 trillion to Citigroup, while Morgan Stanley received $2.04 trillion.

The Royal Bank of Scotland and Deutsche Bank, a German bank, split about a trillion and many other banks received hefty chunks of the $16 trillion.

This is a disgusting and ludicrous situation that will make people recoil in disbelief. But believe it, because it's true, America has been hijacked and our children and grandchildren are being held hostage.

Insider trading is illegal, except for members of Congress. Senators and Congressmen are free to legally trade stock based on nonpublic information they have obtained through their official positions as elected officials, and they do so regularly.

Peter Schweizer's "Throw Them All Out: How Politicians and Their Friends Get Rich off Insider Stock Tips, Land Deals, and Cronyism That

Would Send the Rest of Us to Prison." Schweizer documents many examples of how members of Congress in both parties including Pelosi, Senate Majority Leader Harry Reid and former House speaker Dennis Hastert have used federal earmarks to improve the value of their own real estate holdings. They have done so, by extending a light-rail mass transit line near their property, expanding an airport, cleaning up a nearby shoreline, building roads and bridges, and beautifying land and neighborhoods nearby in each case "substantially increasing values and the net worth of our elected officials, courtesy of taxpayer money."

Perhaps the most disturbing revelations come from Schweizer's investigation into the Energy Department and its infamous "green energy" loan guarantee and grant programs, a program Schweizer calls "the greatest and most expensive example of crony capitalism in American history." The scandal surrounding Solyndra the now-bankrupt Obama connected solar power company that received a federally guaranteed loan of $573 million is well-known. This must end, this must be realized for what it is, criminal. In the loan-guarantee program alone, Schweizer writes, "$16.4 billion of the $20.5 billion in loans granted went to companies either run by or mainly owned by Obama financial backers. Individuals who were what I would call convenient bunglers, members of Obama's National Finance Committee, or large donors to the Democratic Party. That is a staggering 71 percent of the loan money that is criminal by any account.

By all accounts the largest cost to government right behind entitlements and defense are illegal earmarks, lobbyists who bribe the politicians and politicians who steal from the treasury. However we need to also consider the vast theft of our treasury by illegal entitlement fraud and defense contractors that pad our national bill.

The dirty little secret that almost no one in Washington is willing to discuss is the rampant fraud that is set in in the entitlement system. Democrats, led by Obama, Pelosi, and Reid, never discuss the high percentage of fraudulent payments in entitlement programs.

Instead, they continue the mantra that entitlement spending must be preserved even in the face of exploding national debt, and regardless of disturbing signs of rampant fraud.

Increasingly, we hear jaw dropping stories of abuse and fraud that should force our leaders in Washington to put the issue of fraud and abuse within the entitlement system formally on the table. Just last week we learned of the case of the "Adult Baby" , the 30-year old guy, that lives in a diaper, is fed by bottle and thus somehow entitled to taxpayer-supplied, social security disability for his condition. Strangely, this is the entitlement system that most politicians not only insist that we preserve, but are eager to expand.

To collect food stamps, welfare, and those wildly popular cash cards the government won't demand proof of legal residency or even positive identification of the recipients. Fingerprinting and a little database management could prevent redundant payments, ineligible precipitants, and alike. Our politicians can be counted on to obstruct any effort to contain the fraud. The direct deposit of funds into bank accounts allows those on the dole to live anywhere in the world as they collect from as many as 50 states.

The cases of entitlement fraud are a sad sign of just how much fraud is already embedded into our rich entitlement system and how easy it has become for hucksters and fakes to gain access to taxpayer provided benefits. Currently, there are almost 2,000 federal subsidy / entitlement programs, and we know from GAO reports and from anecdotal reporting that fraud is rampant.

Democrats mindlessly push for further expansion of benefits, as the number of those eligible for Food stamps has nearly doubled in during the Obama Administration, costing some $77 billion. Worse yet, politicians see no urgency, and might very well be comfortable, with the disturbing news that food stamps are now being routinely resold at deep discounts to other undeserving recipients

From the glimpses we do get from what lurks behind the curtain, it is becoming increasingly clear that fraud in the entitlement system is likely a trillion dollar problem. Not long ago, we learned that in West Virginia, a Social Security Administrative judge approves almost all applicants seeking Social Security disability claims. Besides, this judge is almost certainly not alone in granting benefits to nondeserving frauds whose real ambition is to gain taxpayer money for fictitious disability claims.

But do not expect anyone to conduct a real inquiry to discover, much less prevent , fraud in the entitlement system.

They do not want Americans to know just how corrupt and easy it is for duplicitous individuals to gain benefits and taxpayer support to which they are not entitled. If Americans were to understand fully rampant entitlement cheating has become, the debate would quickly turn to fixing the corrupt system, and rooting out the frauds and hucksters that are bilking American taxpayers. Some estimates are as high as 30 percent of all expenditures for entitlement programs are spent either on waste or fruad and it all comes from we the people...we the taxpayers.

National security is among the most important roles of the federal government. This does not mean, however, that we should completely abstain from questioning the size of its budget.

As has been reported on several occasions, Secretary of Defense Robert Gates has been one of the most outspoken critics of his own department's budget. Changes in command structures along with other organization adjustments which in aggregate could save billions of dollars over five years are just the beginning. Skeptics see any initiative to curtail spending as a ploy to take the steam out of rising concern for the spiral in defense spending at a time of heightened anxiety over long-term budget deficits.

In truth, cost cutting measures would just nibble around the edge of our vast military establishment, replenished each year by $750 – 800 billion. A 30 percent reduction in the number of contractors will tell Congress how many the Pentagon employs in total even without counting the 150,000 or so who serve as hired help in our two wars. Defense spending actually going up in real terms just by a somewhat lesser amount due to projected cuts.

But there are also concerns over actual fraud and waste in defense spending as well.When it comes to wasting money, the Pentagon has no peer. For one thing, there's the single question of scale. For fiscal year 2010, the Pentagon budget was $465 billion. That's 6 percent of our gross national product, a larger percentage than in virtually any other industrialized nation. In absolute dollars the Pentagon shells out 3 ½ times more than the next largest military spender (Russia), 6 ½ times more than Britain, 7 ½ times more than France, 7 ¼ times more than Japan, 8 ½ times more than Germany.

Our military budget is bigger than the next nine largest military budgets combined, and sixteen times larger than the combined military budgets of all of our "regional adversaries"- Cuba, Syria, Iran, Iraq, North Korea and Libya. It accounts for 40 percent of all military spending on the planet (in comparison, our economy is only 24 percent of the world total.

Lawrence Korb, a military planner under Reagan who's now with the Brookings Institution, says we could have the most overwhelmingly powerful military in the world for around $150 billion a year.In a report called Ending Overkill, the Bulletin of the Atomic Scientists laid out a detailed military budget that includes funding for many programs we think are unnecessary. Even so, its report calls for scaling down the military budget to $215 billion by the year 2010, and states that this would still give us a force "adequate to undertake six or eight Somalia-like operations. At the same time, or to mount a force larger than the American part of Desert Storm."

The Center for Defense Information founded by retired generals and admirals thinks we could get by quite nicely with about a million soldiers, instead of the 2 million we now have, and with a Pentagon budget of about $300 billion.

The average of those three estimates is $255 billion a year-quite a bit less than the $327 billion a year we actually spend.

And remember: that $327 billion doesn't include the $267 billion or more we lay out each year to service debt that's the result of past military programs. Unfortunately, there isn't much we can do about that past debt-except to cut down on present military budgets, so the problem doesn't keep getting worse.

Subtracting $255 billion from $427 billion gives us a figure for current military waste and fraud of $272 billion a year-almost $800 million a day-virtually all of which goes to large corporations and superrich individuals. Sure, some of it pays for ordinary people's salaries, but they'd also be earning money if they were doing something useful. That could buy a lot of medical care, or fill a lot of potholes, or...you name it. After all, it's your money.

Reducing Government

Government agencies and government run corporations are a bad idea and must be dramatically changed in America. Reorganizing at Fannie Mae, Freddie Mac and other companies would be a great step toward getting our country back on track.

The Federal National Mortgage Association commonly known as Fannie Mae was founded in 1938 during the Great Depression as part of the New Deal. It is a government-sponsored enterprise (GSE), though it has been a publicly traded company since 1968. The corporation's purpose is to expand the secondary mortgage market by securitizing mortgages in the form of mortgage-backed securities (MBS), allowing lenders to reinvest their assets into more lending and in effect increasing the number of lenders in the mortgage market by reducing the reliance on thrifts.

As mortgage originators began to distribute more and more of their loans through private label MBS, GSEs lost the ability to monitor and control mortgage originators. Competition between the GSEs and private securitizers for loans further undermined GSEs power and strengthened mortgage originators. This contributed to a decline in underwriting standards and was a major cause of the financial crisis.

Investment bank securitizers were more willing to securitize risky loans because they generally retained minimal risk. Whereas the GSEs guaranteed the performance of their MBS, private securitizers generally did not, and might only retain a thin slice of risk.

Often, banks would offload this risk to insurance companies or other counterparties through credit default swaps, making their actual risk exposures extremely difficult for investors and creditors to discern.

The shift toward riskier mortgages and private label MBS distribution occurred as financial institutions sought to maintain earnings levels that had been elevated during 2001-2003 by an unprecedented refinancing boom due to historically low interest rates. Earnings depended on volume, so maintaining elevated earnings levels necessitated expanding the borrower pool using lower underwriting standards and new products that the GSEs would not (initially) securitize. Thus, the shift away from GSE securitization to private-label securitization (PLS) also corresponded with a shift in mortgage product type, from traditional, amortizing, fixed-rate mortgages (FRMs) to nontraditional, structurally riskier, nonamortizing, adjustable-rate mortgages (ARMs), and in the start of a sharp deterioration in mortgage underwriting standards.

The growth of private-label securitization and lack of regulation in this part of the market resulted in the oversupply of underpriced housing finance that led, in 2006, to an increasing number of borrowers, often with poor credit, who were unable to pay their mortgages - particularly with adjustable rate mortgages (ARM), caused a precipitous increase in home foreclosures. As a result, home prices declined as increasing foreclosures added to the already large inventory of homes and stricter lending standards made it more and more difficult for borrowers to get mortgages.

This depreciation in home prices led to growing losses for the GSEs, which back the majority of US mortgages. In July 2008, the government attempted to ease market fears by reiterating their view that "Fannie Mae and Freddie Mac play a central role in the US housing finance system". The US Treasury Department and the Federal Reserve took steps to bolster confidence in the corporations, including granting both corporations access to Federal Reserve low-interest loans at similar rates as commercial banks and removing the prohibition on the Treasury Department to purchase the GSEs' stock.

Despite these efforts, by August 2008, shares of both Fannie Mae and Freddie Mac had tumbled more than 90% from their one-year prior levels. In October 2010 estimates revealed that the bailout of Freddie Mac and Fannie Mae will likely cost taxpayers $350 billion in total, with over $150 billion already provided.

The Federal Home Loan Mortgage Corporation (FHLMC), known as Freddie Mac is a public government sponsored enterprise (GSE), headquartered in the Tyson's Corner in unincorporated Fairfax County, Virginia. The FHLMC was created in 1970 to expand the secondary market for mortgages in the US. Along with other GSEs, Freddie Mac buys mortgages on the secondary market, pools them, and sells them as a mortgage-backed security to investors on the open market. This secondary mortgage market increases the supply of money available for mortgage lending and increases the money available for new home purchases.

On September 7, 2008, Federal Housing Finance Agency (FHFA) director James B. Lockhart III announced he had put Fannie Mae and Freddie Mac under the conservatorship of the FHFA and becoming a federal takeover of Fannie Mae and Freddie Mac.

Moody's gave Freddie Mac's preferred stock an investment grade rating of A1 until August 22, 2008, when Warren Buffett said publicly that both Freddie Mac and Fannie Mae had tried to attract him and others. Moody's changed the credit rating on that day to Baa3, the lowest investment grade credit rating. Freddie's senior debt credit rating remains Aaa/AAA from each of the major ratings agencies Moody's, S&P, and Fitch.

As of the start of the conservatorship, the United States Department of the Treasury had contracted to acquire US$1 billion in Freddie Mac senior preferred stock, paying at a rate of 10% per year, and the total investment may subsequently rise to as much as US$100 billion. Home loan interest rates may go down as a result and owners of Freddie Mac debt and the Asian central banks that had increased their holdings in these bonds may be protected. Shares of Freddie Mac stock, however, plummeted to about one U.S. dollar on September 8, 2008, and dropped a further 50% on June 16, 2010, when the Federal Housing Finance Agency ordered the stocks delisted. In 2008, the yield on U.S Treasury securities rose in anticipation of increased U.S. federal debt.

What we must do is break up Fannie and Freddie into smaller regional based private companies with the federal government helping make the transition. We have to carefully balance the need to maintain a strong mortgage availability for the country with the need to get taxpayers out of the business. By breaking up these companies to smaller regional concerns they can begin to form relationships with regional banks in order to solidify the new relationship. It has to be a win win situation for all involved.

Labor unions in the United States are legally recognized as representatives of workers in many industries. The most prominent unions are among public sector employees such as teachers and police. Activity by labor unions in the United States today centers on collective bargaining over wages, benefits, and working conditions for their membership and on representing their members if management attempts to violate contract provisions.

Although much smaller compared to their peak membership in the 1950s, American unions also remain an important political factor, both through mobilization of their own memberships and through coalitions with like-minded activist organizations around issues such as immigrant rights, trade policy, health care, and living wage campaigns.

Today most unions are aligned with one of two larger umbrella organizations: the AFL-CIO created in 1955 and the Change to Win Federation, which split from the AFL-CIO in 2005. Both advocate policies and legislation on behalf of workers in the United States and take an active role in politics. Recently unions have become a larger issue within the 2008 "Economic Crisis" with the three largest automakers seeking $50 billion in loans in order to stay viable. According to some Senators 'costly labor agreements' including pension and health plans put the U.S. automakers at a disadvantage to foreign companies resulting in their collapse. Others point out that the United Auto Workers has made extensive concessions to the car companies over the last twenty years in order to help the companies remain competitive, and allege that the automakers' recent troubles are better ascribed to other factors.

Private sector union members are tightly regulated by the National Labor Relations Act (NLRA), passed in 1935. The law is overseen by the National Labor Relations Board (NLRB), an independent federal agency. Public sector unions are regulated partly by federal and partly by state laws. In general they have shown robust growth rates, for wages and working conditions are set through negotiations with elected local and state officials.

The unions' political power thus comes into play, and of course the local government cannot threaten to move elsewhere, nor is there any threat from foreign competition.

Public sector worker unions are governed by labor laws and labor boards in each of the 50 states. Northern states typically model their laws and boards after the NLRA and the NLRB. In other states, public workers have no right to establish a union as a legal entity. About 40% of public employees in the USA do not have the right to organize a legally established union. Increasingly like corporations have done unions have provided a heavy handed influence over American politics. They shower money upon congressman and presidential candidates in order to secure favorable votes. The bailout of General Motors which turned the company into Government Motors was primarily a device to save the UAW and not necessarily what was in the national interest. These payoffs must end and in a political world that does away with all political donations by any organized groups we can put an end to undue influence that creates unintended consequences.

Government regulations have hamstrung our economy and slowed progress to a halt in many areas of the country. Our over regulation brought us Fannie Mae and Freddie Mac, encouraged jobs to leave the country and provided corporate welfare to companies such as GE. They have also cost us becuase of corrupt companies and unions, a FED run amuk and a health care bill that was written by special interests.

Expansive government that has crippled our young people by causing them to become debt slaves by forcing huge student loan debt that is out of control. We must end this foolish over regulation and get the government out of the way of a true free market.

It becomes encumbent upon business and the public and private sector to be virtuous. For their virtue they should be rewarded with success in their endeavors. However for a lack of virtue they must be punished harshly and swiftly.

The Greatest Happiness Principle of John Stuart Mill is a most common adopted criteria. He asserts that the desirability of an action is the net amount of happiness it brings to the largest group of people. In Mill's utilitarianism the moral worth of an action is judged by it's outcome. The true morality of an action can only be determined by knowing all of the consequences.

This type of virtue ethics which focuses on consequences must be applied by everyone in society. Like much of western civilization virtue theory originates from ancient Greek philosophy. The Four Cardinal Virues of wisdom, justice, fortitude and temerance can be found in Plato's Republic.

You can never be sorry for doing the right thing. Morality and virtue are at the heart of successful capitalism. They can never be opposed to one another or else we risk tainting society itself. The golden rule of doing on to others as you would have them due unto you. Establishing good will that will go a log way toward building a virtous respectability. This is why it's encumbent upon the very wealthy to help the very poor, because virtue demands it be so.

A free market that is virtuous, aided by a government policy that gets out of the way of the individual is paramount. By reducing the influence and the size of government and taking away financial insentives to coerse politicians we can achieve much to the benefit of society as a whole. In doing so we can remake the American Empire into the great American Republic that it was always intended to be.

Hundreds of millions have placed their right hand over their heart and said, "I pledge Allegiance to the flag of the United States of America and to the Republic for which it stands, one Nation under God, indivisible, with Liberty and Justice for all." How could anyone who has pledged their devotion to the Constitution, reconcile the violations of the Constitution that are destroying America. For decades, our Government has been meddling in the internal affairs of other countries, without Constitutional authority, which has brought us War and a growing Police State that is repugnant to the Constitution and the General Welfare of a Free People.

We are now gifting and lending taxpayer money and credit to private corporations for decidedly private purposes, which is done asking for no accountability, without any constitutional authority.

We have a fiat currency, in violation of the money clauses of the constitution under the auspices of the Federal Reserve System. We have an absence of well-regulated state militias, and we have federal gun control laws, all in violation of the Second Amendment. For decades, in violation of the sovereignty clauses of the Declaration of Independence, the United States has been entering into treaties and relationships with foreign entities, and giving authority to international bodies. Most all of our international involvement in military treaties, need to be reviewed for constitutionality. The UN, NATO and all other foreign treaties need to be reexamined for their legality and whether they remain in our national interest.

We must stop private land being taken for private purposes in violation of the Fifth Amendment. Our government has become a provider of Health

Care, and about to order the People to purchase a product, powers that are not enumerated in the constitution and therefore not authorized.

Rights of the People

Those who would give up essential Liberty, to purchase a little temporary Safety, deserve neither Liberty nor Safety," wrote Benjamin Franklin. Attempting to gain security by sacrificing liberty is also a foolish action because it only increases the potential for harm. Benjamin Franklin maybe the most prolific writer of the revolutionary era. His ideas and pronouncements are historic and maintain their meanings to this day.

In Neither Liberty Nor Safety: Fear, Ideology, and the Growth of Government, economist and historian Robert Higgs illustrates the false trade-off between freedom and security by showing how the U.S. government's economic and military interventions reduced the civil and economic liberties, prosperity, and genuine security of Americans in the 20th century. Extending the theme of Higgs's earlier books, Neither Liberty Nor Safety stresses the role of misguided ideas in the expansion of government power at the expense of individual liberty. Higgs captures not only many underappreciated aspects of the Great Depression, the two world wars, and the postwar era, but also the government's manipulation of public opinion and the role that ideologies play in influencing political outcomes and economic performance. The use of fear in controlling our population is mighty and frequently used especially by the executive branch. You can almost count on the fact that when any president is in big trouble, they almost always get involved in some kind of national security issue that demands his attention. The resulting fear of the people gets him a repreive of responsibility from whatever crisis has really occurred.

The federal government of the United States was created to secure the individual rights of our citizens and instead now threatens our Life, Liberty and Property through usurpations of the Constitution. Enabled by our lack of responsibility in these matters, government has exceeded its' authority and abandoned our founding principles which have made our nation exceptional and unique.

The passage of the health care reform bill immediately spawned lawsuits by states attorneys general suing to halt its implementation. The financial stimulus package prompted several governors to vow that they would reject federal funds.

Congressional anti-drug regulation has been met in a number of states with the legalization of medical marijuana. In short, the cry of states' rights has returned to political debate. And each of these controversies brings the obligatory references to such historical touchstones as the New Deal, the Civil War, and even South Carolina's 1832 effort to nullify federal law. The left makes states righters out to be confederate boogie men. The right correctly recalls the importance of states rights to our founding principles.

But states' rights does not begin to capture the real essence of federalism, and references to historical moments as mere data points obscure the degree to which early understandings of federalism can help to inform current debates. One of the most interesting and maddening aspects of the idea of federalism is its apparent neutrality.

It has an ability to stand in for whatever particular view one has about the proper structure of governmental authority in the United States.Our States are being directly impacted by the national debt created by Congress. The theft of our finances to pay for unconstitutional and irresponsible constitutional spending on the part of Congress impacts every individual.

The federal budget is totally out of control. With a deficit of $ 1.5 Trillion and total expenditures of nearly $3.8 trillion. By enacting the waste and fraud proposals and consolidating services we can save the $ 1.5 trillion dollars in budget shortfall. By privatizing Social Security and Health Care we can save an additional $ 1 trillion. That would result in nearly eliminating the need for any income tax from individuals earning less than $100,000 and totally eliminating corporate income tax. The perosnal income tax would then simply be 10% on the amount above $100,000 per year.By cutting waste, consolidating programs and privatizing many government programs we can cut our budget to $1.5 trillion and revenues that could support it without punitive taxation.

The uncontrollable spending by Congress effectively steals monies that could otherwise be used for personal growth by the citizens of the various states, thereby creating a quasi welfare/socialist State, where the citizens look to Washington to solve every problem in their lives which our government has encouraged them to do. Its time that we announce that no they can't. That indeed government isn't the solution, they are the problem. The middle class can be saved by this major overhaul in spending and taxation and brighten the future for our children and grandchildren.

In his book *End the Fed,* Ron Paul draws on American history, economics, and fascinating stories from his own long political life to argue that the Fed is both corrupt and unconstitutional. It is inflating currency today at nearly a Weimar or Zimbabwe level, a practice that threatens to put us into an inflationary depression where $100 bills are worthless. What most people don't realize is that the Fed created by the Morgan's and Rockefellers at a private club off the coast of Georgia is working against their own personal interests. Congressman Paul's urgent appeal to all citizens and officials tells us where we went wrong and what we need to do fix America's economic policy for future generations. The impact of this is taken into account as the economy begins to get and stay on course.

It is true to say that the FED can create money out of nothing and inflate the money supply but it is not the whole story. Even if there wasn't a Financial Crisis, the money supply would still need to increase in order to pay the interest to the Banks. Our money supply is dependent on people borrowing money from Banks because our Government's do not create enough money as they leave this task to Private Banks and us - the tax payers; to borrow that money into existence. It is no coincidence that the IRS was created at the same time as the FED. Both institutions are involved in extracting money from the public.

Our Founding Fathers recorded in the founding documents the God-given Rights of Life, Liberty and the Pursuit of Happiness to every citizen. Without Life, there is no Liberty or Pursuit of Happiness. For many decades and over many administrations, both political parties have been violating the Constitution and the states have gone along . "When the people fear their government, there is tyranny; when the government fears the people, there is liberty." These words were written by Thomas Jefferson some 230 years ago and still ring true today. Both federal and state officials should be made to put an end to the violations and restore constitutional governance. "Liberty is the great parent of science and of virtue; and a nation will be great in both in proportion as it is free." More meaningful words from Jefferson that paint a picture of true liberty and true virtue.

James Madison spoke of the abuse of executive power when he said "Liberty may be endangered by the abuse of liberty, but also by the abuse of power." Madison also discussed that war is a tool for tyrants in saying "no nation could preserve its freedom in the midst of continual warfare." The use of fear and continuous war is the favorite weapon of a tyrant. We must demand that our nation's government be returned to the people and that we can live out the true meaning of liberty in America.

Chapter 9 - Restoring Liberty

Individual Liberty

All human beings seek a world of liberty; an existence in which all individuals are sovereign over their own lives and no one is forced to sacrifice his or her values for the benefit of others. Belief in the premise that respect for individual rights is the essential precondition for a free and prosperous world, that force and fraud must be banished from human relationships, and that only through freedom can peace and prosperity be realized. This statement of basic human philosophy is the path to liberty and the best place to start on the road to reconstructing our Republic.

Our society must defend each person's right to engage in any activity that is peaceful and honest, and welcome the diversity that freedom brings. The world we should seek to build is one where individuals are free to follow their own dreams in their own ways, without interference from government or any authoritarian power. That the role of government is first and foremost to be limited in size and scope. The basic principles and enumerated various policy stands derived from those principles are to be articulated in the subsequent pages. Our goal is nothing more nor less than a world set free in our lifetime, and it is to this end that we take these stands. This is the preamble in essence of the Libertarian Party and at the heart of the saving of America.

All individuals have the right to exercise sole dominion over their own lives, and have the right to live in whatever manner they choose, so long as they do not forcibly interfere with the equal right of others to live in whatever manner they choose. These rights to life, liberty and pursuit of happiness are granted not by government, but my natural law. These rights are inalienable which means they are not granted to us by government, they rather are innate to human existence.

Governments throughout history have regularly operated on the opposite principle, that the State has the right to dispose of the lives of individuals and the fruits of their labor. We need only to look at the ancient government models of Monarchy and Authoritarian rule to see the result of the State being of superiority to the individual.

The U.S. Constitution was devised by America's founders to protect individuals from an overly powerful government. In the following two centuries, the federal government has grown so large and so powerful that, if the founding fathers were alive today, they would look back at the reign of George III with a fond yearning.

We've gone from a concept of limited government to one of unlimited government, in which officials are called upon to fix every social ill, assuage every hurt feeling and regulate every human activity in order to assure equality and fairness.

Much of what's still good about America is the residue from the brilliance the founders displayed, and their understanding of the corrosive nature of government. But a residue can only last so long. A free nation can only remain free as long as its people and institutions continue to value and uphold that freedom. As we have seen liberty in America wasn't yanked out from under but rather slowly transferred away from the citizenry.

But from early on with the Alien and Sedition Acts, which gave the federal government police-state authority to silence speech and deport aliens, through the Civil War, where President Abraham Lincoln tested to the limit the crucial checks on states' rights and the rights of men, through the Wilsonian dogma and the socialist New Deal and up to the present time, government officials have twisted the Constitution to give them authority to do all sorts of things that the founders never wanted them to have authority to do.

A Constitution is a written set of rules for a nation. To follow the Constitution's words, and to interpret them within the original intent of the founders, or to follow the founders' method for changing the Constitution the amendment process is said to be by some liberals narrow-minded, literalistic and old-fashioned. When in fact such thoughts that praise our Constitution are intelligent, real and timeless.

If we then look at systems such as Communism, Fascism or even Socialism where we steal from some citizens to spread wealth along with liberty to other people.

We have seen that Communism has destroyed 100 million lives just in the Soviet Union and China alone. Fascism was counted for millions of deaths around the world at the hands of fascist Germany, Japan and Italy in World War II. Throughout the modern world we see the results of the Socialist experiment now seeming to end in fiscal chaos throughout the modern world.

It is a failed system to think that some can be made free at the expense of someone else's freedom. That is at the heart of democratic Socialism that virtually runs most democracies today. The European experiment has failed; after World War II Europe began it's decent into Socialism. Now the fruits of its harvest are here and now resulting in the destruction of the economies of Europe and much of the rest of the world. Socialism is great they say until you run out of other people's money, well that day is here.

Even within the United States, all political parties other than the Libertarian Party grant to government the right to regulate the lives of individuals and seize the fruits of their labor without their consent. The real difference for the most part between a Democrat and a Republican is only around the margins. Both parties are responsible for the huge problems that we Americans suffer from today. The Monarchy has been replaced by a ruling class that manipulates an ever expanding and controlling government by a minority of rulers.

On the contrary we should deny the right of any government to do these things, and hold that where governments exist, they must not violate the rights of any individual. We must particularly safeguard (1) the right to life—accordingly we support the prohibition of the initiation of physical force against others; (2) the right to liberty of speech and action—accordingly we oppose all attempts by government to abridge the freedom of speech and press, as well as government censorship in any form; and (3) the right to property—accordingly we oppose all government interference with private property, such as confiscation, nationalization, and eminent domain, and support the prohibition of robbery, trespass, fraud, and misrepresentation. Your right to life, speech and property all end when it brings force or coercion to another's right to life, liberty and property.

In essence we own our lives, no one person or group can own our lives. This is at the heart of the very foundation of liberty. As such if we lose our life we lose our future, if we lose our liberty we lose our present and the product of our life and liberty is our property. It's the individual's ability to freely develop his talent and brilliance, to exchange with one another that betters us and ultimately all of mankind.

No use of power by fraud or force can be tolerated in a free society. Whether such action is taken by a person or group of persons it can't be tolerated. These rights are inalienable and are found at the very depths of human experience.

No person or government has the right to murder, enslave or steal. Since we own our lives we are also responsible for good or bad for our actions. Virtue can only exist when free choice is present. Achieving a free society requires us to have courage. Especially when it is easier to do nothing, or at least it can seem to be easier until we start to lose our liberty. Since governments, when instituted, must not violate individual rights, we oppose all interference by government in the areas of voluntary and contractual relations among individuals. People should not be forced to sacrifice their lives and property for the benefit of others.

They should be left free by government to deal with one another as free traders; and the resultant economic system, the only one compatible with the protection of individual rights, is the free market.

We need to defend the rights of individuals to unrestricted freedom of speech, freedom of the press and the right of individuals to dissent from government itself. We oppose any abridgment of the freedom of speech through government censorship, regulation or control of communications media. Pornography, as we hold this to be an abridgment of liberty of expression unless claims that it involves rape or assault, or the coercive treatment of anyone gender. We can't abridge the rights of one over another and have a free and open society. So it should be a more local decision to determine what is pornographic in that community.

Individuals should be free to make choices for themselves and to accept responsibility for the consequences of the choices they make.

No individual, group, or government may initiate force against any other individual, group, or government without due process. Our support of an individual's right to make choices in life does not mean that we necessarily approve or disapprove of those choices. For example if I choose to own a gun then I also accept the responsibility and potential punishment for its safe use. Personal freedom cannot be subjective from one individual's choice to another's.

We believe that the private ownership of firearms is part of the solution to America's crime epidemic, not part of the problem. Evidence: law-abiding citizens in Florida have been able to carry concealed weapons since 1987. During that time, the murder rate in Florida has declined 21% while the national murder rate has increased 12%.

In addition, evidence shows that self-defense with guns is the safest response to violent crime. It results in fewer injuries to the defender (17.4% injury rate) than any other response, including not resisting at all (24.7% injury rate).

The people should repeal waiting periods, concealed carry laws, and other restrictions that make it difficult for victims to defend themselves, and end the prosecution of individuals for exercising their rights of self-defense. If gun laws in fact worked, the sponsors of this type of legislation should have no difficulty drawing upon long lists of examples of crime rates reduced by such legislation. That they cannot do so after two centuries plus -that they must sweep under the rug the southern attempts at gun control in the 1870-1910 period, the northeastern attempts in the 1920-1939 period, the attempts at both Federal and State levels in 1965-1976--establishes the repeated, complete and inevitable failure of gun laws to control serious crime.

Attempts at gun law regulation have increased vigorously from the 1980's and over the past thirty years and still there is no evidence that gun laws work to help keep people safe.

It seems rather that even more guns are available for use partially because of these stricter guns laws. When only law abiding people are paying attention to such laws then the laws themselves serve to help arm the criminals. More unintended consequences of trying to regulate society and morality.

In order to support freedom of expression and oppose government censorship, regulation or control of communications media and technology. We favor the freedom to engage in or abstain from any religious activities that do not violate the rights of others. We oppose government actions which either aid or attack any religion. However freedom of expression should end when the rights of another are violated by the action. For example the right to protest at a soldier's funeral is not free expression because the fallen soldier's family likewise has a right to privacy.

Supporting the rights recognized by the Fourth Amendment to be secure in our persons, homes, and property is fundamental.

Protection from unreasonable search and seizure should include records held by third parties, such as email, medical, and library records. Only actions that infringe on the rights of others can properly be termed crimes.

We favor the repeal of all laws creating "crimes" without victims, such as the use of drugs for medicinal or recreational purposes. By de criminalizing drug use we would save billions of dollars in a War on drugs that is lost. We should regulate and tax the sales of drugs, prostitution, gambling and other so called morally questionable activities.

The regulated legalization system would probably have a range of restrictions for different drugs, depending on their perceived risk, so while some drugs would be sold over the counter in pharmacies or other licensed establishments, drugs with greater risks of harm might only be available for sale on licensed premises where use could be monitored and emergency medical care made available. Examples of drugs with different levels of regulated distribution in most countries include: caffeine, nicotine ethyl alcohol and antibiotics.

Full legalization is often proposed by groups who object to drug laws on moral grounds, while regulated legalization is suggested by groups such as Law Enforcement Against Prohibition who object to the drug laws on the grounds that they fail to achieve their stated aims and instead greatly worsen the problems associated with use of prohibited drugs, but who acknowledge that there are harms associated with currently prohibited drugs which need to be minimized.

Not all proponents of drug re-legalization necessarily share a common ethical framework, and people may adopt this viewpoint for a variety of reasons. In particular, favoring drug re-legalization does not imply approval of drug use.

The resulting savings to the taxpayer would be huge when we consider the reduction in crime, prison population and societal costs of protecting ourselves against such crimes.

There are numerous economic and social impacts of the criminalization of drugs. Prohibition increases crime (theft, violence, corruption) and drug price and increases potency. In many developing countries the production of drugs offers a way to escape poverty. Milton Friedman estimated that over 10,000 deaths a year in the US are caused by the criminalization of drugs, and if drugs were to be made legal innocent victims such as those shot down in drive by shootings, would cease to come about. The economic inefficiency and ineffectiveness of such government intervention in preventing drug trade has been fiercely criticized by drug-liberty advocates. The War on Drugs of the United States, that provoked legislation within several other Western governments, has also garnered criticism for these reasons.

The War on Drugs has failed, a high-level commission comprised of former presidents, public intellectuals and other leaders studying drug policies concluded in a recent report. Efforts to crack down on drug producers and consumers and to try to reduce demand have had devastating consequences for individuals and societies around the world, according to a report from the Global Commission on Drug Policy. The commission, which includes former U.N. Secretary-General Kofi Annan and Virgin Group founder Richard Branson, challenges the conventional wisdom about drug markets and drug use.

The theory that increasing law enforcement action would lead to a shrinking drug market has not worked. To the contrary, illegal drug markets and the organized criminal organizations that traffic them have grown. Countries such as Mexico suffer from widespread drug-related violence. More than 40,000 people have been killed in Mexico in the past four years as rival cartels battle each other over lucrative smuggling corridors and as the army fights the cartels. This violence is beginning to spill over the border to the U.S. The commission's findings add more high-profile voices to a growing movement calling for a radical approach to drugs.

Some leaders, such as former Mexican President Vicente Fox, have called for drug legalization as part of a solution to his country's woes. Its time that the U.S. decriminalize drugs in order to take out the profit and put the drug cartels out of business.

Protecting the rights and interests of victims should be the basis of our criminal justice system. Victims should have the right to be present, consulted and heard throughout the prosecution of their case. In addition we should do more than just punish criminals. We should also make them pay restitution to their victims for the damage they've caused, including property loss, medical costs, pain, and suffering. If you are the victim of a crime, the criminal should fully compensate you for your loss.

Drug prohibition does more to make Americans unsafe than any other crime factor. Just as alcohol prohibition gave us Al Capone and the mafia, drug prohibition has given us the Crips, the Bloods and drive-by shootings. Consider the historical evidence: America's murder rate rose nearly 70% during alcohol prohibition, but returned to its previous levels after prohibition ended. Now, since the War on Drugs began, America's murder rates have doubled.

The cause/effect relationship is clear. Prohibition is putting innocent lives at risk. What's more, drug prohibition also inflates the cost of drugs, leading users to steal to support their high priced habits. It is estimated that drug addicts commit 25% of all auto thefts, 40% of robberies and assaults, and 50% of burglaries and larcenies. Prohibition puts your property at risk. Nearly one half of all police resources are devoted to stopping drug trafficking, instead of preventing violent crime.

By ending drug prohibition we would double the resources available for crime prevention, and significantly reduce the number of violent criminals at work in your neighborhood. Anyone who harms another person should be held responsible for that action. By contrast, the Democrats and Republicans have created a system where criminals can get away with almost anything. Politicians have actually created an industry out of the so called War on Drugs.

Jail sentences seldom mean what they say. Fewer than one out of every four violent felons serves more than four years. We should dramatically reduce the number of these early releases by eliminating their root cause - prison over-crowding. Since nearly six out of every ten federal prison inmates are there for non-violent drug-related offenses, it's clear that drug prohibition is the primary source of over-crowding. It has been estimated that every drug offender imprisoned results in the release of one violent criminal, who then commits an average of 40 robberies, 7 assaults, 110 burglaries and 25 auto thefts. Early release of violent criminals puts you and your family at risk.

It is a maxim of the law that there can be no crime without a criminal intent; that is, without the intent to invade the person or property of another. But no one ever practices a vice with any such criminal intent. He practices his vice for his own happiness solely, and not from any malice toward others. Unless this clear distinction between vices and crimes be made and recognized by the laws, there can be on earth no such thing as individual right, liberty, or property; no such things as the right of one man to the control of his own person and property, and the corresponding and coequal rights of another man to the control of his own person and property.

For a government to declare a vice to be a crime, and to punish it as such, is an attempt to falsify the very nature of things. It is as absurd as it would be to declare truth to be falsehood, or falsehood truth. Any society that lets kids grow up dependent on government welfare, attending government schools that fail to teach, and entering an economy where government policy has crushed opportunity, will be a society that breeds criminals.

No permanent solution to crime will be found until we address these root causes of crime.

Sexual orientation, preference, gender, or gender identity should have no impact on the government's treatment of individuals, such as in current marriage, child custody, adoption, immigration or military service laws. Government does not have the authority to define, license or restrict personal relationships. Consenting adults should be free to choose their own sexual practices and personal relationships.

Whatever your personal belief is regarding gay marriage is your business between your god and you. Not your government and you. Therefore as long as government just stays out of the question of gay marriage that is enough. It's kind of ridiculous to think that good people with good backgrounds can't adopt a child because of their sexual orientation while we have generations of children legally having children. On the other hand it is certainly my right to not approve of gay marriage on religious grounds as well. I should be able to disapprove of gay marriage for myself as long as my disapproval doesn't harm or injure another. To say otherwise would condemn people who hold religious beliefs that are different from our own. If Catholics don't want to recognize gay marriage that is their religious right, just as it is your right to join a different religion that reflects your values system.

Recognizing that abortion is a sensitive issue and that people can hold good-faith views on all sides, we believe that government should be kept out of the matter, leaving the question to each person for their conscientious consideration. Having said that while abortion is a women's right to choose it also recognizes that public funds can never be used for it. To do so would diminish the rights of those who believe that Abortion is wrong. The moral choice to terminate life via abortion is a private matter and should be kept between the women and her doctor and no one else. We don't need the government or quasi government agencies to advise us abort what to do. Our family, friends and churches in our local community can help us make our choices.

We would condemn state-funded abortions. It is particularly harsh to force someone who believes that abortion is murder to pay for another's abortion. It is the right of the woman, not the state, to decide the desirability of prenatal testing, Caesarean births, fetal surgery, and/or home births.

Government exists to protect the rights of every individual including life, liberty and property. Criminal laws should be limited to violation of the rights of others through force or fraud, or deliberate actions that place others involuntarily at significant risk of harm. Punishments should be harsh for actions of force or fraud. Much more than they are today.

For example if who rob someone at gunpoint you should get twice as harsh a sentence under this new system. If you commit fraud over another in a business transaction you should get the same kind of treatment. Enough of the Wall Street criminals and their light sentences. Individuals retain the right to voluntarily assume risk of harm to themselves. We support restitution of the victim to the fullest degree possible at the expense of the criminal or the negligent wrongdoer. Not only should the guilty party pay with his time as in prison, but also financially.

They should have to pay court costs and not be able to profit from their crimes. We oppose reduction of constitutional safeguards of the rights of the criminally accused. The rights of due process, a speedy trial, legal counsel, trial by jury, and the legal presumption of innocence until proven guilty, must not be denied. We assert the common-law right of juries to judge not only the facts but also the justice of the law.

The only legitimate use of force is in defense of individual rights — life, liberty, and justly acquired property — against aggression. This right inheres in the individual, who may agree to be aided by any other individual or group. We affirm the individual right recognized by the Second Amendment to keep and bear arms, and oppose the prosecution of individuals for exercising their rights of self-defense.

We oppose all laws at any level of government requiring registration of, or restricting, the ownership, manufacture, or transfer or sale of firearms or ammunition.

As was said by George Washington in his time that happiness and moral duty are inseparably connected. No words more true were ever spoken. This compels us to act in an ethical and moral way to follow the golden rule of do onto others as you would have them do unto you. Under this new paradigm we are faced with the greatest test of all and that is to be reasonable toward others and with ourselves.

If we always remember that while Europe was created by history and Wars, America was created by philosophy. It was created by the philosophy of faith in the declaration of independence and loyalty to the constitution.

It's been 235 years since some of the greatest intellects ever on our continent or possibly the world gathered in the city of Philadelphia.

With the backdrop of an oppressive government and an insurrection, they debated the high ideals of a free society, one disgarding the absolute power of a monarch. My how times have changed: Go to an airport and be groped by a government thug from the Transportation Security Administration. The Patriot Act, Warrantless wiretaps, No-knock, predawn government raids by thugs with machine guns and wearing black balaclavas. Popular referendums to enact freedom-restricting laws such as smoking in private places, restricting gambling, blocking same-sex marriages and Confiscatory tax codes.

We Americans, as a whole, clearly are not as free as we once were. Have no misconceptions about the freedoms of the founding era that were labored for. While the freedoms then, in many respects, were wider, the number of Americans to whom they applied was by magnitudes smaller.

Today, we find ourselves in the same sinking ship of liberty. Sure and most of us probably believe that we are free, that America is the land of the free. And to some extent, that is correct. Every society, in fact, has some level of freedom. But here in the so-called land of the free we are missing real freedom, the kind of freedom our Founders fought a bloody revolution to win. Today, after those brave men told King George III that we wouldn't sit still any longer for tyranny, those same great thinkers would hang their heads in disgust at what our country has become.

Economic Roadmap

We should want all members of society to have abundant opportunities to achieve economic success. A free and competitive market allocates resources in the most efficient manner. Each person has the right to offer goods and services to others on the free market. The only proper role of government in the economic realm is to protect property rights, adjudicate disputes, and provide a legal framework in which voluntary trade is protected. All efforts by government to redistribute wealth, or to control or manage trade, are improper in a free society.

Property rights are entitled to the same protection as all other human rights. The owners of property have the full right to control, use, dispose of, or in any manner enjoy, their property without interference, until and unless the exercise of their control infringes the valid rights of others. We oppose all controls on wages, prices, rents, profits, production, and interest rates. We advocate the repeal of all laws banning or restricting the advertising of prices, products, or services. We oppose all violations of the right to private property, liberty of contract, and freedom of trade. The right to trade includes the right not to trade — for any reasons whatsoever. Where property, including land, has been taken from its rightful owners by the government or private action in violation of individual rights, we favor restitution to the rightful owners.

We deserve a clean and healthy environment and sensible use of our natural resources. Private landowners and conservation groups have a vested interest in maintaining natural resources. Pollution and misuse of resources cause damage to our ecosystem. Governments, unlike private businesses, are unaccountable for such damage done to our environment and have a terrible track record when it comes to environmental protection. Protecting the environment requires a clear definition and enforcement of individual rights in resources like land, water, air, and wildlife.

Free markets and property rights stimulate the technological innovations and behavioral changes required to protect our environment and ecosystems.

We realize that our planet's climate is constantly changing, but environmental advocates and social pressure are the most effective means of changing public behavior.

The conservative principle of the rule of law both requires and is required for economic freedom. Friedrich Hayek argued that the certainty of law was one of the biggest factors to the prosperity of the West.

Other important principles of the rule of law are the generality and equality of the law, which require that all legal rules apply to everybody. These principles can be seen as safeguards against severe restrictions on liberty, because they require that all laws equally apply to those with political and coercive power as well as those who are governed.

With property rights protected, people are free to choose the use of their property, earn on it, and transfer it to anyone else, as long as they do it on a voluntary basis and do not resort to force, fraud or theft.

In such conditions most people can achieve much greater personal freedom and development than under a regime of government coercion. A secure system of property rights also reduces uncertainty and encourages investments, creating favorable conditions for an economy to be successful. Economist Milton Friedman sees property rights as "the most basic of human rights and an essential foundation for other human rights."

Evidence suggests that countries with strong property rights systems have economic growth rates almost twice as high as those of countries with weak property rights systems, and that a market system with significant private property rights is an essential condition for democracy. According to Hernando de Soto, much of the poverty in Third World countries is caused by the lack of Western systems of laws and well-defined and universally recognized property rights. De Soto argues that because of the legal barriers poor people in those countries can't utilize their assets to produce more wealth.

Free market advocates argue that political and civil liberties have simultaneously expanded with market-based economies, and present empirical evidence to support the claim that economic and political freedoms are linked. In *Capitalism and Freedom* (1962), Friedman developed the argument that economic freedom while itself an extremely important component of total freedom, is also a necessary condition for political freedom.

He commented that centralized control of economic activities was always accompanied with political repression. In his view, voluntary character of all transactions in a free market economy and wide diversity that it permits are fundamental threats to repressive political leaders and greatly diminish power to coerce. Through elimination of centralized control of economic activities, economic power is separated from political power, and the one can serve as counterbalance to the other.

Economist Ludwig von Mises argued that economic and political freedom was mutually dependent: "The idea that political freedom can be preserved in the absence of economic freedom, and vice versa, is an illusion.

Political freedom is the corollary of economic freedom. It is no accident that the age of capitalism became also the age of government by the people." In The Road to Serfdom, Hayek argued that "Economic control is not merely control of a sector of human life which can be separated from the rest; it is the control of the means for all our ends." Hayek criticized socialist policies as the slippery slope that can lead to totalitarianism.

For example our government, at the federal, state, and local levels, is the single greatest polluter in the land. In addition, our government doesn't even clean up its own garbage! In 1988, for example, the EPA demanded that the Departments of Energy and Defense clean up 17 of their weapons plants which were leaking radioactive and toxic chemicals—enough contamination to cost $100 billion in clean-up costs over 50 years! The EPA was simply ignored. No bureaucrats went to jail or were sued for damages. Government departments have sovereign immunity. We can't have one set of rules for the public and another for government. By turning to government for environmental protection, we've placed the fox in charge of the hen house. Governments, both federal and local, control over 40% of our country's land mass. Unfortunately, government's stewardship over our land is gradually destroying it.

While energy is needed to fuel a modern society, government should not be subsidizing any particular form of energy. We oppose all government control of energy pricing, allocation, and production. Allow the market to determine the resources to be consumed and a free market will bring us a large supply of lower cost energy as the market will bear.

All persons are entitled to keep the fruits of their labor. We should repeal the income tax, the abolishment of the Internal Revenue Service and all federal programs and services not required under the U.S. Constitution. We should oppose any legal requirements forcing employers to serve as tax collectors. Government should not incur debt, which burdens future generations without their consent. We support the passage of a "Balanced

Budget Amendment" to the U.S. Constitution, provided that the budget is balanced exclusively by cutting expenditures, and not by raising taxes.

Today, buying a decent home is no more than a dream for many hard-working American families. Something has caused your family's budget to be cut. Something is going to destroy your family's future unless you act to stop it. That something is the Federal government and its policy of taxation and inflation. Let's take a look at a median income family of four in the 1950s. At that time, the Federal income tax amounted to only 2 percent of the family budget. Americans enjoyed the highest standard of living in the world. By contrast, today the Federal income tax takes 25 percent of income for the same family of four. Taxes at all levels—federal, state, and local; hidden and visible—take about 50 percent of a family's income.

During those same years, the government has increased the money supply—producing inflation. Whether the inflation rate is 12 percent or 3 percent, the result is the same: groceries cost more; clothing costs more; your car costs more. You work harder every year for less purchasing power. The Federal government is driving your family into bankruptcy. The government hasn't stopped there. They have borrowed so much money that your children will be sacrificing their entire economic lives to pay the Federal debt.

It seems that no matter who we elect to public office, the government budget gets bigger and the family budget gets smaller. All too often we have only two choices in an election: a Democrat or a Republican. And no matter which one you vote for, you get higher taxes, bigger deficits, and broken promises. It is astounding that so many Americans think the government should enact heavy taxes on the rich to redistribute wealth, which is patently un-American. Less surprising is that 71 percent of Democrats think that way.

Another disturbing figure from Gallop's 2011 Economics and Finance poll is that 31 percent of Americans say there are too many rich people in the country. In addition to showing how large the green-eyed monster has become in this country, it shows the ignorance people have of how the economy works and how government is funded.

In a free society, one based on capitalism and the free-market system, the number of wealthy citizens is a sign of a healthy economy. Unless you are living off government entitlement programs, your paycheck is likely coming from a wealthy person, a company owned by a wealthy person, or a corporation owned by wealthy people. And, as the IRS tells us, if you are living on government entitlement programs, that money also comes from the wealthy.

The top 1 percent of wage earners in this country earn somewhere between 21.4 percent and 23.5 percent of the income but pay about 40 percent of federal income taxes. The top 1 percent actually pays more in federal income tax than the bottom 95 percent. In fact, 51 percent of wage earners in this country pay no federal income tax.

We should favor free-market banking, with unrestricted competition among banks and depository institutions of all types. Individuals engaged in voluntary exchange should be free to use as money any mutually agreeable commodity or item. We support a halt to inflationary monetary policies and unconstitutional legal tender laws. By ending the FED and getting our money back by something again we can return to financial soundness within a decade. A soundness and security that will last forever.

From the Great Depression, to the stagflation of the seventies, to the current economic crisis caused by the housing bubble, every economic downturn suffered by this country over the past century can be traced to Federal Reserve policy. The Fed has followed a consistent policy of flooding the economy with easy money, leading to a misplacement of resources and an artificial "boom" followed by a recession when the Fed-created bubble bursts.

Though the Federal Reserve policy harms the average American, it benefits those in a position to take advantage of the cycles in monetary policy. The main beneficiaries are those who receive access to artificially inflated money and/or credit before the inflationary effects of the policy impact the entire economy.

Federal Reserve policies also benefit big spending politicians who use the inflated currency created by the Fed to hide the true costs of the welfare-warfare state. It is time for Congress to put the interests of the American people ahead of special interests and their own appetite for big government. Abolishing the Federal Reserve will allow Congress to reassert its constitutional authority over monetary policy.

Returning to a constitutional system will enable America to return to the type of monetary system envisioned by our nation's founders: one where the value of money is consistent because it is tied to a commodity such as gold. Such a monetary system is the basis of a true free-market economy. We should defend the right of individuals to form corporations, cooperatives and other types of companies based on voluntary association. We seek to divest government of all functions that can be provided by non-governmental organizations or private individuals. We oppose government subsidies to business, labor, or any other special interest. Industries should be governed by free markets.

We support repeal of all laws which impede the ability of any person to find employment. We oppose government-fostered forced retirement.

We support the right of free persons to associate or not associate in labor unions, and an employer should have the right to recognize or refuse to recognize a union. We oppose government interference in bargaining, such as compulsory arbitration or imposing an obligation to bargain.

Education, like any other service, is best provided by the free market, achieving greater quality and efficiency with more diversity of choice. Schools should be managed locally to achieve greater accountability and parental involvement. Recognizing that the education of children is inextricably linked to moral values, we would return authority to parents to determine the education of their children, without interference from government. In particular, parents should have control of and responsibility for all funds expended for their children's education.

Also by eliminating government supplied so called public education we could begin the dismantling of an educational system gone haywire. Where most of our property taxes and federal taxes that pay for education end up going for salaries and benefits of school employees. This system would end and the private free market will cost less and produce better results.

We favor restoring and reviving a free market health care system. We recognize the freedom of individuals to determine the level of health insurance they want, the level of health care they want, the care providers they want, the medicines and treatments they will use and all other aspects of their medical care, including end-of-life decisions. People should be free to purchase health insurance across state lines.

As recently as the 1960s, low-cost health insurance was available to virtually everyone in America - including people with existing medical problems. Doctors made house calls. A hospital stay cost only a few days' pay. Charity hospitals were available to take care of families who could not afford to pay for healthcare. Since then the federal government has increasingly intervened through Medicare, Medicaid, the HMO Act and tens of thousands of regulations on doctors, hospitals and health-insurance companies.

Today, more than 50 percent of all healthcare dollars are spent by the government. Health insurance costs are skyrocketing. Government health programs are heading for bankruptcy. Politicians continue to pile on the regulations. We know the only healthcare reforms that will make a *real* difference are those that draw on the strength of the free market. We could deposit tax-free money into a Medical Savings Account (MSA). Whenever you need the money to pay medical bills, you will be able to withdraw it.

For individuals without an MSA, the Libertarian Party will work to make all healthcare expenditures 100 percent tax deductible.

We should repeal all government policies that increase health costs and decrease the availability of medical services. For example, every state has laws that mandate coverage of specific disabilities and diseases. These laws reduce consumer choice and increase the cost of health insurance. By making insurance more expensive, mandated benefits increase the number of uninsured American workers.

We should replace harmful government agencies like the Food & Drug Administration (FDA) with more agile, free-market alternatives. The mission of the FDA is to protect us from unsafe medicines. In fact, the FDA has driven up healthcare costs and deprived millions of Americans of much-needed treatments. For example, during a 10-year delay in approving Propanolol Propranolol (a heart medication for treating angina and hypertension), approximately 100,000 people died who could have been treated with this lifesaving drug. Bureaucratic roadblocks kill sick Americans.

Retirement planning is the responsibility of the individual, not the government. Libertarians would phase out the current government-sponsored Social Security system and transition to a private voluntary system. The proper and most effective source of help for the poor is the voluntary efforts of private groups and individuals.

We believe members of society will become more charitable and civil society will be strengthened as government reduces its activity in this realm.

Politicians in Washington are stealing your future. Every year, they take 12.4% of your income to prop up their failed Social Security system - a system that is heading toward bankruptcy. If you are an American earning the median income of $31,695 per year, and were given the option of investing that same amount of money in a stock mutual fund, you would retire a millionaire - without winning the lottery or a TV game show.

Those million dollars would provide you with a retirement income of over $100,000 per year - about four times what you could expect from Social Security. Even a very conservative investment strategy would yield three times the benefits promised by Social Security. We believe you should be able to opt out of Social Security and invest your money in your own personal retirement account. An account that you own and control, one that politicians can't get their hands on. Republicans and Democrats say it can't be done - that your Social Security taxes are needed to pay benefits to today's retirees. Instead of letting you invest in your own future, they want you to have faith that someone else will pay your benefits when it comes time for you to retire.

Although most won't admit it publicly, their "solutions" to the Social Security crises all come down to some combination of tax increases and benefit cuts. Countries like Chile, Mexico, Britain, and Australia have successfully made the transition from their failed Social Security systems to healthy systems based on individual retirement accounts. In Chile, over 90% of workers have opted out of the government-run system. It's time America did as well.

The federal government owns assets worth trillions of dollars - assets that it simply doesn't need to perform its Constitutional functions.

By selling those assets over time, we can keep the promises that were made to today's retirees, and to those nearing retirement, while freeing the rest of America from a failed Social Security system.

We should introduce and support legislation to give you that choice, and put you in control of your own retirement future.

In the last few decades, the federal government has exploded in size. No area of your life or business is free from the meddling of politicians—especially your wallet. **It doesn't have to be that way.** With less government and lower taxes, you could keep more of what you earn. It would be easier to start new businesses, build new homes, and fuel stronger economic growth.

If government's role were limited to protecting our lives, rights and property, then America would prosper and thrive as never before. Then the federal government could concentrate on protecting our Constitutional rights and defending us from foreign attack. **A federal government that did** *only* **those two things could do them** *better* **and at a small fraction of the cost.**

Instead of tending to the basics, government has grown into a bloated conglomerate of political services that gets larger every year—with no end in sight. For example, politicians spend millions of dollars to urge people not to smoke—while spending more millions to subsidize tobacco farmers. They send billions overseas for foreign aid, while the federal deficit swells. They spend millions to subsidize public art ,while working families struggle to pay their taxes. Politicians also run trains, bail out savings and loans, construct houses, sell insurance, print books, and build basketball courts—you name it! **But the fact is, every service supplied by the government can be provided** *better and cheaper* **by private business.**

Military expenses are over $250 billion a year! A large percentage of this is spent overseas to defend wealthy countries like Germany and Japan—who then wallop us in international trade.

Let's take them off military welfare. **We can defend America better and save at least $100 billion a year in taxes.**

No one has the right to cover his losses at taxpayer expense—and yet wealthy corporations demand exactly that. The federal government has bailed out railroads, banks, and other corporations with your tax dollars. The bulk of your welfare tax dollars goes to pay the handsome salaries of well-educated welfare workers.

The poor get little from government welfare except meager handouts and a cycle of despair. Let's get government out of the charity business. **Private charities and groups do a better and more efficient job of helping the truly needy get back on their feet.**

Before 1913, federal income taxes were rare and short-lived. America became the most prosperous nation on earth. The U.S. Government did not try to police the world or play "nanny" to everyone from cradle to grave. People took responsibility for themselves, their families, and their communities. That is how the founders of America thought it should be. We know that 100% of all personal "income" taxes extorted by the IRS goes to the "Federal" Reserve Banking System and does not fund a single function of the government. So, let's take the people's blood and sweat off the table.

What other revenues does the government collect? Corporate taxes, social security taxes, constitutional revenues such as excise taxes on cigarettes, alcohol, tobacco, firearms, tires, etc., tariffs on trade, military hardware sales, and some minor categories. Let's say that those revenues will total $900 billion dollars. The politicians want $1.7 trillion to spend on their favorite welfare programs, wars and foreign welfare, but have a short fall of $800 billion dollars. This is called the deficit and the deficit, created by the spending of Congress, creates the "national debt.

Because the politicians are $800 billion dollars short, they simply call up Al Greenspan and borrow your children's and grand babies' futures. The

"Federal" Reserve Banks don't loan anything of value to Congress. They aren't banks; they're really an overpaid, powerful, private accounting service. When that $800 billion dollars worth of ink is transferred to the Treasury, it gets piled onto the existing national debt.

Congress overspends because no one is making them accountable. In other words, Congress basically pays the bills with social security and borrowed ink from the "Fed." Americans have been bred to a welfare dependent mentality. Special interest groups who have no interest in the Constitution, demand that billions be spent on their pet interests.

Billions upon billions of dollars have been unconstitutionally thrown to foreign governments, some days our friend, a week later our enemies. They are only our friend as long as the U.S. throws money at their corrupt governments. Billions of dollars have unconstitutionally been spent on grants to colleges and universities, which in turn sell their research to the highest bidder, paid for by the sweat off the back of the little guy out in America. No, they don't return any back to the little guy who funded these studies and research programs.

As long as the American people themselves condone continued unconstitutional spending by Congress, the longer they will violate their oath of office, and continue to fund unconstitutional expenditures, placing your children and grand babies in a state of unpayable, massive debt. America became the greatest, debt free nation on earth by a resourceful, independent, self reliant people. Sadly, today we have a large percentage of our population who can't get through the day without a government memo telling them how, step-by-step, with a redistribution of average, ordinary Americans assets into the hands of the unproductive. A very sad commentary to what made our nation great and prosperous.

America functioned very well without an income tax throughout the history of this Republic. The answer to the question of funding without a direct tax is found is Article 1, Section 9 of the Constitution since 1787.

It provides for Congress to pass a legislative bill for tax money to be paid by each state in proportion to its population. Proper, constitutional funding will allow large amounts of money to fund a limited form of Republican government. To continue on the path of this massive and unconstitutional spending will bring a final and total collapse of the economy. Make no mistake about it.

Securing our Legacy

Foreign aid is little more than welfare for nations with the same disastrous effects as domestic welfare programs. It merely serves to keep people enslaved to the aide. There is an old proverb that if you give a man a fish you feed him today, if you teach him to fish you feed him forever.

The U.S. currently spends about $15 billion per year on foreign aid, far less than most people believe, but still a large sum. Since the end of World War II, the United States has spent more than $400 billion on aid to other countries.

But there is little evidence that any of these programs has significantly improved the lives of the people in countries receiving this aid. Instead, foreign aid has typically slowed economic development and created dependence.

Indeed, the U.S. Agency for International Development itself admits, "Only a handful of countries that started receiving U.S. assistance in the 1950s and 1960s have ever graduated from dependent status." In fact, despite massive amounts of international aid, the average annual increase in per capita GNP has declined steadily in developing nations since the 1960s, with many of the Third World's heaviest aid recipients actually suffering negative economic growth.

Since the post World War II foreign aid has delivered more international funds to Africa. Yet, the continent remains the world's poorest and has had almost no per capita GNP growth in the past fifty years.

During the past fifteen years inflation averaged 15% and energy and agricultural production declined dramatically.

A recent study by Peter Boone of the London School of Economics and the Center for Economic Performance confirmed that U.S. economic aid does not promote economic development. Studying more than 100 countries, Boone concluded that "Long-term aid is not a means to create economic growth."

There are many reasons for the failure of foreign aid. First, foreign aid has a widespread record of waste, fraud, and abuse. U.S. aid programs have built tennis courts in Rwanda, sent sewing machines to areas without electricity, and constructed hospitals in cities where a dozen similar facilities already sat half empty. It's all a case of a system run amuck.

Frequently, the aid is stolen by corrupt foreign leaders. As new have seen just recently in Egypt and other Arab Spring nations the aid is stolen by the leaders in order to line their pockets. The Agency for International Development admitted in that much of the investment financed by aid in the past fifty years has disappeared without a trace. Even when aid reaches its intended beneficiaries, the results are often counterproductive. Just as domestic welfare prevents Americans from becoming self-sufficient; foreign aid keeps entire nations dependent. According to one internal aid audit, "Long-term feeding programs . . . have great potential for creating disincentives for food production."

Specific examples of counterproductive aid policies are easy to come by. For example, following a devastating earthquake in Guatemala, farmers trying to sell their surplus grain found the market flooded by the U.S. Food for Peace program.

As a result, according to the Institute for Food and Development Policy, "food aid stood in the way of development." According to journalist Michael Maren, a long-time volunteer with such groups as the Peace Corps, Catholic Relief Services, and AID, aid to Somalia aggravated the country's famine, disrupted local agriculture, and turned nomadic tribesmen into "relief junkies." Similar results have been documented in countries as diverse as Colombia, Haiti, and India. Moreover, foreign aid has often been used to prop up failing Socialist economies, preventing countries from moving to free-market economic policies. Yet, an examination of world economies clearly shows that those countries with free markets experience the greatest economic prosperity. As a result, Alex de Waal, president of the human rights group, Africa Rights, concludes that foreign aid is "structurally bad because it undermines the incentive to take responsibility. The more aid a country receives, the less the government of that country has to answer to the people."

If Americans truly want to help other countries, they can best do so not through failed foreign aid programs, but by improving the U.S. economy, so that U.S. businesses have funds to invest abroad, and pursuing free trade policies. As the Congressional Budget Office recently admitted, "Critics rightly argue that the broad policies of the major Western countries—trade policies, budget deficits, growth rates, and the like—generally exert greater positive influence on the economies of developing countries than does aid."

Probably the most important role for the federal government is to provide for the defense of its citizens. The defense of our nation is the highest and best use of government. Our nation spends way too much on what we call defense, but what looks like to many is empire. With over 100,000 troops around the world on so called peace missions, bases and securing other countries our present system is neither economically feasible or desirable by the citizenry. We need to bring our troop's entire home, not only from Afghanistan and Iraq, but all over the world. By bringing home all of our troops we are delivering the message loud and clear that we are no longer the policeman of the world.

All of our alliances on a military basis need to be reexamined to determine their viability. Since we will be moving from the imperialist military posturing to hands off neutrality position all treaties would need to be re stated. The message to all current allies is we support you and we will trade with you, but we will not lose American lives anymore. The message to any potential enemies is that we are not involved in hating anyone, but we will speak softly and carry a very big stick.

In other words as long as our people are not threatened by a potential foe we will not attack. However if we are threatened then our policy is not one for war, but rather the total elimination of the problem at hand. In other words rather than wage war that will cause the death of too many Americans and possibly innocent civilians we choose not to fight that war. We will determine how to deal with our foes including all means at our disposal. If that means total nuclear annihilation then so be it, it will be the policy of our defense to use assured destruction as an option to deal with any foe.

As Americans we must have the rights guaranteed to us by our bill of rights. That means that no kind of Patriot Act or alien and sedition act can ever exist in this nation. When we deny some rights to some, we deny all rights to all. We must carefully regard American rights and not necessarily extend them to foreigners especially foreign combatants.

American foreign policy should seek an America at peace with the world. Our foreign policy should emphasize defense against attack from abroad and enhance the likelihood of peace by avoiding foreign entanglements. In other words no mutual defense treaties, but we should set an example for how other nations should act. By becoming a friend to all we can truly utilize the talents of our best and brightest to help us become more financially strong than ever.

Of course where there exists human suffering we must try to help with food and medical aid for countries that have extremely critical needs.

However no more billions for foreign dictators and evil allies, for too long these arrangements have bled our people. We must also support free trade and free migration to the United States. Of course we have a right to use excise taxes and tariffs to help our own companies and raise some revenue for our substantially reduced federal government.

The incentive to move jobs away from America will disappear when government hurdles don't exist in the way they do now. Of course we need regulation for the safety of our people but too much regulation has pushed jobs away from our shores.

On the immigration front we need to have sensible immigration laws that for the most part exist now. We can do some tweaking to protect our citizens to the maximum. On the other hand it's ridiculous to make criminals out of a workforce that has been needed in our country for many years. We should establish a good program that would include guest workers instead of illegal aliens. In this way we can make legal millions of immigrants and hundreds of businesses in America. This country is a country not of territory or ethnic trait, it's a country founded on principles and not where you were born. Let the rest of the world use their foolish need for ethnic righteousness rule them.

In European countries foreigners are welcomed, tolerated and eventually sent home. In America what has always worked is that we welcome foreigners, we woo them and then we make them citizens or we deport them.

America needs to staple a green card to every diploma we hand out to foreign students so that they can help to perpetuate our American dream. We are a nation of immigrants and that is the foundation of our very being.

Permanent military alliances have been ruiness to our country. From World War I until the present we have had too many military alliances. We should be trading partners with the world and not its policeman.

We had no national security issue in World War I; it was simply a first major move in imperialism by President Wilson and others to feed a war machine. World War II happened because we were attacked by Japan at Pearl Harbor. While I believe that the war was justified, I also believe that most wars aren't. For example Korea was a virtual money pit for the past sixty years. Our war there without any real national interest costs tens of thousands of lives and 341 billion dollars in treasure over those years.

The Vietnam War is another instance of war by choice and not by need. We had no national interest in whether Vietnam was Communist or not. Yet we lost tens of thousands of men and spent 748 billion dollars in prosecuting that war. Almost every war except for the American Revolution and World War II could have been avoided; possible exception of course would be Afghanistan.

The first Persian Gulf War in 1990-1991 cost us 102 Billion dollars in a very short war. The total cost of the Iraq war of 783 Billion and Afghanistan war of 321 Billion has done much to undermine our economy and our society. Instead of invading Iraq and Afghanistan we should have gone after al-queda and focus all of our energies on that mission. If we have learned any lesson from Iraq and Afghanistan it's that we can't be the watchdog for the world anymore.

If we state loudly and firmly a new neutralism in foreign entanglements we will flourish as a society and trading partner. We can return millions of jobs back to America and live out the true meaning of our national creed. That is our right as free people to life, liberty and property.

Government should not deny or abridge any individual's rights based on sex, wealth, race, color, creed, age, national origin, personal habits, political preference or sexual orientation. In short government can't deny rights because they are not theirs to deny. A truly free society can only be free if all of their citizens are free as well.

We need to end any tax-financed subsidies to candidates or parties and to repeal of all laws which restrict voluntary financing of election campaigns. We oppose laws that effectively exclude alternative candidates and parties, deny ballot access, gerrymander districts, or deny the voters their right to consider all legitimate alternatives.

We are under a kind of two party tyranny in the United States, where power resides with Democrat and Republican national organizations. We should move to eliminate the two party system and replace it with a multi party system. The two-party domination of the election process severely limits our citizens to voting for either a Democratic candidate or a Republican candidate, each committed to a party platform of political ideology. However, you literally have no choice. One of them will be elected to represent you. Such limitations are not unlike denying or abridging a citizen's right to vote because of race, sex or failure to pay a poll tax in violation of the Constitution. The two-party political environment in the Congress and the Presidency excludes many people and other nonpartisan or small party citizens speech and right to vote, and that the two-party system has escalated to hostile levels, dangerous to the survival of our Constitution, our government and the republic itself. Society has been assaulted by selfish interests and battered by the failures of good intentions. The two-party system has alienated the people from their government and caused the people to become cynical and apathetic. Under these adverse conditions, representative government has failed the millions of citizens across the nation.

It should be noted that all state governments have followed the lead of the United States in that they are also dominated and controlled by the two-party system with similar adverse effects upon their people.

As concerned citizens of the United States, we have the responsibility to do something about this serious problem... Time is of the essence in this matter of vital national importance.

Whenever any form of government becomes destructive of individual liberty, it is the right of the people to alter or to abolish it, and to agree to such new governance as to them shall seem most likely to protect their liberty. If ever there was a time and place for restructuring our government this is the time and America is the place.

BIBLIOGRAPHY

Badger, Anthony J. FDR: The First Hundred Days. Hill and Wang 2008

Barnett, Randy. Restoring the Lost Constitution:The Presumption of Liberty. Princeton University Press. 2003

Bastiat, Fredric. The Law. Foundation for Economic Education, 1950

Bickell, Alexander M. Morality of Consent. Yale University Press, 1975.

Boaz, David. The Libertarian Reader, Editor, Free Press 1997.

Bovard, James. Freedom In Chains: The Rise of the State and the Demise of the Citizen. St. Martin's Press, 1999

Browne, Harry. How I Found Freedom in an Unfree World: A Handbook for Personal Liberty. Liamworks, 1988

Crisp, Roger; Slote, Michael Virtual Ethics, Oxford University Press, 1997

Diggins, John Patrick. Ronald Reagan: Fate, Freedom, and the Making of History. WW Norton, 2007

Ely, John Hart. Democracy and Distrust. Harvard University Press. 1980

Fogel, Robert W. The Fourth Great Awakening & the Future of Egalitarianism. University Of Chicago Press; May 2000

Folsom, Burton. New Deal or Raw Deal? : How FDR's Economic Legacy has Damaged America. Threshold Editions 2008

Friedman, Milton. Capitalism and Freedom. University of Chicago Press, 1982

Friedman, Milton. Freedom to Choose: A Personal Statement. Harvest Books, 1990

Goldston, Robert. The Great Depression: The United States in the Thirties The Bobbs-Merrill Co.,. 1968

Greenstein, Fred I. The George W. Bush Presidency: An Early Assessment . Johns Hopkins University Press, 2003

Hayek, Friedrich A. The Road to Serfdom, University of Chicago Press, 2007

Hayek, Friedrich A. The Constitution of Liberty, University of Chicago Press, 1960

Hess, Karl. Dear America. William Morrow and Company, 1975

Hicks, John D. Republican Ascendancy, 1921-1933. Harper Torchbooks, 1960

Higgs, Robert Neither Liberty Nor Saftey, Independent Institute, 2007

Hooks Gregory. The Military Industrial Complex: World War II's Battle of the Potomac. University of Illinois Press, 1991

Hospers, John. Libertarianism: A Political Philosophy for Tomorrow. Nash Pub, 1971

Johnston, David Cay Free Lunch, Penguin Publishing, 2008

Kallen, Stuart A. The Roaring Twenties. Greenhaven Press, 2001

Kelly, Brian Adventures In Porkland, Villard, 1992

Mill, John Stuart On Liberty, Penguin Publishing, 1982

Murray, Charles. Losing Ground: American Social Policy, 1950-1980: Basic Books; 10th edition February 1995

Murray, Charles. What It Means To Be A Libertarian. Broadway, 1997

Narveson, Jan. The Libertarian Idea. Broadview Press, 2001

Nock, Albert J. Our Enemy, The State. Hallberg Publishing Corp, 1983

Optiz, Rev. Edmund Optiz. The Libertarian Theology of Freedom. Hallberg Publishing Corp, 1999

Paul, Ron End The Fed,

Pestritto, Ronald J. Woodrow Wilson:The Essential Political Writings. Lexington Books, 2005

Phelps, Edmund S. Rewarding Work: How to Restore Participation and Self-Support to Free Enterprise. Harvard University Press, 1997

Pilling, Geoffrey. The Crisis of Keynesian Economics A Marxist View. Croom Helm, 1987

Rand, Ayn. Capitalism: The Unknown Ideal. Signet, 1986

Rand, Ayn. Anthem. Plume, 1999

Reagan, Ronald. An American Life. New York: Simon and Schuster, 1990

Richman, Sheldon. Separating School & State: How to Liberate America's Families. Future of Freedom Foundation, 1994

Rockwell, Llewellyn H. Jr. Speaking of Liberty, Ludwig Von Mises Institute, 2003

Rothbard, Murray. Egalitarianism as a Revolt Against Nature and Other Essays. Ludwig von Mises Institute, 2000

Rothbard, Murray. For a New Liberty. Ludwig von Mises Institute, 2006

Scheizer, Peter Throw Them All Out, Houghton Miflin Harcourt Trade, 2011

Smith, Gene. The Shattered Dream: Herbert Hoover and the Great Depression. Pub. William Morrow, 1970.

Spooner, Lysander. An Essay On The Trial By Jury. Book Jungle, 2009

Stiglitz, Joseph. The Roaring Nineties. W.W. Norton, 2003

Taylor, Richard An Introduction to Virtue Ethics, Prometheus Books, 2002

Thorton, Mark. The Economics of Prohibition. Ludwig von Mises Institute, 2007

Tuccille, Jerome. Radical Libertarianism: A Right Wing Alternative. Cobden Press, 1985

Unger, Irwin. The Best of Intentions: the triumphs and failures of the Great Society under Kennedy, Johnson, and Nixon: Doubleday, 1996

Vatter, Howard. The U.S. Economy in World War II. Columbia University Press, 1985 .

Von Mises, Ludwig. The Anti-Capitalist Mentality. D. Van Nostrand Company, Inc., 1956

Von Mises, Ludwig. Planning for Freedom and Other Essays and Addresses. Libertarian Press, 1962

Weinberger, Sharon Imaginary Weapons, Nation Boooks 2006